From Ukraine with Love for Chess

From Ukraine with Love for Chess

**Contributions by Vasyl Ivanchuk,
Ruslan Ponomariov,
Mariya and Anna Muzychuk
and many, many others**

New In Chess 2022

© 2022 New In Chess

Published by New In Chess, Alkmaar, The Netherlands
www.newinchess.com

All photos: New In Chess archives, unless indicated otherwise. Every reasonable effort has been made to trace copyright, but the publisher welcomes any information that clarifies the copyright ownership of any unattributed material displayed and will endeavour to include corrections in reprints.

Cover design: Buro Blikgoed
Translation and editing: Steve Giddins
Production: New in Chess editorial team

Have you found any errors in this book?
Please send your remarks to editors@newinchess.com. We will collect all relevant corrections on the Errata page of our website www.newinchess. com and implement them in a possible next edition.

ISBN: 978-94-93257-57-3

Contents

Preface

First of all, thank you very much for purchasing this book. All funds from the sales will be used to help the Ukrainian people. By doing something good, I hope you can also enjoy and share a passion for chess with us.

I remember well the day of February 24 when I woke up, as usual, to prepare my kids for school and start the working day. But the morning was not happy at all. My smartphone was already receiving messages in non-stop mode – the war in Ukraine had started.

I was deeply shocked and depressed for the first week. What to do? How to help? Leave my family safe and join the military forces?

When Peter Boel contacted me on 7th March with an idea to make a book on Ukrainian chess, I didn't think for long. At least now I could do something. And chess is what I have dedicated my whole life to.

In your hands is the work of many authors and contributors. It was not a simple task, as it would be in normal circumstances. Some of them had fled from their homes without knowing what would happen on the next day. Some were hiding in a bomb shelter, trying to survive. But we managed to do it!

This book is not an Encyclopedia of all Ukrainian chess players. I am sure, for example, Vasyl Ivanchuk could write a book just with his own best games. But I hope that everyone can find something interesting here: middlegame ideas, complex positions for calculating, psychological tricks over the board, etc. What's the secret of the 'Ukrainian chess school'?

When I just started to learn chess as a small kid, replaying annotated brilliancies over the board was always inspiring for me, and it helped me to study and play better myself.

I hope we can meet one day in happier circumstances, and we can discuss chess in person or, if you are a book collector, all contributors could sign your copy of the book.

Well, farewell, my dear reader.

Ruslan Ponomariov
Getxo, April 2022

Acknowledgments

This book is a tribute to Ukrainian chess. It is far from complete, as it was assembled in haste, but these stories and games provide a wonderful picture of the richness and strength of Ukrainian chess players.

The book celebrates the older generation of Stein and Savon, who played most of their games within the Soviet Union. Vasyl Ivanchuk chose to annotate his favorite game of Stein.

There are numerous games from the next generation, the first one playing for the yellow-and-blue flag of an independent Ukraine. Ivanchuk, who won dozens of elite tournaments, leads the pack. This generation was very successful at the Chess Olympiad, winning two times, in 2004 and 2010.

The Ukrainian women won the Olympiad, in 2006. The female successes further include the World Championship in classical chess by Anna Ushenina and Mariya Muzychuk and in rapid and blitz by her sister Anna.

This book started with an email by Steve Giddins, chess author, translator, and contributor to New In Chess. He wanted to share his desire to help the Ukrainian chess community in the terrible times after the invasion of Ukraine by Russia. If New In Chess was planning to publish anything by Ukrainian chess players, Steve offered to translate their writings for free.

We embraced his idea and decided to publish a book to support Ukrainian chess and Ukrainians in need. All proceeds (all revenue minus costs such as printing and distribution) will go to Ukrainian charities. At the end of 2022, we will share the results via email with all New In Chess customers.

Peter Boel, our book editor, suggested an anthology of games from the best Ukrainian players. The next step was asking Ukrainian top GM Ruslan Ponomariov. The FIDE World Champion has been a frequent contributor to our New In Chess Yearbooks and we know him well. Ruslan immediately joined our efforts and offered to reach out to his countrymen and -women and coordinate their contributions. All players he asked were prepared to cooperate, insofar as they could find the time. Some players were busy with other tasks; Natalia Zhukova, for example, is a member of the city council in Odessa. She permitted us to reprint her game notes from *New In Chess* magazine.

We have added excerpts from *New In Chess* magazine, written by editor-in-chief Dirk Jan ten Geuzendam, highlighting the victories of the Ukrainian teams at the Chess Olympiads of 2004, 2006, and 2010.

Grandmaster Oleg Romanishin goes into great detail about his secret training matches with World Champion Mikhail Tal, the magician from Riga. Last but not least, Dutch Grandmaster Jan Timman showcases some of his favorite endgame studies by Ukrainian composers, a story that was also published in New In Chess magazine 2020#3.

Steve Giddins translated and edited the games. Dutch design studio Buro Blikgoed created the cover without sending us any invoice. Everyone from the editorial team at New In Chess has been working on this book in their spare time, especially our designer Anton Schermer. Chess journalist Colin McGourty from Chess24 helped with some of the biographies. Our printers in Poland and the USA have printed the book at a huge discount.

Thank you all!

Remmelt Otten
Publisher *New In Chess*
Alkmaar, April 2022

CHAPTER I

The Pioneers

Leonid Stein

The chess career of Leonid Stein (born 1934 in Kamenets-Podolskiy) developed much slower than usual. He earned the Grandmaster title in 1962. His first successes came only in his late twenties: two-time Ukrainian Champion (1960-62); three-time Soviet Champion in 1963 (winning a play-off with Spassky and Kholmov), 1965 and 1966/67; two times team gold at the Olympiads of 1964 and 1966 (board gold and silver).

Stein was the strongest player never to participate in a Candidates Tournament. Twice he fell victim to the FIDE rule that the number of participants from any one country should not exceed three, and in 1967, after a play-off with Reshevsky and Hort, where all tied on 4 points.

His two outstanding tournament victories were both achieved in Moscow (50th anniversary of the 1917 October Revolution in 1967 and the Alekhine Memorial in 1971, tying with Karpov).

In 1973 he died of a heart attack in the Rossija Hotel in Moscow just when he was expected to take the world by storm. He was considered the favourite for the Petropolis Interzonal later that year.

Ray Keene wrote a classic biography on Leonid Stein called *Master of Attack* (1976). When Kotov praised Stein with a fine game in the Soviet tradition, Stein replied: 'But I'm a Ukrainian!' He was buried in Kyiv.

NOTES BY
Vasyl Ivanchuk

Game 1   Sicilian Defence
Leonid Stein
Semyon Furman
Moscow tt 1959

1.e4 c5 2.♘f3 e6 3.d4 cxd4 4.♘xd4 ♘c6 5.♗e3
A very rare move, but quite typical of the original attitude to opening preparation of Leonid Stein. We can also remember his famous game against Lajos Portisch at the Stockholm interzonal 1962, where Leonid played 5.♘d2!? after 4... a6. Also, it's important to understand that Semyon Furman was one of the best theoretical experts in the Soviet Union. Because of this, it was very logical to not play more popular lines against him like 5.♘c3 ♕c7, 5.♘b5 d6 6.c4, or 5.c4 ♘f6 6.♘c3 ♗b4 7.♘xc6 bxc6 8.♗d3.
5...♘f6 6.♗d3!?
6.♘c3 ♗b4 7.♗d3 d5 (7...♘e5!? 8.0-0 0-0 looks like a good alternative

for Black too) 8.exd5 ♘xd5 9.♘xc6
♘xe3!? (9...bxc6 10.♗d2! leads to a
roughly equal position) 10.♘xd8
♘xd1 11.♖xd1 (11.♘xf7?? ♘xb2!)
11...♔xd8 12.♗xh7+ ♔c7 13.♗e4
♗d7 (or even 13...f5!? 14.♗f3 ♗d7;
13...♖h4 is interesting to check
too) 14.♗xb7 ♖ab8 gives Black
good enough compensation for two
sacrificed pawns.

6...d5
There is nothing wrong with
6...♕c7!? 7.♘c3 (7.0-0 ♘e5!)
7...a6! – the game transposes to the
Taimanov Variation.

7.exd5
7.♘d2 was possible as well, but
in that case, Black has a pleasant
choice between 7...♘e5!? and
7...♗d6.

7...♘xd5!?
After this capture with the knight,
the position starts to remind me of
a famous game Tiviakov-Sutovsky
from the Alapin-system (Plovdiv
Ech 2008): 1.e4 c5 2.♘f3 e6 3.c3 d5
4.exd5 ♕xd5 5.d4 ♘f6 6.♘a3 ♘c6
7.♗e3 cxd4 8.♘b5 ♕d8 9.♘xd4 ♘d5.
  A) By the way, Black has a wide
and practically (!) tough choice
among several possibilities here:

7...♘xd4 8.♗xd4 ♕xd5 9.♗xf6!
(9.0-0 ♗d7! 10.♗xf6 ♘c6! 11.♕g4
gxf6 12.♘c3 ♕g5 is totally safe for
Black) 9...gxf6 (9...♕xg2?? 10.♗b5+)
10.0-0 was an option to reach a
double-edged position, where both
opponents have their trumps;
  B) 7...exd5 with the idea of ♗d6
and 0-0 looks like an improved
version of the last game between
Fischer and Spassky in Reykjavik
1972. I mean 1. e4 c5 2.♘f3 e6 3. d4
cxd4 4.♘xd4 ♘c6 5.♘c3 a6 6.♗e3
♘f6 7.♗d3 d5!? 8.exd5 (8.0-0!?, as in
Ivanchuk-Benjamin, Munich 1994,
with the idea 8...♗d6 9.♘xc6! bxc6
10.f4, may be more precise) 8...exd5
9.0-0 ♗d6!;
  C) The option 7...♕xd5 8.♘xc6
♕xc6 (8...♕xg2?? 9.♗e4!) 9.0-0 b6
10.♘c3 a6 11.♗e2 ♗b7 12.♗f3 ♕c7
can be considered as well.

8.♘xc6 bxc6
8...♘xe3? 9.♘xd8 ♘xd1 10.♘xf7! was
not playable, of course.

9.♗d4 ♘b4?!
Furman wants to create concrete
threats, but I am not sure that
he chose the best method in this
position. For example, it's very
logical and solid to play 9...c5!
10.♗e5 ♗d6! 11.♗xd6 ♕xd6 12.0-0
♗h7! with approximately equal
chances (of course not 12...0-0??
13.c4!+−).
9...♗d6? immediately, however, is
bad because of 10.♕g4!.

10.♗e4 ♗a6
10...f5?! 11.a3! can hardly be
recommended for Black.

11.a3

11.c3!? looks like another interesting possibility for White in this position. But probably, Leonid Zakharovich decided that the weakness of the d3-square can be more important in some variations than the possibility of an attack with ♕d1-a4.

11...♘d5 12.♘d2

12... f5?

Again, Black plays the sharpest move, but unfortunately for him, it is not totally correct, because it is White who has the development advantage here!

It was much more solid to play 12...♖c8! 13.♕f3 (13.c4 ♘b6 looks acceptable for Black, or 13...♘f6!?) 13...c5 14.♗e5 ♗d6 15.♗xg7 (15.♗xd6 ♕xd6 16.♕g3 is possible and gives White a small advantage) 15...♖g8 16.♗xd5 (16.♗c3!?) 16...exd5 17.♗f6 ♗e7 18.♗xe7 ♕xe7+ 19.♔d1 is not totally clear. Black has enough compensation for the pawn in my opinion.

13.♕h5+!

Probably Semyon Abramovich missed the idea with ♕h5+ and ♕h3! in his calculations. Other options like 13.♗d3 ♗xd3 14.cxd3

♘f4 or 13.♗f3 e5! look totally playable for Black.

13...g6

14.♕h3! ♘f4

This is not really good, but it's very hard to propose a reasonable alternative here.

14...♖g8 15.♕xh7! fxe4 (15...♘e7 16.♗f6!) 16.♕xg8 ♘f4 17.♗g7 ♘xg2+ 18.♔d1 is obviously bad for Black.

15.♗xc6+?!

15.♕c3! was even stronger here in my opinion!

15...♔f7 16.♕e3 ♗h6 17.♕e5!

Now both black rooks are attacked. The 'traps' 17.0-0-0?? ♕xd4! or 17.♗xa8? ♘d3+! 18.cxd3 ♗xe3 19.fxe3 e5! 20.♗xe5 ♖e8 are too primitive for Grandmaster level, of course.

17...♖c8

17...♘e2!? 18.♘b3 ♘xd4 19.♘xd4 ♖c8 may have been the best chance for Black.

18.♕xh8 ♕xh8 19.♗xh8 ♖xc6 20.g3 ♘h3?!

20...♘d5! was certainly more stubborn! At least the black pieces would have been much better coordinated than in the game, but the position after 21.c4 ♗xc4

22.♘xc4 ♖xc4 23.0-0 looks winning for White anyway.

21.c4! ♗xd2+

21...♗xc4 22.♘xc4 ♖xc4 23.♗c3 is equally hopeless.

22.♔xd2 ♘xf2 23.♖hc1 ♗xc4 24.♗d4!+−

24.b3?! ♖d6+ 25.♔e3 ♘g4+ 26.♔f4! may be winning as well, but it is not necessary for White to calculate such variations.

24...♘e4+

24...♘g4 25.b3! and the game is over! **25.♔e3 e5 26.♗xe5 ♖e6 27.♖xc4 ♖xe5 28.♖c7+ ♔f6 29.♖xa7 ♘xg3+ 30.♔d3 ♘e4 31.♖xh7 f4 32.♖f1 g5 33.h4 ♔f5 34.hxg5 ♘xg5 35.♖h8 ♖e3+ 36.♔c4 ♖e4+ 37.♔b5 ♖e5+ 38.♔a4 f3 39.♖f8+ ♔g4 40.♖g1+ ♔h5 41.♖xg5+ 1-0**

Vladimir Savon

Vladimir Savon (1940-2005) was born in Chernihiv but soon moved to Kharkiv and lived there for the rest of his life. He became a Grandmaster in 1973, the first grandmaster ever from Kharkiv. As an International Master (a titled he earned at the age of 18 already), he had already won the Ukrainian Chess Championship in 1969 and the very strong USSR Championship in 1971, finishing 1½ points ahead of Tal and Smyslov and 2 points ahead of Karpov This was a sensational result at the time. It earned him the Grandmaster title, and a place on the USSR Olympiad team in 1972. As a coach, Savon worked with many children, the most successful of them being Alexander Moiseenko, who wrote a book as a tribute to his coach – the game analysis below is a fragment from it. Savon died in Kharkiv at the age of 65.

NOTES BY
Vladimir Savon and Alexander Moiseenko (indicated in **bold**)

Game 2   Sicilian Defence
Vladimir Savon
Lev Polugaevsky
Leningrad ch-USSR 1971 (3)

─────────────────────────

1.e4 c5 2.♘f3 d6 3.d4 cxd4 4.♘xd4 ♘f6 5.♘c3 a6

6.♗e2
This move has been successfully employed by Grandmasters Efim Geller and Vasily Smyslov. I prefer 6.♗g5, but I was afraid of 6...e6 7.f4 b5, a line developed by Polugaevsky. **6...e6 7.f4 ♗e7 8.0-0 0-0 9.♗e3 ♕c7 10.a4**

Black has played the opening very smoothly, without yet showing his development plan. With the text move, White tries to bring clarity in the positioning of Black's forces.

10...♞c6 11.♞b3 b6

Aimed against the unpleasant 12.a5.

12.♝d3

12.♝f3 ♝b7 13.♛e2 ♞d7 14.♜fd1 ♜ab8 15.g3 ♜fd8 16.♝g2 ♞c5 17.♞d4 ♝f6 18.f5 ♞xd4 19.♝xd4 ♞d7 20.♛f2 ♝c6 21.g4 ♝xd4 22.♜xd4 ♞e5, with a slight advantage for Black, in De Firmian-Kasparov, New York 1995 (½-½, 58).

12...♝b7 13.♛f3 ♞b4

In this variation, the white queen often moves to h3, so it is necessary to take the bishop on d3 under fire.

14.♞d4

Preventing the dangerous undermining of the centre by ...e6-e5 or ...d6-d5.

Less good was 14.♛h3, due to 14...e5! and White's knight on b3 remains out of action.

14...g6!

The great master of the Sicilian Defence at work. Black prepares ...e6-e5, chasing away White's most dangerous piece from the centre, which should be the first step towards taking the initiative.

15.♜ad1 e5 16.♞de2

Worse was 16.fxe5 dxe5 17.♞de2 ♞h5!, after which Black's position is more promising.

16...d5 17.fxe5 dxe4

When in the Sicilian Defence Black has the liberating ...d6-d5 advance, he usually has no difficulties, and this position is no exception, but Black's last move is inaccurate. Correct was 17...♛xe5 when White gets approximate equality with 18.♛g3 ♛xg3 19.♞xg3 ♞xd3 20.cxd3 dxe4 21.dxe4 or 18.♝d4 dxe4 19.♞xc4 ♝xe4! 20.♝xe5 ♝xf3 21.♜xf3 ♝c5 22.♝d4.

18.♞xe4 ♛xe5

19.♛xf6!!!

The start of some very interesting tactics, where White's and Black's pieces come under attack simultaneously.

Alexander Moiseenko: An absolutely fantastic attack, fundamentally changing the situation on the board and the psychological situation in the game. It would seem that Black has handled the opening better, with a planned breakthrough in the centre, but suddenly this unexpected blow turns everything upside down.

19...♘xd3!

Polugaevsky is alert.

Alexander Moiseenko: Dangerous was 19...♗xf6 20.♘xf6+, and now:

A) 20...♔g7 21.♗d4 and Black has nothing better than to resort to the move in the game: 21...♘xd3 22.♘d7.

B) 20...♔h8 21.♗d4 ♕e6 (21...♘xd3! 22.♘d7) 22.♘f4 ♕d6 23.c3 ♘xd3 24.♖xd3, with strong threats – note the computer score of +4.

Black cannot accept the queen sacrifice.

20.♗d4!

The only move that maintains the tension, otherwise the initiative could pass to Black.

Alexander Moiseenko: An important decision, keeping the initiative alive. The computer gives its favoured score of 0.00

and regards the moves 20.♕xe5, 20.♖xd3 and 20.♗d4 as almost equal. In reality, the move 20.♗d4 poses difficult problems to Black. Bad was 20.cxd3 ♗xf6 21.♘xf6 ♔h8 22.♘g4 (22.♗d4 ♕xe2) 22...♕d5 23.♗d4 f6, when Black is better. After 20.♕xe5 ♘xe5 21.♘f6 ♗xf6 22.♖xf6 ♘g4 23.♖xb6 ♘xe3 24.♖d3 play is equal.

20...♗xf6

After 20...♗xe4 21.♗xe5 ♗xf6 22.♗xf6 ♘c5 23.♘c3! ♗xc2 24.♘d5 White preserves the initiative.

21.♘xf6+ ♔g7

22.♘d7!

The best move, maintaining the tension!

Alexander Moiseenko: The computer prefers 22.♗xe5 ♘xe5 23.♘d7 ♘xd7 24.♖xd7 ♗c6 25.♖c7 ♗xa4 26.b3 ♗e8 27.♘f4, with some compensation for the pawn.

22...♕xd4+ 23.♘xd4 ♘xb2 24.♖b1 ♖fd8

Alexander Moiseenko: Easier was 24...♘xa4!? (if you understand chess like Savon did!) 25.♘xf8 ♖xf8 26.♖b4 b5 27.c4 ♘c3 28.cxb5 ♘xb5 with a draw, because in this type of endgame the extra exchange is not enough to convert to a win.

25.♘e5!

After 25.♘xb6 ♖ab8 Black has the better chances.

25...♖xd4 26.♖xf7+

26...♔h6?

The first inaccuracy. After 26...♔g8 27.♖xb7 ♘xa4 28.♘d7 ♖f4 29.♖f1 ♘c5! this complicated game would have ended in a draw.

27.♖xb7 ♘xa4

Alexander Moiseenko: Better was 27...♘c4 28.♘f3 ♖e4 29.♖d1! ♘e5 30.♖xh7 ♔xh7 31.♘g5 ♔h6 32.♘xe4 ♖f8 and Black has good chances to draw.

28.♖b3!!!

It seems to me that exactly this move was not taken into account when Black played 26...♔h6. Now Black comes under a very strong attack.

28...♖d1+

Losing was 28...♘c5 29.♖h3 ♔g5 30.♘f3.

29.♔f2 ♖d2+ 30.♔g3 ♘c5 31.♘g4+ ♔g5

32.♖e7!

The last difficult move in this game. The mating net around the black king is closed!

32...♖xg2+ 33.♔xg2 ♘xb3

After 33...♔xg4 White has a nice choice between 34.♖xb6 ♖d8 35.♖b4+ ♔f5 36.♔g3 and 34.♖g3+ ♔f5 35.♖xh7, with a winning position.

34.♔g3

Study-like. White creates a mating net with a minimum of material!

34...♔f5 35.♖e5 Mate.

Alexander Moiseenko: An absolutely phenomenal game! Lev

Abramovich Polugaevsky, then at the height of his form, was a very strong chess player, with profound opening knowledge, erudition, tactical talent and dedication to chess. In this game we see him equalizing the position in an opening that he knew better than his opponent, gaining a comfortable game. In reply, Savon posed enormous practical problems by sacrificing his queen. Polugaevsky didn't get confused and defended strongly. Just one real mistake, 26...♚h6? (not wanting to retreat his king to the 8th rank), led to a completely unexpected mating final. Bravo, Vladimir Andreyevich!

Gennady Kuzmin

Gennady Kuzmin (1946-2020) was a Grandmaster (since 1973) and trainer. Born in Mariinsk, he reached his peak strength in the early to mid-1970s. Kuzmin won the Ukrainian Chess Championship three times, all shared, in a period spanning thirty years: 1969 at Ivano-Frankivsk (shared with Vladimir Savon), 1989 at Kherson (shared with Igor Novikov), and 1999, when the title was shared several ways at Alushta. He won the bronze medal as a reserve (12½/15) for the USSR team that won the Nice Olympiad in 1974, and came first in many tournaments.

Later, Kuzmin became a successful chess coach who worked, among others, with the strong women players Maia Chiburdanidze, Lydia Semenova and Kateryna Lagno, and also with Ruslan Ponomariov. He was the head coach of the Ukraine women's team until 2003.

NOTES BY
Alexander Moiseenko

Game 3   Sicilian Defence
Gennady Kuzmin
Semyon Furman
Orel ch-USSR st 1966

1.e4 c5 2.♘f3 ♘c6 3.d4 cxd4 4.♘xd4 e6 5.♘c3 d6 6.♗e3 ♗e7 7.f4 ♘f6 8.♕f3 e5 9.♘xc6 bxc6

10.fxe5
More popular nowadays is 10.f5, after which Black has a wide choice. An interesting duel between Anand and Khalifman went 10...d5 11.exd5 cxd5 12.0-0-0 0-0 13.♘xd5 ♘xd5 14.♗c4 ♗xf5 15.♗xd5 ♕c8 16.♕f2 ♖b8 17.♗xa7 ♖b5 18.♗e3 ♗e6 19.♗xe6 ♕xe6 20.♔b1 ♖a8 21.b3 ♖ba5 22.a4 ♖b8 23.♗c1 ♖xa4 24.♗b2 ♖aa8 draw (while Black is better), Anand-Khalifman, Zurich 2009 (rapid). Instead of Black's last move, he could have played 24...♖xb3!! 25.cxb3 ♕xb3. Sychev-Kobalia, Yaroslavl 2018, saw 10...h5 11.0-0-0 ♕a5 12.♗c4 ♗b7 13.♗b3 ♖d8 14.♗g5, with a slight advantage for White, who in the end lost (0-1, 83).
10...dxe5 11.♗c4 0-0

12.h3

12.0-0 allows 12...♘g4 13.♖ad1 ♘xe3, and now:

A) 14.♗xf7+ ♔h8 15.♕xe3 ♕b6 16.♕xb6 axb6 17.♗c4 ♗g4, with compensation for the pawn;

B) The sharp 14.♖xd8 ♗xd8 15.♗xf7+ ♔h8 16.♖f2 ♘g4 17.♖f1 ♘h6 18.♕h5 ♗g4 19.♕xe5 ♗b6+ 20.♔h1 ♘xf7 led to a non-standard position with Black being outplayed in Najer-Morozevich, Moscow 2014 (1-0, 50);

C) 14.♕xe3 ♕b6 15.♕xb6 axb6, with an advantage for Black, in Gufeld-Furman, Tallinn 1965 (0-1, 50).

12...♗b4

Too ambitious. Black wants to destroy White's structure but ignores the dynamic factors of the position.

Later, the well-known theorist Semyon Furman, who was also the coach of the USSR national team, worked out a variation that resulted in a win for the ex-World Champion Tigran Petrosian with the black pieces:

12...♗e6! 13.♗xe6 (13.♗b3 c5 14.♕e2 ♖b8 15.♗xe6 fxe6 16.b3 c4! 0-1, 53, Tal-Balashov, USSR 1973) 13...fxe6 14.♕e2 ♖b8 15.0-0 ♖xb2 16.♖ab1 ♖b4 17.♕a6 ♕c7 18.a3 ♖xb1 19.♖xb1 ♖a8 20.a4 h6 21.a5 ♔h7 22.♕b7 ♕xa5! 23.♕xa8 ♕xc3 24.♕xa7 ♘xe4 25.♖f1 ♗h4 26.♖f7 ♗f6 27.♔h2 ♕xc2 28.♕d7 ♕b3 29.♗f2 ♕d5 30.♕a7 ♕d2 31.♕e3 ♕c2 32.♗e1 c5 33.h4 c4 34.♖c7 ♕d3 35.♕f3 ♕b1 36.♕e3 ♘d6 37.♕d2 ♘f5 38.♖xc4 e4 39.♕c2 ♕xe1 40.♖xe4 ♗e5+ 0-1, Hübner-Petrosian, Seville 1971.

13.0-0 ♗e6 14.♗b3 ♕a5 15.♗g5

15...♗xc3?

It was not too late to go back, at the cost of a tempo, to a normal position with 15...♗e7.

16.bxc3 ♕c5+ 17.♔h2 ♘d7 18.♕g3 ♔h8

Black should have exchanged the bishops and played 19...f6. From now on, White never gives him a second chance.

19.♖ad1! ♘b6

20.♖f6!!!
A fantastic winning move! Of course, Black cannot take the rook.
20...♘c4
20...♗xb3 21.axb3 ♖ae8 22.♕h4 ♕xc3 23.♖h6 f6 24.♖xh7+ ♔g8 25.♕h5, with inevitable mate.
21.♕h4!
This was White's idea. Taking advantage of the rook's immunity, he quietly creates the threat 22.♖h6, after which there is no protection from checkmate.

21...♖g8
Trying to cover g7.

22.♖d3!
Bringing on the other rook for the attack!
Also winning was the immediate 22.♖h6 gxh6 23.♗f6+ ♖g7 24.♕xh6 ♕f8 (24...♖g8 25.♕xg7+ ♖xg7 26.♖d8+ ♕f8 27.♖xf8 mate) 25.♖d3 ♔g8 (25...♘d6 26.♖xd6 and wins) 26.♗xg7 ♕xg7 27.♖g3.
22...♘d6 23.♗xe6 fxe6

24.♖h6!
Black resigned, as after 24...gxh6 25.♗f6+ ♖g7 26.♗xg7+ ♔xg7 27.♕e7+ he will be mated.

Vladimir Tukmakov

Vladimir Tukmakov (born 1946 in Odessa) has always been an exemplary team player. His career first took flight when he was a member of the World Student Team Championships from 1966 to 1972, winning nine gold medals along the way for the USSR. He also took team gold in his only Olympiad appearance in 1984 and won two individual gold medals in the European Team Chess Championships in 1973, 1983 and 1989.

Tukmakov did well in many top-class tournaments, but often ended in second place (behind Fischer in Buenos Aires 1970, behind Karpov at Madrid 1973). The same applied for his ten attempts to become Soviet Champion. He came very close on three occasions; at Riga 1970, Baku 1972 and Moscow 1983, where he finished behind Kortchnoi, Tal and Karpov respectively. He did, however, become Champion of Ukraine in 1970.

Arguably Tukmakov's greatest claim to fame is leading the Ukraine team to victory at the 36th Chess Olympiad in Calvia (2004) as a non-playing captain. In the same year he was awarded the title of FIDE Senior Trainer. In this field, he is best known for his work with Anish Giri since 2014.

In recent years Tukmakov has become a prolific book author with titles such as *Modern Chess Preparation – Getting Ready for Your Opponent in the Information Age* (New In Chess 2012). He also wrote a book about the Candidates Tournament in Yekaterinburg 2020.

NOTES BY
Vladimir Tukmakov

Game 4   Nimzo-Indian Defence
Vladimir Tukmakov
Viktor Kortchnoi
Riga ch-USSR 1970 (4)

Notes in inverted commas are from Tukmakov's book *Profession: Grandmaster*.
'The game was played in the fourth round in the USSR Championship; in fact Kortchnoi had a 100% score and I was behind by a half-point. Because the tournament was just beginning, the sporting significance of the games for the leaders should not be overestimated. But a duel with Kortchnoi is always a challenge!'
1.d4 ♘f6 2.c4 e6 3.♘c3 ♗b4 4.e3 0-0 5.♗d3 c5 6.♘f3 d5 7.0-0 dxc4 8.♗xc4 ♘bd7 9.♕b3
9.♕e2 is the main move nowadays.
9...a6 10.a4 ♕e7

'While preparing, I concentrated on the game Portisch-Kortchnoi (Belgrade 1970) in which there was 10...♗a5 11.♖d1 cxd4 12.exd4 ♕b6 13.♕c2 ♕c7 14.♗d3 h6 15.♗d2 ♗b4 16.♕b3. White's position suited me. Kortchnoi probably wasn't happy about anything in that game.'
10...b6 11.d5 ♗xc3 12.dxe6 ♗a5 13.exd7 ♕xd7 14.♖d1 ♕c7 15.♗d2 is a common line now.

11.♖d1 ♗a5

11...♖d8 12.♗d3 ♗a5 13.♗d2 h6 14.♖ac1±.

12.♕c2 cxd4

'Kortchnoi continues with the same line he played in the game with Portisch; however worth considering was 12...h6 or 12...♘b6.'

13.exd4 ♘b6

14.♗a2!

It seems that Viktor Lvovich underestimated the variation with the direct attack on the black king. After 14.♗d3 h6 Black wouldn't have experienced any special problems.

14...h6 15.♘e5 ♗d7 16.♗b1 ♖fd8?

Better was 16...♖ac8 17.♖d3 ♘bd5.

17.♖d3! ♖ac8

17...♗c6.

18.♖g3!?

This had been previously planned. Still, very strong would have been the immediate 18.♗xh6! gxh6 19.♕d2 (19.♖g3+ ♔f8 20.♕c1 ♔e8 21.♕xh6 ♗c6 22.♖g7+−) 19...♔f8 (19...♖xc3 20.bxc3 ♘e4 21.♕xh6+−) 20.♕xh6+ ♔e8 21.♖f3 (21.♕h8+ ♕f8 22.♕xf6 ♘d5) 21...♗xc3 22.bxc3 ♘bd5 23.♘g6!+−.

18...♔f8

18...♔h8 19.♗xh6 (19.♕g6!+−) 19...gxh6 20.♕d2 ♘g8 21.♕d3 ♘f6 22.♖g6!+−.

19.♕d2!?

19.♗xh6! gxh6 20.♕c1! (20.♘g6+!? fxg6 21.♕xg6 ♕f7 22.♕xh6+ ♔e7 23.♖g7 ♖g8 24.♖xf7+ ♔xf7 25.♘e4 ♘xe4 26.♗xe4+−) 20...♕b4 21.♕xh6+ ♔e7 22.♖f3 ♘bd5 23.♘xd5+ ♘xd5 24.♖xf7+ ♔d6. During the game, Tukmakov rejected this line because he could not see a decisive continuation here, but after 25.♗f5! ♔c7 26.♘xd7 ♖xd7 27.♖xd7+ ♔xd7 28.♕xe6+ White wins.

19...♘bd5

19...♘c4 20.♘xc4 ♖xc4 21.♖xg7 ♔xg7 22.♕xh6+ ♔g8 23.♗g5 ♕f8 24.♕h4.

20.♗g6?

Preparing the queen sacrifice, but missing the reply 20...♗c7! (see following note). Stronger was 20.♖xg7! ♔xg7 21.♕xh6+ ♔g8 22.♗g5! (22.♘xd5! ♖xc1+ 23.♕xc1 ♘xd5 24.♖a3+−) 22...♗xc3 23.bxc3 ♖xc3 24.h3!+− ♖b3 25.♗h7+ ♘xh7 26.♗xe7 ♘xe7 27.♕h4 f6 28.♕g4+.

20...♗e8?

20...♗c7! 21.♗xf7 ♗xe5 22.dxe5 ♗c6 23.♘xd5 ♖xd5 24.exf6 ♕xf6 25.♕e1 ♔xf7 26.♗d2±.

21.♕xh6! ♕b4

21...gxh6 22.♗xh6+ ♔g8 23.♗e4+ ♔h8 24.♗g7+ ♔g8 25.♗xf6+ ♔f8 26.♘xd5 exd5 27.♗xe7+ ♔xe7 28.♗f5+−; 21...fxg6 22.♕h8+ ♘g8 23.♗g5 ♘df6 24.♘e4+−; 21...♘xc3 22.♕h8+ ♘g8 23.bxc3 ♖xc3 24.♗h7+−.

22.♕h8+ ♔e7

23.♕xg7?!

Not the strongest.

23.♗g5! ♕xd4 24.♘xf7+−; 23.♗xf7 ♕xd4 24.♗xe8 ♖xe8 25.♕xg7+.

23...♕xd4

23...♘xc3 24.bxc3 ♖xd4 25.♗g5!.

24.♘d3

24.♘f3!.

24...♗xc3?!

24...♘xc3 25.bxc3 ♗xc3 26.♖b1±.

25.bxc3 ♘xc3 26.♗a3+ ♔d7 27.♖e1 ♔c7

27...♖c7 may have been a better practical chance, but Black is losing anyway.

28.♗e7 ♘cd5 29.♗xd8+ ♔xd8 30.♗e4 ♕xa4 31.♗xd5 ♘xd5 32.♕g5+ ♔c7 33.h4+− ♗b5 34.♖c1+ ♔c6 35.h5 ♕d4 36.♘e5 f6 37.♘xc6 bxc6 38.♕g7+ ♔d6 39.h6 ♘f4 40.♕g4 ♕d2 41.♖d1 1-0

Game 5   Slav Defence
Viktor Kortchnoi   2630
Vladimir Tukmakov   2580
Reggio Emilia 1987/88 (1)

**1.♘f3 d5 2.c4 c6 3.e3 ♘f6 4.♘c3 e6
5.d4 ♘bd7 6.♕c2 ♗d6 7.♗e2 0-0
8.0-0 dxc4 9.♗xc4 b5 10.♗b3**
Effectively this was a novelty at the
time.
  A) 10.♗e2 ♗b7 11.a3 a6 12.♖d1 c5;
  B) 10.♗d3 ♗b7 11.e4 e5 12.dxe5
♘xe5 13.♘xe5 ♗xe5 14.h3 ♖e8
15.♗e3 ♕e7 16.♖ae1 a6 17.♘e2 c5!
18.♗xc5 ♕c7 19.♗d4.
10...♗b7 11.e4
11.♖d1.

11...c5! 12.♘xb5?!
Played quickly, but probably a
mistake.
  A) 12.c5 ♗xf3 (12...c4 13.exd6
cxb3 14.♕xb3 ♗xf3 15.gxf3 ♕b6)
13.exd6 (13.♘xb5) 13...cxd4 (13...c4
14.gxf3 ♕b6 15.♗e3 cxb3 16.♕xb3
a6) 14.♘xb5 ♗e4;
  B) 12.dxc5 ♗xc5 13.e5 ♘g4 14.♗g5
g6 15.♘xe6 (15.♘ce4) 15...♕h4
16.♗f4 fxe6 17.♗xe6+ ♔h8 18.♗g3
♕h5 19.♘e4! (19.♗xd7 ♖xf2)
19...♗xe4 20.♕xe4 ♘gxe5 21.♖ad1
♖ae8 22.♕d5 ♗xf2+ 23.♗xf2

♖xf2 24.♖xf2 ♖xe6 25.♖ff1 with a
balanced position.
12...♗xe4 13.♕e2
13.♕c3 ♗e7 (13...cxd4!? 14.♕xd4
♗c5) 14.dxc5 ♘xc5∓;
13.♕d1 ♗e7∓.
13...♗xf3!

14.gxf3
Forced because of 14.♕xf3 ♗xh2+
15.♔xh2 ♕b8+ 16.♕g3 ♕xb5 and
Black is slightly better.
14...♗b8! 15.f4!?
15.dxc5 ♘xc5 16.♖d1 ♘d5!∓.
15...a6!
This is stronger than 15...♕b6
16.dxc5 ♘xc5 17.♗c4.
16.♕f3 ♗xf4!?
16...axb5!? 17.♕xa8 c4 18.♗c2 ♘d5
with good compensation for Black.
17.♗xf4 axb5 18.♗d6 cxd4!?
18...c4!? 19.♗xf8 ♘xf8 (19...cxb3?
20.♗e7!) 20.♗c2 b4∓.
19.♗xf8 ♕xf8
19...♘xf8!?.
20.♖ac1 ♖d8! 21.♖c7?!
  A) 21.♖fd1 ♘c5 (21...♘e5 22.♕g3
♘g6) 22.♕c6 ♘xb3 23.axb3 e5
24.♕xb5 ♕e7∓;
  B) 21.♕c6 b4 (21...♘e5!? 22.♕xb5
♘f3+ 23.♔g2 ♘h4+ 24.♔h1 ♕d6)
22.♖fd1 e5.

21...♘c5
The computer's 21...♘e5 22.♕f4 ♘d3
23.♕g3 (23.♕d2 ♕d6) 23...♘xb2
24.♖b1 ♘a4∓ was even stronger.
22.♖c1
22.♖d1 h6.
22...♘fe4! 23.♖e1
23.♕f4 was more tenacious: 23...d3
(23...h6) 24.♗d1! (24.f3 d2 25.♖d1
♘f2) 24...d2 25.♖c2 f5 26.♕h4 and
the situation is unclear.
23...♘d2
23...♘g5!? 24.♕c6 ♘d3 25.♖e2 h6∓.
24.♕c6 ♘d3
24...♘cxb3!? 25.axb3 h6.

25.♖d1?
Missing a great practical chance:
25.♖xf7! ♕xf7 26.♗xe6 ♘xe1
27.♗xf7+ ♔xf7 28.♕c7+ ♔e8
29.♕xg7 and the exposed black king
gives White chances.
25...♘e5 26.♕c5 ♘df3+
Six consecutive knight moves!
27.♔g2 d3 28.h3
28.♕xf8+ ♔xf8 29.♖c5 ♖d4!
30.♖xb5 ♘g4+ 31.♔h1 ♖h4 32.♔g2
♖xh2+ 33.♔f1 ♘g4-+.
28...g5! 29.♕xf8+ ♔xf8 30.♖b7
30.a3 ♖d4 (30...♘d4 31.♗a2) 31.♖c5
g4.
30...♘d4 31.♖c1?
31.a3 ♘g6! (31...♘xb3 32.♖xb5)
32.♗a2 ♘f4+ 33.♔h2 h5-+.

31...♘xb3 32.axb3 d2
White resigned.
If 33.♖d1 ♘d3.

Alexander Beliavsky

Alexander Beliavsky (born 1953 in Lviv) not only won the World Junior Chess Championship in 1973, he was victorious in the USSR Chess Championship no fewer than four times (in 1974, 1980, 1987 and 1990).

Beliavsky won four gold team medals with the USSR: 1982, 1984 (top board), 1988 and 1990. Later he also played for Ukraine in 1992 and since 1996 ten times for Slovenia where he is currently living.

In 1983 he made it to the Candidates matches, losing to the eventual winner Garry Kasparov in the quarterfinals.

For decades, Alexander the Great was one of the most active and successful tournament players, winning numerous tournaments. In November 2009, he was the oldest person among the world's top 100 active players, and in 2013 he tied for 1st-8th places in the European Individual Chess Championship in Legnica, thus qualifying for the FIDE World Cup 2014.

Beliavsky shares the record with Paul Keres and Viktor Kortchnoi for having defeated the most undisputed World Champions. He has defeated nine – every undisputed World Champion since Vasily Smyslov except Bobby Fischer. He also wrote several books in collaboration with Adrian Mikhalchishin. His autobiography, published in 1998, is called *Uncompromising Chess*.

NOTES BY
Alexander Beliavsky

Game 6   Queen's Gambit Declined
Boris Gelfand   2700
Alexander Beliavsky   2640
Linares 1991 (7)

1.♘f3 d5 2.d4 ♘f6 3.c4 e6 4.♘c3 ♗e7 5.♗f4 0-0 6.e3 c5 7.dxc5 ♗xc5 8.♕c2
At Belgrade 1993, Vladimir Kramnik played 8.a3 ♘c6 9.♖c1 against me, but after 9...d4 10.♘xd4 e5! (10...♘xd4 11.b4!?) 11.♘b3 ♗xa3 12.bxa3 exf4 13.♕xd8 ♖xd8 14.exf4 ♗e6 Black gained good compensation for the pawn.
8...♘c6 9.a3 ♕a5
Since the variation where White castles queenside is considered dangerous for Black, 9...♗e7 comes into consideration, when after 10.0-0-0 (10.♗d3 dxc4 11.♗xc4 a6 12.0-0 b5 13.♖fd1 ♕b6 14.♗d3 ♗b7 15.♘e4 ♘xe4 16.♗xe4 f5 17.♗d3

♖ac8 18.♕e2 ♗f6 with mutual
chances, Radjabov-Beliavsky,
Moscow 2002) he gains an important tempo to launch a counter-
attack on the c-file by 10...♗d7,
since if 11.cxd5? ♘xd5 12.♘xd5
exd5 13.♖xd5 ♖c8 with a clear
advantage.

analysis diagram

Here Boris offered a draw, which I
accepted. However, this game was
'continued' at the 1996 Olympiad.
Vladimir Akopian did not offer a
draw, and I decided to prevent the
threatened check at f6 by 20...f5,
after which I was considerably
surprised by the reply 21.♘f6+!.
It turned out this move had been
analysed in one of the issues of *New
In Chess*, which I had not seen. The
game continued 21...♖xf6 22.♕c7
♕h6 23.♖d8+ ♖f8 24.♖xf8+ ♔xf8
25.♖d1 ♗d7 26.♖xd7 b5 27.♔b1 ♖e8,
and when Akopian failed to find the
best continuation 28.♕d6+ (28.♖f7+
♔g8 29.♕d7 ♖d8! (29...♖f8 30.♖e7)
30.♖xg7+ ♕xg7 31.♕xd8+ ♔f7=)
28...♔g8 29.♖a7± and played instead
28.♕e5? ♖e7, I managed to escape
from the vice.

10.0-0-0
This variation was devised by
grandmasters Mikhail Gurevich
and Grigory Kaidanov.

10...♗d7
In later games of mine there were
some amusing developments in
the alternative variation 10...♗e7
11.g4. The following year in Linares
I played against Gelfand 11...dxc4
12.♗xc4 a6?! (more vigorous is 12...
e5, as played in Van Wely-Short,
Wijk aan Zee 1997: 13.g5 exf4
14.gxf6 ♗xf6 15.♘d5 ♘e7 16.♘xf6+
gxf6 17.♖hg1+ ♔h8 18.e4 b5 19.♗d5
♘xd5 20.exd5 b4 21.axb4 ♕a1+
22.♔d2 ♕a6 23.♕c6 ♖d8 24.♔c3!?
♗b7 25.♕xa6 ♗xa6, and Black
maintained the balance) 13.g5 ♘h5
14.♗d6 ♗xd6 15.♖xd6 ♘e5 16.♗e2
♘xf3 17.♗xf3 ♕xg5 18.♘e4 ♕f5
19.♗xh5 ♕xh5 20.♖g1.

The best defence against the
check at f6 is probably 20...♔h8 or
20...♕h6, but of course this does
not solve all Black's problems.

11.g4
This may not have been the best
move.
11.♔b1!?, as played against me
by Chernin in a rapid game

(Aubervilliers 1996), not only moves the king to a safer square, but also threatens the d5-pawn. It is not possible to win it immediately: 11.cxd5 ♘xd5 12.♘xd5 exd5 13.♖xd5? ♗xe3+.

11...♖fc8 12.♔b1

12...b5!?

12...♗f8 13.g5 ♘h5 14.♗g3 ♘e7 15.♘e5 ♗e8 16.♗e2 and White had the initiative in Gelfand-Beliavsky, Linares 1990.

13.cxb5

A) After 13.♘xb5 a6 White is drawn into forcing play, where Black's attack develops of its own accord:

A1) 14.♘bd4 ♘xd4 15.♘xd4 (15. cxd4 ♗xa3 16.bxa3 ♕xa3) 15...♗a4 16.♕d2 ♕b6 17.♖c1 ♘e4 with dangerous threats;

A2) 14.♗c7 ♖xc7 15.♘xc7 ♖b8! 16.cxd5 ♗xa3;

A3) 14.♘c3 ♗xa3! 15.bxa3 ♕xa3 16.♕b2 ♖ab8 17.♗xb8 ♖xb8 18.♘b5 ♕a5 and Black regains his piece with a continuing attack.

B) White also cannot be satisfied with 13.cxd5 ♗xa3!, when he comes under a fierce attack after both 14.dxc6 ♗xc6 and 14.♗xb5 ♘b4.

If 13...b4 14.dxc6 ♗xc6 15.♘e5! (15.axb4 ♗xb4 16.♗e2 ♗xc3 17.bxc3 ♗e4 18.♖d3 ♖ab8+−+) 15...♗xh1 16.♘c4 ♕a6 17.♘d6 ♕c6 (17...♕a5 18.♘c4 ♕a6=) 18.♗b5 ♕f3 19.♘xc8 ♖xc8 20.♗a6 ♖e8 21.g5 bxc3 22.gxf6 is unclear;

C) The inclusion of 13.g5 ♘h5 and now 14.cxb5 runs into 14...♘xf4! (not 14...♘e7? 15.♗e5 a6 16.b4 ♕xa3 17.bxc5 axb5 18.♕b2, when White parries the threats, retaining his extra piece) 15.exf4 (both 15.bxc6 ♗xc6 16.exf4 d4 17.♘e4 ♗a4 and 15.♕a4 d4! also favour Black) 15...♘e7 16.♘e5 ♗e8, when Black gains the advantage.

13...♘e7 14.♘d2

White threatens a fork, but 14.♖c1!? and 14.♕a4!? were also interesting

14...♕d8!

Against the threat of 14...♗xa3 there follows 15.♘b3 ♕b4 16.♖d4.

15.♘b3

15.♗e2 was simpler, completing his development.

15...♘e4!?

Attacking the c3-knight which is covering the queen.

White was hoping after 15...♗b6 to develop his bishops more actively by 16.♗d3 ♘g6 17.♗g5. However, disillusionment awaits him.

16.♘xc5

Now if 16.♘xe4 there follows 16...♗xe3 17.♕xc8 (17.♘ec5 ♗xf4∓) 17...♖xc8 18.♗xe3 dxe4 with advantage to Black, while if 16.♗e5 Black diverts the bishop with 16...♗d6! 17.♗xd6 ♘xd6, gaining the advantage.

16...♖xc5 17.♗e5 ♘xc3+

The simplest.

If 17...♘g6 18.♗d4 ♘xc3+ 19.♗xc3! (19.bxc3 ♖xb5+ 20.♗xb5 ♗xb5 with compensation) 19...♗xb5 20.♗xb5 ♖xb5 21.h4 and White stands better.

18.♗xc3 ♗xb5 19.♗xb5

Of course, not 19.b4 ♗a4!.

19...♖xb5 20.h4

The situation appears to have clarified, but apparent simplicity is deceptive. White's king is less securely covered, and he has to reckon with the possible manoevre of the knight to c4, from where it attacks the a3- and b2-pawns. White hopes by the advance of his h-pawn to lengthen the a1-h8 diagonal for his bishop, but even so I was more afraid of 20.f4!? with the idea of f4-f5.

20...♖c8?!

Too slow. After 20...♘c8! the knight could have gone via b6 or d6 to c4 with dangerous threats: 21.h5 ♘d6 22.h6 ♘c4 23.♔a1 (23.♕xh7+ does not work: 23...♔xh7 24.hxg7+ ♔g6 25.♖h8 ♘xb2 26.♗xb2 ♖xb2+ 27.♔xb2 ♕f6+) 23...g6 24.♕d3 ♖ab8 25.f4 ♕b6.

Things are even worse for White after 21.♕a4 ♘d6 22.♕d4 f6 23.g5 e5 24.♕g4 f5 25.♕g3 ♘c4 26.♗xe5 ♕b6.

21.h5 ♕d6 22.♕a4

While defending the a3-pawn, White removes a defender from the b2-pawn.

A) Gelfand did not like 22.h6 ♕xa3 23.hxg7 ♘g6 24.♖d3 ♕a6! with the threat of 25...♖a5, when Black's attack gets there first: 25.♕e2 (or 25.♕d1 e5 26.g5 d4! 27.♕h5 ♘h4! 28.♖xh4 ♖xb2+ 29.♔xb2 ♕xd3) 25...♖b3 26.♖c1 d4!;

B) The simplest was 22.♔a1!?, with less predictable consequences.

22...♕b8! 23.♗e5 ♕b7 24.g5?

The immediate 24.♖c1 was better, although after 24...♘c6 25.h6 (25.♔a1!±) 25...d4! 26.♗xd4 ♖b8 Black's initiative is very dangerous.

24...♘c6 25.♖c1

25...d4! 26.♗xd4 ♖b8 27.♗c3 ♖xb2+ 28.♔a1 ♖b6 29.g6

After 29.♕c2 ♕a6 30.♔a2 Black wins by 30...♖b4 31.g6 hxg6 32.hxg6 (or 32.h6 ♖a4 33.h7+ ♔h8 34.♗xg7+

♔xg7) 32...♖a4 33.gxf7+ ♔xf7 34.♕g6+ ♔xg6 35.♖cg1+ ♔f5.
29...♖a6 30.gxf7+ ♔xf7 31.♕f4+ ♔g8 32.♕d6

32...♘d4!
White resigned.

CHAPTER II

Oleg Romanishin's secret training matches with Mikhail Tal

In 1976, Mikhail Tal approached a rising star from Lviv and invited him to play a training match, attracted as he was by the young man's 'tasty chess'. **Oleg Romanishin** writes about this and a second training match with 'the Magician from Riga', reliving a dear memory from which he emerged with a positive score.

Oleg Romanishin crossed swords with eight World Champions. The largest number of official games (23) he played against Mikhail Tal.

As a young boy, I grew up surrounded by a love for chess. My father was an electrical engineer by profession, with a passion for the game. He was a first-category player and had participated in the Lviv championships in the 1930s and '40s. His best result, I believe, was third place. He stopped playing competitive chess when his children were born, but he taught all of us the rules. My older siblings quickly lost interest, but I, the youngest, liked the game.

I learned to play at the age of five, and my father started playing handicap matches against me. He began by giving me queen and two rooks, and when I quickly scored my first win, the next handicap was queen, rook and minor piece. And so he continued. Next was queen and rook, then queen and minor piece. Whenever I started winning, he would reduce the odds.

By the time we played our first normal game, I was seven years old. We recorded the score. I lost the first 99 games with equal material, and then, in the 100th game, I made a draw! I think he did this on purpose. He wanted to teach me to lose. He wanted me to be ready to lose a game. Of course, this approach also contained a risk. You must overcome your losses, but you mustn't get used to losing – or tire of the game. Still, despite those 99 losses I didn't lose interest and continued to be ready to fight. Most children would have lost interest, and that would be it, but I still wanted to win. Some 40 years ago, when I was a grandmaster, a Polish journalist asked me what had been my first success. I said, when I scored this first draw against my father. And that was true.

Glued to the radio

We had a lot of chess books at home, and I devoured them. Everybody in our family knew how to play, and we all followed the important tournaments on the radio and in the newspapers. My father made cross-

Lviv legend Leonid Stein instructs budding talents. Opposite Stein sits a very young Alexander Beliavsky, next to him (seen on the back) Oleg Romanishin.

tables of the Interzonals and the Candidates tournaments. We looked at the games of the World Championship matches between Botvinnik and Smyslov in 1957, and Botvinnik and Tal in 1961, as they were published in the newspapers. Starting with the title match between Botvinnik and Petrosian in 1963, it was possible to follow the games on the radio. We wrote down the moves as we listened, analysed the positions and tried to guess the next moves. I didn't have a favourite player at the time, but already in 1959, during the Candidates tournament in Yugoslavia, while the other members of my family were rooting for Keres, I was rooting for Tal. I wanted Tal to win – which he did, ahead of Keres – but I don't recall why.

Autographs

In 1962, the annual traditional friendly match between the USSR and Yugoslavia was held in Lviv. Every day I went there to collect autographs from Gligoric, Ivkov, Matanovic, Taimanov and Stein, who was from Lviv. Of course, I didn't dare to speak to them, because I was too shy, and unfortunately I no longer have those autographs. But already then, at the age of 10, I knew the names of all the famous chess players. And like every child I had dreams. I dreamed that one day I would participate in such tournaments and cross swords with these great players.

Later, these childhood dreams started coming true. In 1971, I was lucky to play in a tournament (a round-robin!) in Gothenburg with Spassky, Hort, Szabo and Pomar. In the space of just a couple of years, such tournaments became normal, and I was fortunate to play many games against almost all the great grandmasters of the previous generation: Petrosian, Smyslov, Bronstein, Kortchnoi, Geller, Gligoric, Larsen, Portisch, and many more. Unfortunately, I 'missed' Keres by one year. His last USSR championship was in 1973, while I made my debut in 1974.

All in all, I played eight World Champions from different generations. From Smyslov to Kramnik and Anand (I am only considering the winners of title matches), a total of 73 games with a total score of +16 -20 =37. But the largest number of games, 23 in official competitions, I played against Mikhail Tal.

Getting to know Tal

The first time I saw Tal in the flesh was in Riga in 1968, during the Soviet Cup, when I played on one of the junior boards for my club Avantgarde, while he played for Daugava, his club from Riga. Six years later, in 1974, I played my first game against him in my first Soviet Championship in Leningrad. Tal won that championship together with Beliavsky. With two rounds to go, Tal was one point ahead of Beliavsky, who he would play against as White in the penultimate round. But he was afraid of Vaganian, who was playing against me with Black and who was the runner-up at that point. Tal was afraid I could lose to Vaganian and paid more attention to our game than to his own, and didn't know what to go for. Everybody knows that this is a big mistake. You have to play your own game and not take other games into account – which is easier said than done, of course. By the time he realized that I was winning against Vaganian, he was already in trouble against Beliavsky and lost. They ended up sharing first and second place, while I won my last three games to share 5th place.

Tal and I got to know each other better in 1975, when we were both sent to a festival of the Communist newspaper of Germany [West-Germany at

Tal and Romanishin at the start of their first-round game in the 1975 Soviet Championship in Yerevan.

the time – ed.], *Unsere Zeit* (Our Time), in Düsseldorf. This was how it went in those years. We were obliged to go there, give a simul and talk to the people, and we did not receive any payment for this, except expenses and some pocket money.

Our reception at the airport of Frankfurt was slightly comical. They met us, embraced us and then asked us who we were. I told them that we were chess players and that Tal was a former World Champion. They said OK, and a few minutes later they started calling him Spassky! Because Spassky was the chess player they mostly read about.

When they took us to our hotel, Tal shocked them by telling them that he wanted to buy a lot of things for his little daughter, who was one year old. This was another funny episode. Tal never talked about the price, but just entered a shop and pointed at what he wanted to buy: this, this and this. He didn't care about the price; he just wanted to buy it. And the Germans couldn't understand this.

Then, in the evening, Tal wanted to go to a chess club. He always wanted to do something with chess, wherever he was. The organizers were not very eager and said it was complicated and impossible. So in the hotel Tal asked for the telephone book, found a chess club and just called them. Of course they were happy to have Tal, and they organized a blitz tournament for us that evening. I don't remember, but I suppose Tal won. He was a fantastic blitz player.

First training match

We are slowly getting close to what I wanted to write about: the two 'secret' training matches that I played against Tal – matches that you won't find in the databases. Tal invited me to play the first training match at the end of the 1975 Soviet Championship in Yerevan, after the closing dinner. In that championship, we had played an interesting game in the first round that ended in a draw. Tal told me later that he had been impressed by my decision in the following position:

Game 7
Romanishin-Tal

Yerevan ch-USSR 1975

position after 20...♞xb7

Here I played 21.♕g4!?, offering a queen swap (which was accepted), despite the fact that I was an exchange down.

In that same championship, I had also introduced two home-prepared strong novelties; moves that won me two games and that have stood the test of time till this day: a pawn sacrifice in the Ruy Lopez against Geller and the following manoeuvre against Petrosian:

Game 8
Romanishin-Petrosian

Yerevan ch-USSR 1975

position after 5.♗d3!?

Petrosian won the championship, and this was the only game he lost. Tal and I were amongst four players who shared second place half a point adrift. Attracted by my play, Tal invited me to a training camp that he planned to have in Jurmala in the summer of 1976, where he wanted to prepare for the upcoming Interzonal in Biel. As Genna Sosonko confided to me many years later, Tal had told him that 'Romanishin plays tasty chess'. Maybe that was why he found it difficult to play against me. This is quite common when you appreciate someone's play.

Jurmala is a seaside resort on the Baltic Sea, and we were staying close to the beach at a resort of the Ministry of Health. We had all our meals at the hotel, but it was a kind of sanatorium, and very dull, so we didn't want to be lodged there and stayed in a different building. We could eat there because the president of the Latvian chess federation was the Minister of Health of Latvia. He had arranged this for Tal. As usual, Tal had his family with him; he liked to travel with his family. He was with his wife, his third one, Gela (Angelina), and their daughter Zhanna. They had a suite where we played our match. We talked a lot during our meals, which I found interesting, because he was a very educated person. We spoke about life, but also about openings, some positions, how to prepare... during our conversations we didn't speak much about politics. Tal was not a Communist, nor was he like Spassky, who maybe talked too much. But I learned many political jokes from Tal. Political jokes were normal in the Soviet Union in the '70s and '80s. In the '50s or '40s they could have got you into prison or before the firing squad, but in the '70s and '80s, intellectuals had stopped believing in any of these Communist ideas. Of course no one could expect that the Soviet Union would collapse so soon, but everyone understood what was going on and that it was propaganda. So we spoke like normal people and we trusted each other.

A lot of improvisation

As it turned out, our training match consisted of five games. Somehow we didn't manage to play more. The games were played in the afternoon. Before lunch we were busy with other things. In the evening, we would analyse the game together, including the adjourned positions, if there were any. The time-control was the usual one at that time, 2.5 hours for 40 moves.

Please don't criticize the level of the games, particularly in the opening, too harshly. They were played in the 'pre-computer' era. There was a lot of improvisation on both sides. If there was any preparation, it was mostly 'in the mind'.

The first two games ended in wins for me. In the first game, I won

material with a tactical trick, but Tal missed chances to fight for a draw. The second game was my best effort.

Game 9 English Opening
Oleg Romanishin
Mikhail Tal
Jurmala 1976 (secret match, 2)

1.c4 e5 2.♘c3 ♘f6 3.♘f3 ♘c6 4.g3 ♗c5

This system hadn't been played very often; only in a few games up to that time. Tal's great opening erudition and wide chess knowledge allowed him to play various rare lines, often things he

A cartoon showing that Romanishin and Tal shared first place in Leningrad 1977.

40

had seen played by someone else somewhere... and he didn't use these ideas in training games only... of the current grandmasters with a similar approach, I would mention Vasyl Ivanchuk, with the main difference that Ivanchuk prefers to prepare first.

5.♗g2 0-0 6.0-0 d6 7.d3

I wasn't sure whether I wanted to push the pawn to d4 at all.

7...h6 8.e3

8...a6

Also possible is 8...♗g4!? 9.h3 ♗h5, or 8...♖e8!?. And 8...a5 is playable too, even though it slightly weakens the queenside.

9.a3 ♗a7 10.b4

10...♗g4

10...♗e6 11.♘d2, with the idea of ♘d5, was Kortchnoi's recommendation here.

Lajos Portisch played another plan after 10...♗c6, preventing the bishop on g2 from being exchanged and opening the b-file by pushing the a-pawn: 11.♖e1 ♕d7 12.♖b1 ♖ad8 13.♕c2 ♘e7 14.a4. Maybe it isn't necessary to put the bishop on b2 if you don't intend to push d3-d4 or if Black doesn't play ...d6-d5. From d2, the bishop would defend the e3-pawn against a counter-attack. I would prefer 10...♗f5, saving a tempo (compared to the game) and preventing ♘d2.

11.h3

Miton-David, Greece tt 2014, saw 11.♕c2 ♕d7 12.♗b2 ♗h3.

11...♗e6

The alternative was 11...♗h5.

12.e4!?

An unexpected decision. White switches to active play on the king-side after having smothered Black's activities in the centre. The black bishop on a7 shouldn't cause White any problems. Also possible was the traditional 12.♗b2!?, when 12...e4 13.♘xe4 ♘xe4 14.dxe4 ♗xc4 15.♖e1 would be clearly in White's favour.

12...♘d4 13.♗e3 ♕d7

Another idea was 13...c6.

14.♗xd4

14.♔h2? would be a mistake: 14...♘xf3+ 15.♕xf3 ♘g4+! 16.hxg4 ♗xg4 17.♗h3, and this saves the queen, but ends up losing a pawn after 17...♗xh3.

14...exd4

It would probably have been better to refuse the pawn offer and exchange the 'bad' bishop with 14...♗xd4 15.♘xd4 exd4 16.♘e2 ♗xh3 17.♘xd4, although White gets some space advantage, of course.

15.♘e2 ♗xh3 16.♗xh3

There was no reason to recapture the d4-pawn and activate the a7-bishop. White now gets a piece majority for an attack on the kingside and the open h-file.

16...♕xh3 17.♘f4 ♕d7 18.♔g2 b5

Trying to get counterplay, but creating additional weaknesses.

19.cxb5 axb5 20.♖h1

20...♖fe8?

It was better to bring a second rook to the defence of the kingside with 20...♖ae8. The rook on a8 is doing nothing there.

21.♘h5 ♘g4?

Missing a tactic. Better was 21...♖e6. Black is lost now.

Oleg Romanishin and Mikhail Tal answer questions from members of the Jurmala Chess Club. Next to Tal sit a Latvian official and former draughts World Champion Iser Kuperman.

22.♘h4 ♖e5 23.♘xg7

23...♖g5
Since 23...♔xg7 runs into 24.♘f5+
♖xf5 25.♕xg4+, and White wins.
**24.♘gf5 ♔f8 25.♕d2 ♕e6 26.♕f4
♕f6 27.♘f3 ♖g6 28.a4**

Exploiting the poor position of rook
a8. White also gets a passed pawn.
**28...♗b6 29.a5 ♗a7 30.♖ac1 c5
31.bxc5 ♗xc5**
31...dxc5 is also met by 32.♖h4.
**32.♖h4 ♘e5 33.♘xe5 dxe5 34.♕d2
♗e7 35.♖c7 ♗d8 36.♕b4+ ♔g8
37.♖d7 ♕e6 38.♖d6**

**38...♕xd6 39.♘xd6 ♗xh4 40.♕c5
b4 41.♘xf7 1-0**

In the third game, we repeated the
opening of the first game, a sub-line
of the French Defence. I deviated
with a daring pawn push on move
5, which led to more interesting
play. That game ended in a draw,
but I should have lost.

Game 10   French Defence
Mikhail Tal
Oleg Romanishin
Jurmala 1976 (secret match, 3)

———————————————————

**1.e4 e6 2.d4 d5 3.♘c3 ♗e7 4.e5 c5
5.♕g4 g5!?**
An adventurous move and more
interesting than 5...g6, which I
had played in the first game. Some
people prefer 5...♔f8 here

6.♕h5
I have found only one other game in
which 5...g5 was played; it continued
6.dxc5!? h5 7.♕d1 ♘c6 8.♘f3 g4
9.♘d4 ♘xe5 10.♘db5 a6 11.♘d6+
♗xd6 12.cxd6 ♕xd6 13.♗e3 ♗d7
14.♕d2 0-0-0 15.0-0-0 f6, and Black
was a pawn up in Young-Driessens,
European Clubs 2013.

6...cxd4 7.♘b5

7...a6?

Better was 7...♘c6 8.♘f3 first, and only then 8...a6 9.♘bxd4 (or 9.♘xg5!? ♘xe5 10.♘xe6 ♗xe6 11.♕xe5 ♗f6 12.♘c7+ ♔d7 13.♘xe6 fxe6, with a complicated position) 9...♘xd4 10.♘xd4, but after 10...♕c7 11.f4 ♗b4+ 12.♔d1 gxf4 13.♗xf4 White is better anyway.

8.♘xd4 ♕b6 9.♘gf3 ♘d7 10.♗d3 h6

Now Black would be OK after 11.0-0? ♘gf6!. But:

11.♗g6!

A very unpleasant surprise. Taking loses the queen, and the pawn on f7 cannot be defended.

11...♔d8 12.♗xf7 ♘xe5 13.♗xg8 ♘xf3+ 14.♘xf3 ♕b4+ 15.♗d2 ♕e4+ 16.♔d1 ♖xg8 17.♗a5+ ♔d7 18.♖e1

Tal flashed out all these moves.

18...♕a4 19.♕f7 ♔d6 20.♕xg8 ♕xa5 21.♘d4 ♕d8 22.♕f7 ♕f8

As long as White has his rook on a1, Black still has some chances.

23.♖xe6+ ♗xe6 24.♕xe6+ ♔c7 25.♔e2!

Finally. White is two pawns up, and now all he needs to do is deploy his rook.

25...♗c5 26.♕xd5 ♔b6 27.c3 ♖d8 28.♕c4 ♕d6 29.♘b3 ♖c8 30.h3 ♕e5+ 31.♔f1 ♕h2

32.♖d1?

Missing a winning continuation:
32.♘xc5! ♖xc5 33.♕b4+ ♖b5 (or
33...♔c6 34.♕e4+ ♔b6 35.♖d1 ♖e5
36.♕d4+, and wins) 34.♕d4+ ♔c7
35.♖d1, and Black is lost. Now Black
saves the game:

**32...♕h1+ 33.♔e2 ♖e8+ 34.♔d2
♖d8+ 35.♘d4 ♕xg2 36.♔c2 ♗xd4
37.cxd4 ♕xf2+**

The pawns are equal again.
**38.♔b3 ♕f3+ 39.♖d3 ♕d5 40.♖e3
♕b5+ 41.♕xb5+ ♔xb5**
Draw.

The fourth game was adjourned
after 42 moves. Tal, playing as
Black, was about to lose a pawn
and had to fight for a draw. But we
didn't find time to resume play.
The fifth game was the last one we
played and this time, Tal won.

Game 11   French Defence
**Mikhail Tal
Oleg Romanishin**
Jurmala 1976 (secret match, 5)

1.e4 e6 2.d4 d5 3.♘c3 ♗e7 4.♗d3
After 4.♘f3 ♘f6 5.♗d3 Black
continues with 5...c5 or 5...dxe4.

4...♘c6 5.♘f3 ♗b4 6.♗e2
White achieves nothing with 6.0-0
♘xd3, but could try to include
6.♗b5+ c6 7.♗e2.
**6...dxe4 7.♘xe4 ♘f6 8.♘xf6+ ♗xf6
9.c3 ♘d5 10.0-0 0-0 11.♕c2 b6
12.♕e4**

12...♖b8
And not immediately 12...♗b7? in
view of 13.♗d3 g6 14.♗h6 ♖e8 15.c4
♘b4 16.♕xb7 ♘xd3 17.♕e4 ♘b4
18.a3, and White is clearly better.
13.♗d3 g6 14.♗h6 ♗g7

15.♗g5!

White should keep his pieces, use his space advantage and threaten sacrifices on g6 and e6, while attacking the black king.

15...♘e7 16.♖fe1

16.♕h4? would have been a mistake in view of 16...f6 17.♗h6 ♗b7 18.♘d2 ♘f5.

16...h6 17.♗h4 ♗b7

17...f5?! only favours White after 18.♗xe7 ♕xe7 19.♕e3.

18.♕g4

18...♕e8

Maybe Black should have tried 18...g5!?, as the sacrifices on g5 are not that clear.

19.♕h3 c5 20.dxc5 bxc5 21.♘e5 ♘d5 22.♗g3 ♖d8 23.♖ad1

23...♘f6?!

Black should have prevented White from moving his bishop to the c1-h6 diagonal. But that is easier said than done.

24.♗f4 g5 25.♗e3!?

Very clever, first luring the queen to e7.

25...♕e7 26.♗c1

Now White's pieces are ready to launch an attack.

26...♖d5 27.f4 ♖fd8 28.fxg5 hxg5 29.♗xg5 c4 30.♗h7+ ♔f8 31.♖xd5 ♖xd5 32.♕e3 ♕c7 33.♗c2 ♕b6 34.♕xb6 axb6

35.♗xf6?

White should not have fallen for the temptation to grab a second pawn. 35.♗c1, or even 35.h4!?, would have been good enough.

35...♗xf6 36.♘xc4

36...♖g5?

Oleg Romanishin

1952	Born in Lviv, when Ukraine was part of the Soviet Union
1973	European Junior Champion
1974	Board 4 (8 out of 9) of winning Soviet team at World Student Team Championship
1975	Soviet Championship, shared 2nd behind Petrosian
1976	International Grandmaster
1976/77	Hastings, 1st
1977	Leningrad, shared 1st (with Tal)
1978	Olympiad Buenos Aires, 2nd with Soviet team (behind Hungary)
1979	Gausdal, 1st
1979	Tilburg, 2nd (behind Karpov)
1980	Polanica Zdroj, 1st
1983	Jurmala, 1st
1984	Member of Soviet team in USSR-Rest of the World match in London
1985	Moscow, 1st
1986	Reggio Emilia, shared 1st (with Andersson and Ljubojevic)
1990	Hungarian Open, 1st
1993	Peak rating of 2615
1998	Elista Olympiad, 3rd with Ukrainian team
2000	Istanbul Olympiad, 3rd with Ukrainian team
2005	Rome, 1st

A further mistake.
After 36...b5 Black would have had chances of a draw due to his active pieces: 37.♘a5 ♖d2 38.♘xb7 ♖xc2 39.♖b1 ♗e7.
37.♗e4 ♗a6 38.♘xb6 ♗d8 39.♘a4 ♗b5 40.b3 ♖e5 41.♖d1 ♗a5 42.♖d4 f5 43.♗d3 ♗xa4 44.♖xa4 ♗xc3

Here the game should have been adjourned, but Black resigned.

The second training match
At the beginning of November 1976, just four months after our training camp in Jurmala, I received another phone call from Tal. This time he invited me to come to Riga to play a short training match at the chess club there. He wanted to prepare for the upcoming USSR Championship in Moscow with a very strong line-up, which included Karpov [who would win convincingly; Tal finished 7th, Romanishin 9th – ed.]. Anyone who was at the club could come and watch, but as with the first match, the games were not published. And I was the only one who kept scoresheets. Tal was famously careless in such matters, and I don't think he kept his.

In this second match, we played four games. In all of them Tal had a clear advantage, and I had to defend resourcefully. Tal's play was spectacular, but not quite reasonable enough, so he didn't win any of the games. Perhaps he was not really bothered...

In the final game, I managed to escape with a nice trick.

Game 12
Oleg Romanishin
Mikhail Tal
Riga 1976 (match, 4)

position after 37.♖xa8

37...♗xf2
Tal thought this would be an easy win, but he had overlooked a neat detail.

He could have tried 37...♗c5!?, when it's impossible for White to attack the a2-pawn with his bishop. On the other hand, how should Black improve his position after 38.♖a6 ?
38.♔xf2 ♖h1

And Black wins, doesn't he? Well, not after
39.♗d1!.
An amusing riposte, and suddenly White is really defending.
39...♖xd1
And draw agreed.

CHAPTER III

We are Ukrainian

Vasyl Ivanchuk

The Sphinx from Lviv (Vasyl Ivanchuk, (born 1969 in Kopychintsi)) burst into the chess scene by winning the 1986/87 European Junior Championship. Next year he got his Grandmaster title and tied for first (behind Joel Lautier) in the World Junior in Adelaide.

First prize at the New York Open 1988 was only the beginning. Possibly his best result ever was victory in Linares 1991, beating the reigning World Champion Garry Kasparov in the process.

But the list goes on and on: Linares (3x outright), Biel, Wijk aan Zee, Tal Memorial, Gibraltar, the European Championship 2004; the World Blitz 2007; the World Rapid 2016.

On the Olympiad – four team golds, twice for the USSR (1988 and 1990) and twice for Ukraine (2004 + 2010 where he took gold on board 1 as well).

Ivanchuk consistently ranked among the top 10 from July 1988 to October 2002 and was ranked second on three FIDE listings.

He is regarded as a true chess genius by his peers. Along with Keres and Kortchnoi, surely he was the strongest player never to become World Champion, and the greatest Ukrainian chess player ever.

His style is original, unpredictable and all-inclusive, and he is constantly in search for the truth in chess. Chess is his life. 'He lives on Planet Ivanchuk' is a typical expression.

NOTES BY
Vasyl Ivanchuk

Game 13   Sicilian Defence
Vasyl Ivanchuk   2769
Maxime Vachier-Lagrave   2686
Istanbul Olympiad 2012 (9)

1.♘f3 c5
I was ready to play the Anti-Grünfeld too after 1...♘f6 2.c4 g6 3.♘c3 but my opponent chose the Najdorf Variation.

2.e4 d6 3.d4 cxd4 4.♘xd4 ♘f6 5.♘c3 a6 6.♗g5

6...e6

Here, 6...♘bd7!? became extremely popular only after my game against Radjabov during the tournament in Bazna.

6...♘c6 7.♕d2 leads to the Rauzer Attack.

7.f4 ♕c7

A little surprise from Maxime. During my preparation before this game I mainly considered 7...♕b6 or 7...h6 8.♗h4 ♕b6.

8.♗xf6 gxf6

9.♕d2

Other promising lines here are:

  A) 9.f5!?;

  B) 9.♕f3;

  C) Vugar Gashimov played 9.♘b3?! but after 9...h5! Black is totally OK!;

  D) 9.♕h5?! ♕c5! is fine for Black;

  E) 9.♗e2!? ♘c6 10.♘b3! is possible too.

9...b5

This move is very standard for the Najdorf Variation and is quite committal here, because in the structure after ♗xf6 gxf6 Black usually tries to castle queenside. It is obvious that, after ...0-0-0 in future, the black pawn looks like a better defender for its king on b7 than on b5.

9...♗d7 10.0-0-0 ♘c6 11.♔b1 0-0-0 12.♗e2 h5 is a safer possibility for Black according to theory.

10.♗d3 ♗b7 11.0-0

Where to castle? Of course, it is a matter of taste. The advantage of short castling is that White can consider the option of a2-a4 b5-b4 ♘c3-a2 in the future.

After 11.0-0-0 ♘d7 12.♔b1 (12.a3!? is more precise, maybe) 12...b4 13.♘ce2 d5 Black has counterplay.

11...♘c6

  A) 11...♕b6 12.♔h1! ♘d7;

  B) or immediately 11...♘d7! was very logical, of course, e.g. 12.♔h1 (12.♖ae1 ♕b6) 12...b4 13.♘ce2 d5;

  C) 11...b4 12.♘a4 d5 13.♖ae1 dxe4 14.♗xe4 ♗xe4 15.♖xe4 ♘c6 16.♘xe6 fxe6 17.♖xe6+ ♗e7 18.♕d5 ♖c8 19.♖fe1 ♔f8 20.♔h1 looks very dangerous for Black, however, or even 20.♘c5!? ♕b6 21.♔h1 ♕xc5 22.♖xf6+.

12.♘b3

12.♘xc6 was natural and good, but I preferred to keep more pieces on the board.

12...h5

12...0-0-0 13.♔h1 b4 (13...♔b8 14.a4! b4 15.♘b5!? axb5 16.axb5 with a strong attack!) 14.♘a4 d5 15.exd5 ♖xd5 16.♕e3! cannot be recommended for Black but 12...♘e7!? 13.♔h1 d5 was interesting.

13.♔h1! h4 14.h3 ♗e7

14...♘e7?? is too late already, because after 15.♗xb5+! axb5 16.♘xb5 Black doesn't have a check from b6, but 14...0-0-0 15.a4 b4 16.♘b5 axb5 17.axb5 ♘b8 was worth considering. I am not sure that White has a decisive attack there.

15.♖ae1

15...b4?

A highly provocative move in a situation when the standard sacrifice ♘d5 is hanging in the air.

  A) 15...♘a5? 16.♘d5! exd5 17.♘xa5;

  B) 15...0-0-0 16.♘d5! (16.a4 b4 17.♘d5 exd5 18.exd5 ♘e5 19.fxe5 dxe5 20.♗e4 is possible too) 16...exd5 17.exd5, when Black cannot save his extra piece: 17...♘e5! (17...♘b8? 18.♗f5+; 17...♘a7 18.♕e3!) 18.fxe5 dxe5 19.c4 (19.♗e4!?) gives White a dangerous attack without any material concessions;

  C) But in my opinion 15...♔f8! was the best attempt for Black here: 16.a3 (16.♘d1!? with ideas like ♘d1-e3 or c2-c4, is also

reasonable, in the style of Vishy Anand; 16.♘d5 exd5 17.exd5 ♘a7 is possible for White, but of course, Black has much better chances for a successful defence than in the game) 16...b4 (16...♘a5!? is possible too, because 17.♘d5? (17.♘d4 ♘c4 (17...♖c8!?) 18.♗xc4 ♕xc4 leads to a very complicated game) 17...♘xb3! doesn't work with the black king on f8!) 17.axb4 (17.♘d5!? exd5 18.exd5) 17...♘xb4 18.♘b5 axb5 19.♕xb4 d5 20.♕xb5 dxe4 21.♗xe4 ♗xe4 (21...♗a6 22.♕a4 ♖a7 23.♖a1 ♗xf1 24.♕xa7 ♕xf4) 22.♖xe4 ♕xc2 I thought acceptable for Black during the game.

16.♘d5!

Of course!

16...exd5 17.exd5 ♘a7 18.♘d4 ♗xd5

Also after 18...0-0-0 19.♕xb4 ♕c5! 20.♕a4! Black is under a very dangerous attack again (but not 20.♕xc5+ dxc5 21.♘c6 ♗xc6! 22.♖xe7 ♗d7!=).

19.♘f5 ♘c6

19...♗e6? 20.♘xe7! ♔xe7 21.f5 is simple and strong for White. 19...♘c8 20.♗e4 ♗xe4 21.♖xe4 doesn't look like an improvement for Black either.

20.♗e4!

After this important bishop exchange, White has total domination on the board.

20...♗xe4

20...♗e6 21.♘xe7 ♔xe7 22.f5 is hopeless for Black.

21.♖xe4 ♔f8

It's easy to see that Black cannot defend his position after 21...0-0-0 22.♕d5 or 22.♖c4!.

22.♖fe1 ♖e8 23.♕e2 ♖h7 24.♕g4 d5 25.♖4e2

25...♕b6

25...d4 26.g3! ♕b7 27.♖g2! is totally hopeless for Black.

26.g3! ♘d4 27.♘xe7!

27.♖xe7 ♖xe7 28.♘xe7 ♘e6! was less convincing.

27...♘xe2 28.♕g8+ ♔xe7 29.♖xe2+ ♔d6 30.♖xe8

30...hxg3

30...♕f2 31.♕f8+ ♔c6 32.♖c8+ ♔b5 33.a4+! ♔xa4 (33...bxa3 34.♕e8+) 34.♕e8+ ♔a5 35.♕d8+ ♔a4 36.♕d7+ ♔a5 37.♕xd5+ ♔a4 38.♕a2+ ♔b5 39.♖b8+ ♔c5 40.♕a5+ leads to an unavoidable mate.

31.♕f8+ ♔c6 32.♖c8+ ♔d7 33.♕e8+ ♔d6 34.♖d8+ ♔c5 35.♕e3+ ♔c6

35...♔b5 36.♖xd5+.

36.♖d6+

Black resigned.

Ruslan Ponomariov

Ruslan Ponomariov (born 1983 in Horlivka) was a true chess prodigy. At twelve, he already won the European Under-18 Championship, and at thirteen he took the Under-18 World title. He became a grandmaster at fourteen in 1998, the youngest grandmaster ever at the time. He won many strong tournaments and earned the gold medal on board two for Ukraine at the Istanbul Olympiad in 2001 (8½ out of 11). In 2002, at eighteen, Ponomariov became the FIDE World Champion by beating his fellow countryman Vasyl Ivanchuk in the final. He held this world title for two years. He has been living in Spain since 2012. In April of this year Ponomariov had a nice comeback, ending shared third in the European Championship in Terme Catez. Ponomariov was an important and faithful contributor to New In Chess Yearbooks from 2018 to 2022.

NOTES BY
Ruslan Ponomariov

Game 14   Slav Defence
Ruslan Ponomariov   2699
Vladimir Malakhov   2722

Danzhou 2017 (7)

1.d4 d5 2.c4 c6 3.♘f3 ♘f6 4.♘c3 a6!?
This is a modern piece of chess theory: the so-called Chebanenko Variation. My opponent has played many games with it, and he is one of its specialists. True, his choice was not difficult to predict, and it was easy for me to prepare for the game.
5.c5 ♘bd7 6.♗f4 ♘h5 7.♗d2 ♘hf6 8.♗f4
The time control gets faster every year, and if I can, I don't mind gaining some time on the clock by repeating moves.
8...♘h5 9.♗d2
Now Black has to repeat moves:

9...♘hf6
If 9...g6 10.e4 dxe4 11.♘xe4 ♗g7 12.♗c4 0-0 13.0-0 ♘df6 14.♘xf6+ ♘xf6 15.♕b3 ♘d5 16.♖fe1 (Podgaets-Ponomariov, Odessa 2005), White's position is much easier to play. He has free development and more space for his pieces to manoeuvre.
10.♕c2 g6 11.g3
My opponent and I had already played this variation at the World Cup semi-finals. That game went 11.h3 ♕c7 12.♗g5 ♗g7 13.e3 e5 14.0-0-0 0-0 15.♗h4 exd4 16.exd4 b6 17.♗g3 ♗h6+ 18.♔b1 ♗f4 19.cxb6 ♘xb6 20.♗xf4 ♕xf4

21.♗d3 Ponomariov-Malakhov, Khanty-Mansiysk 2009. The opposite-side castling guarantees a complex game with chances for both sides.

11...♗g7 12.♗g2 0-0 13.0-0

13...♖e8

Later in the same tournament, Vladimir tried to improve Black's play by 13...b6 14.b4 a5 15.a3 ♖e8 (Yu Yangyi-Malakhov, Danzhou 2017), and now by analogy 16.♖ad1 makes little sense, since Black can profitably open the position by 16...axb4 17.axb4 bxc5 18.bxc5 e5 with good play, e.g. 19.dxe5 ♘xe5 20.♘xe5 ♖xe5 21.e4 ♗a6 22.♗f4 ♖e8 23.♖fe1 ♕a5.

But White can also play more strongly: 14.cxb6!? ♘xb6 15.♘e5 ♗f5 16.e4 dxe4 (16...♘xe4 17.♘xe4 ♗xe5 18.dxe5 dxe4 19.♗h6 ♖e8 20.♗xe4 ♗xe4 21.♕xe4 ♕d5 22.♖fe1±) 17.♘xc6 ♕d7 18.♘xe4 ♘xe4 19.♗xe4 e6 20.♖ac1 ♖fc8 21.♗xf5 gxf5 22.♗a5 ♘d5 23.♕a4 ♗xd4 24.♕xd4 ♖xc6 25.♖xc6 ♕xc6 26.♗d2 ♕b6 27.♕xb6 ♘xb6 28.♖c1.

In both cases, he has a small but persistent advantage without the slightest risk of losing.

14.♖ad1

A slightly mysterious rook move to a closed file. But in fact, White must constantly ask himself what Black wants. It is obvious that Black has less room for his pieces and to somehow free himself he must play either ...e7-e5 or ...b7-b6, which is what White is preparing for. In general, the opening manuals and statistics promise an advantage for White, but everything is not so simple.

14...b5

Now on 14...b6 15.b4 a5 there is 16.b5 ♗b7 17.♘e5 with uncomfortable pressure: 17...♘xc5 18.dxe5 ♘d7 19.bxc6 ♗xc6 20.♘xd5. It is clear that White is now better prepared to open the position.

15.♗g5!?

A new idea. At the same time, the move is far from the first that the engines suggest.

In the event of the natural 15.b4 a5 16.a3 axb4 17.axb4 ♘f8 18.♘e5 ♗f5 19.♕b3 ♕c8 it is not so easy to break through Black's position, which was shown in the game Fressinet-Malakhov, Tromsø 2013.

15...a5

Ruslan Ponomariov in Dortmund in 2014.

Played after long thought. In a practical game, it is not so clear which move to choose:

A) It is clear that White is very well prepared for the showdown 15...e5 16.e4;

B) 15...h6 16.♗f4 g5 17.♗c1 only leads to additional weakening on the kingside;

C) For tactical reasons, Black cannot just complete his development by 15...♘f8 16.♘e5 ♕c7 17.♗xf6! ♗xf6 18.♘xc6 (it turns out that the move ...b7-b5 has its drawbacks) 18...♗f5 19.♘xd5 ♕xc6 20.♕c3 and Black cannot avoid additional material losses;

D) Perhaps best was 15...b4!? 16.♘a4 ♖a7! (16...a5 17.♘e5 ♘xe5 18.dxe5 ♘g4 19.♘b6 ♖a7 20.e4) 17.a3 (17.♘e5 ♘xe5 18.dxe5 ♘g4) 17...a5, maintaining the semi-closed nature of the position. However, I would have been pleased with this as well. The black pawn on b4 has broken away from the rest of its pieces, which provides an additional object for attack.

The move played by Black in the game is quite principled, forcing White, in fact, to go for subsequent complications.

16.e4 b4 17.exd5!

This was also one of the ideas behind the move 15.♗g5. Now the bishop on d2 is not attacked.

17...bxc3 18.dxc6 ♘f8 19.bxc3

This position is what I aimed for in my home preparation. It seems to me that the three pawns, although tripled, would be stronger than

Black's minor piece. How often it happens that analysing everything at home is impossible, and the position remains hard to play.

19...♗f5

20.♕b3

I wanted to somehow consolidate my position and start pushing the passed pawns.

First I planned 20.♕c1 but then I didn't really like it over the board:

A) 20...♕d5 (attacking the white pawns) 21.♘h4 (White can regain the piece with 21.♗xf6 ♗xf6 22.♘h4 ♗e4 23.c4 ♕xc6 24.d5 ♕xc5 25.♗xe4 ♖ac8 26.♗d3 ♗xh4 27.gxh4 e6, but then Black has a rather simple game. An extra pawn looks like little consolation for such a bad pawn structure on the kingside.) 21...♗e4 (21...♕xa2 22.♘xf5 gxf5 23.d5 ♕c4 24.d6 with a White initiative) 22.f3 ♗f5 23.♘xf5 gxf5 looks unclear. Such complications are rather in Black's favour;

B) Perhaps the strongest move is the computer recommendation 20.♕d2!?, for example: 20...♘e4 (20...♗e4 21.♗xf6 ♗xf6 22.d5; 20...♕d5 21.♗xf6 ♗xf6 22.♘e5;

20...♘e6 21.♗xf6 ♗xf6 22.♖fe1)
21.♕e3 ♘xg5 22.♘xg5 and then
White can finally start pushing his
pawns. But in a practical game, it
is not so easy to understand the
difference between the various
retreats of the queen.

20...a4

Black also had the alternative
20...♖b8 21.♕a3 ♘e6 22.♗e3 ♘d5
(22...♗e4 23.c4) 23.c4 ♘xe3 24.♕xe3
♖b4 25.d5 ♘c7 26.♘d2 ♗c2 27.♖c1
♖b2, still with a complicated
position. But it seems to me that it's
easier to play with White here.

21.♕a3

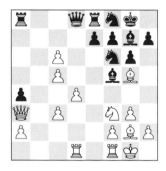

21...♘e4?!

A miscalculation, perhaps. Here
the knight is very unstable, and
temporary attacks are not so
difficult to refute.

  A) 21...♕a5, saving the move ...♘e4
as a threat, looks more logical
at first, e.g. 22.♘d2 ♗d3 23.♖fe1
♘e6 24.♗xf6 ♗xf6 25.♖e3 ♗c2
26.♖de1±;

  B) But even stronger is 21...♗c2!?
luring the white pieces into sub-
optimal positions: 22.♖d2 ♗e4
23.d5 e6 24.c4 (24.dxe6 ♕e7)
24...♕a5 25.♖fd1 exd5 26.♗xf6

(26.cxd5 ♘xd5 27.♖xd5 ♗xd5
28.♖xd5 ♕b5) 26...♗xf6 27.cxd5
♖ad8 and the white pawns won't be
going any further...

22.♗e3 ♕a5 23.♖c1!

Perhaps Black underestimated this
move, and he had been hoping only
for 23.c4 ♕c3 with counterplay. The
move in the game not only protects
the pawn, but also the c3-square.

23...♕a6

If 23...♖ac8, then 24.♖fd1 ♖xc6
25.♘d2 ♖e6 26.d5±.

24.c4 ♕xc6

Black has finally taken the most
advanced passed pawn, but now the
e4-knight falls under a deadly pin.

25.♘g5

Even stronger was 25.♘d2 ♖ab8
26.g4! (over the board I thought I
had to play 26.♘xe4 ♗xe4 27.d5
♗b2 28.♕xb2 ♖xb2 29.dxc6 ♗xg2
30.♔xg2 ♘e6 when White is better,
but I wanted more) 26...♕d7 27.gxf5
♘xd2 and now I did not notice the
quiet move 28.♖fd1! with a large
and probably decisive advantage for
White.

25...e6

My idea was that after 25...♖ab8
26.d5 ♗b2 27.♕xb2 ♖xb2 28.dxc6

the knight on d2 is not under attack and I can save the pair of bishops: 28...♘xg5 29.♗xg5 ♘e6 30.♗e3 ♖xa2 31.♖fd1 a3 32.♖d7 ♖b2 33.♖b7 ♖b8 34.♖a1 a2 35.♖xa2 ♖b1+ 36.♗f1 ♖8xb7 37.cxb7 ♖xb7 38.f3+−.

26.g4 h6 27.gxf5 hxg5 28.f6!

With this tactical shot, White wins back the piece, remaining with an extra pawn and a pair of active bishops. It seemed that the game had already been decided. But my resourceful opponent, despite time trouble, finds opportunities to play on.

28...♗xf6 29.♕d3 ♖ad8

I expected 29...♘xc5 30.dxc5 ♕c8 31.♗xa8 ♕xa8 32.♖fd1 ♕f3 33.♗d4, easily stopping the attacks by the black queen, with a further simple technical stage of converting the material advantage. The move in the game, which puts pressure on the d4-pawn, looks more unpleasant from the practical point of view.

30.♗xe4 ♕c8

31.♕c3

I was not so sure about straight-forwardly beginning to advance the pawns: 31.d5 ♘d7 32.c6 ♘e5 33.♕d1

exd5 34.cxd5 ♘g4 (Black activates his pieces) 35.♗g2 ♘xe3 36.fxe3 ♗e5 37.♕xa4 ♕c7. Despite the two minus pawns, Black has good counterplay on the dark squares. With the queens on the board, the white king also feels uncomfortable.

31...♗g7 32.♗g2 f5 33.♖cd1

I did not want to return the extra pawn, but at the same time, I wanted to avoid unnecessary complications after let's say 33.f3 f4 34.♗f2 e5!? 35.d5 e4 36.♗d4 ♗xd4+ 37.♕xd4 e3 38.♖b1 ♘e6 39.♕f6 ♕xc5.

33...f4 34.♗c1 ♕xc5 35.dxc5 ♗xc3

36.♗c6?!

There were four more moves before the time control. Before that, the play had been more or less forced. By inertia, I wanted to calculate some concrete lines and was afraid to make a mistake and spoil my position.

But I should have calmed down and played the simpler 36.c6! ♖b8 37.♗a3 ♗e5 38.h3, slowly improving my position and keeping all the pieces on good squares. Black is unable to defend all of his weaknesses.

36...♖xd1 37.♖xd1 ♖c8 38.♗xa4 ♖xc5 39.♗b5 ♖c8 40.a4

Better was 40.♖d3, immediately forcing the black bishop to decide where to go: 40...♗b4 41.a4 e5 42.♖d5 etc.

40...e5

41.♖d5

The time trouble phase is over, but the position has not become easier, as material is equal. It is clear that White should try to move his passed pawns forward as quickly as possible. But at the same time, he must watch out for Black's possible counterplay.

  A) For example, after the straight-forward 41.c5 ♗d4 (41...♖xc5 42.♗a3 ♖c8 43.♖c1+−) 42.c6 ♘e6, White's pawns are stopped. And Black, on the contrary, can improve his position. So after much deliberation, I decided to try to keep my rook active;

  B) Even stronger with the same idea was 41.♖d6! e4 (41...♗b4 42.♖d5) 42.♗a3 ♔g7 43.h3, gradually starting to advance the passed pawns, but also keeping an eye on Black's possible active play.

41...♘h7 42.♖d6 ♔g7

The natural move: protecting the pawn and activating the king in the endgame.

But Black had an interesting chance here: 42...♗b4!? (material is not as important as the activity of the pieces) 43.♖b6 (43.♖xg6+ ♔f7 44.♖c6 ♖d8) 43...♖d8 44.♔g2 g4 45.♖xg6+ ♔f7 46.♖xg4 ♔e6 47.♖g7 ♘f6. White has two extra pawns, but it's too early to talk about any clarity, since all his pieces are poorly coordinated. However, it's quite difficult to find all these moves in a practical game.

43.♗a3 ♗d4 44.♖c6

Eventually the white pawns move faster. Black lacks just a little bit to start his counterplay on the kingside.

44...♖a8

44...♖xc6 45.♗xc6 ♘f8 46.♗d6 ♘e6 47.a5+−.

45.♖c7+ ♔h6 46.c5 ♘f6 47.♖f7 ♘e4!?

Again, the players were already in time trouble. Here too Black finds an opportunity to set a trap.

48.c6

Tempting was 48.♗c6 ♖a6 49.♗xe4 ♖xa4 50.c6 ♖xa3 51.c7

♖c3 52.♗b7? (52.h3! ♗b6 53.♖f6!
♗xc7 54.♖xg6+ ♔h5 55.♖g7 g4
56.hxg4+ ♔h4 57.g5+−), but then
52...♖c1+ 53.♔g2 g4 and White
can't win. If 54.c8♕ f3+ 55.♖xf3
♖xc8 56.♗xc8 gxf3+ 57.♔xf3.

48...♗xf2+ 49.♔g2 g4

49...♗c5 50.♗xc5 ♘xc5 51.c7 ♖c8
52.♖e7+−.

50.c7 f3+ 51.♔f1

Unfortunately, Black cannot create
more threats.

51...g3

51...♗b6 52.♖f8.

**52.hxg3 ♗b6 53.♖f8 ♘xg3+ 54.♔e1
f2+ 55.♔d1 f1♕+ 56.♗xf1 ♗xc7
57.♖xa8 ♘xf1**

58.a5

The passed rook's pawn is especially
strong against the knight.

**58...♘e3+ 59.♔e2 ♘d5 60.a6 ♗b6
61.♔f3 ♘c7 62.♖c8**

And here at last, Black resigned. A
tense game from start to finish!

Pavel Eljanov

Pavel Eljanov (born 1983 in Kharkiv) is the son of an International Master, and became a Grandmaster himself in 2001. He won many strong tournaments, like the Aeroflot Open in 2012, the Reykjavik Open in 2013 and the Poikovsky tournament in the same year. In 2010 he was the No. 1 of Ukraine and the No. 6 in the world with a 2761 rating. Eljanov worked as a second for Boris Gelfand in his run-up to the World Championship match with Anand (which Gelfand lost only in the rapid playoffs), and also for Magnus Carlsen and Mariya Muzychuk.

In the FIDE World Cup in Baku, 2015, he reached the semifinals. One year later, Eljanov won the super-strong Isle of Man Open after beating Fabiano Caruana in the tiebreak.

NOTES BY
Pavel Eljanov

Game 15   Ruy Lopez
David Navara
Pavel Eljanov
Baku Olympiad 2016 (10)

1.e4 e5 2.♘f3 ♘c6 3.♗b5 ♘f6 4.d3 ♗c5 5.c3 0-0 6.0-0 ♖e8 7.♗g5 a6!?
The normal move here is 7...h6, although it could transpose to the same position we got in the game.

8.♗c4!?
A very interesting concept. Instead of going back with 8.♗a4, White transposes to the Giuoco Piano with the extra move ...♖e8. But it looks as if this rook move would favour White.
8...h6 9.♗h4

9...d6
Here the normal and typical reaction would be 9...♗e7, but after 10.a4 d6 11.♘a3 ♘h5 12.♗g3! White

is ready to open the f-file in the event of ...♘xg3, when the rook on e8 is very much misplaced.

It was also dangerous to push forward immediately, since after 9...g5 10.♗g3 g4 White has a pleasant choice between 11.d4!? and 11.♘fd2.

10.a4

10...g5

My first intention was to play 10...♕e7 11.♘bd2 ♗e6, with a pretty solid position of course, but White has some initiative in any case after 12.b4 ♗a7 13.♖e1 ♗xc4 14.♘xc4 ♕e6 15.b5 ♘e7 16.♗xf6 ♕xf6 17.♖b1.

11.♗g3 ♗a7

After 11...g4 White has the strong reply 12.♗h4!.

12.♘bd2 ♗g4

I was happy to play this, because I had already tried this plan against Giri in a similar situation in Stavanger at Norway Chess 2016. Now I have two ideas for the price of one: my bishop is not only pinning White's knight, but will also cover the very important g6- and f7-squares.

13.h3 ♗h5 14.♖e1 ♕d7 15.b4

Maybe it was more to the point to start the typical knight transfer 15.♘f1 ♘e7, and now 16.♗h2!, when probably White is slightly better in this complicated position.

15...♘d8!

Now I'm in time and have decent counterplay.

16.d4

Interesting, but not necessary. After 16.a5 ♘e6 17.♗b3 c6 the position is unclear.

16...exd4 17.♕c2 ♗g6

Also interesting was 17...♘c6!?.

18.cxd4 ♘c6

Here I was optimistic because I didn't see how White would get full compensation for one of the pawns that I will capture eventually. But David found a strong move sequence:

19.♕c3!
After 19.d5 ♘xb4 20.♕c3, 20...♘h5! favours Black.
19...♘xe4 20.♘xe4 ♖xe4 21.b5 ♘e7 22.♖xe4 ♗xe4 23.♖e1
23.bxa6 bxa6 24.♗xa6? runs into 24...♕c6, and Black is clearly better.

23...♗g6!
Avoiding 23...♘d5 24.♕b3 ♘f6 25.bxa6 bxa6 26.♖xe4! ♘xe4 27.♕b7, which is fine for White.
24.♘h2?!
Not a big mistake, but the first step in the wrong direction. White would still have enough compensation after 24.bxa6 bxa6 25.a5.
24...♘f5 25.♘g4 ♔g7

26.♖e4?

But now the must-play move was 26.♗d3! ♖f8 27.♗xf5 ♗xf5 28.bxa6 bxa6 29.♘e3 ♗e4, with some compensation for the pawn deficit, but White already has to prove it.
26...♖f8! 27.d5+ f6
Now all my pieces are very well placed and after a quick counter-attack everything comes to an end.
28.♖e6 ♗d4 29.♕e1 ♖f7

30.♗d3
White's position is also lost after 30.♘e3 ♗xe3 31.fxe3 ♘xg3 32.♕xg3 ♖f8.
30...♘xg3 31.♗xg6 ♔xg6 32.♕b1+ ♔g7 33.♕d3 h5 34.♕xd4

34...♕xe6!
A nice final touch.
35.dxe6 ♘e2+ 0-1

Zahar Efimenko

Zahar was born in 1985 in the Donbas region of Ukraine, studied at the famous Kramatorsk chess school, and showed his talent when he won the U14 World Youth Championship in 1999. In 2006 he won the Ukrainian Championship, and he went on to finish 1st or shared 1st in events such as the Gibraltar Masters (2005), the Isle of Man Masters (2007), the Bosna International (2010) and the Abu Dhabi Masters (2013).

The highlight of Zahar's career came in 2010, when he crossed the 2700 mark and helped Ukraine claim gold at the Khanty-Mansiysk Olympiad. Zahar won the crucial game as Ukraine held a 2:2 draw against Russia, while his unbeaten 8½/11 gave him individual silver on Board 4. He also won bronze with Ukraine at the World and European Team Championships, while as a coach he has worked for 14th World Chess Champion Vladimir Kramnik and Kazakhstan rising star Zhansaya Abdumalik. Zahar married Ukrainian WIM Maria Tantsiura in 2015.

NOTES BY
Zahar Efimenko

These events took place at the Chess Olympiad in Dresden in 2008. Thanks to this victory, the Ukrainian team beat Russia with a score of 2½-1½.

Game 16   French Defence
Zahar Efimenko   2680
Alexander Morozevich   2787
Dresden Olympiad 2008 (9)

___

1.e4 e6 2.d4 d5 3.♘d2 ♗e7!?
Morozevich often used this particular system in the French Defence. Black provokes the development of the knight to f3.

But in these positions the knight is much more elastic on e2.

A) 3...c5!? 4.exd5 ♕xd5 5.♘gf3 cxd4 6.♗c4 ♕d7 7.♘b3 ♘c6 8.0-0 ♘f6 9.♘bxd4 ♘xd4 10.♘xd4 a6 11.♗g5 ♗e7 12.♖e1;

B) 3...♘f6!? 4.e5 ♘fd7 5.♗d3 c5 6.c3 ♘c6 7.♘e2 cxd4 8.cxd4 f6 9.exf6 ♘xf6 10.0-0 ♗d6 11.♘f3 ♕c7 12.♗d2 0-0, both with counterplay.
4.♗d3!?
White is still ready to move into the main position. Therefore, he is in no hurry to develop the knight; 4.♘gf3!? ♘f6 5.e5 ♘fd7 6.♗d3 c5 7.c3 ♘c6 8.0-0 g5 9.dxc5 g4 10.♘d4 ♘dxe5 11.♗b5 ♗d7 12.♘2b3 h5 with chances for both sides.
4...c5

4...♘f6 5.e5 ♘fd7 6.♘e2 c5 7.c3 ♘c6 8.0-0 0-0 9.♘f3 f6 10.exf6 ♘xf6 11.♖e1 ♗d6 12.♗f4 ♘g4 13.♗xd6 ♕xd6 14.♘g3±.

5.dxc5 ♘f6 6.♕e2!?

White improves the position of his queen and does not allow its exchange. After 6.♘gf3 dxe4 7.♘xe4 ♘xe4 8.♗xe4 ♕xd1+ 9.♔xd1 ♗xc5 10.♔e2 ♘d7 11.♗f4 ♘f6 12.♘d2 0-0 13.♖hd1 ♗e7, a comfortable endgame arises for Black.

6...♘c6

6...0-0 7.♘gf3 a5!? 8.0-0 ♘a6 9.e5 ♘d7 10.c4 ♘axc5 11.♗c2 b6 12.b3 (12.♘d4 ♗a6 13.b3 ♖c8 14.♗b2 with counterplay) 12...♗b7 13.♗b2 ♕c7 14.♖fe1 ♖fd8 15.♘d4 ♘f8 16.♕g4 ♘g6 17.♘2f3 dxc4 18.bxc4 ♖ac8 19.♖e3 ♗xf3 20.♘xf3 ♘d7 21.♗b3 ♘c5 22.♗d4 ♘xb3 23.axb3 ♗c5 24.♗xc5 ♕xc5 25.h4 ♘e7 26.♕e4 ♘f5 27.♖d3 ♘g3 28.♖xd8+ ♖xd8 29.♕c2 ♘f5 30.♖d1 ♘d4 31.♕e4 ♘xf3+ 32.♕xf3 ♖xd1+ 33.♕xd1 h5 34.♕d8+ ♔h7 35.♕d7 ♔g6 36.♕d8 ♔h7 37.♕d6 ♔g6 38.♕d3+ ♔h6 39.♕g3 g6 40.♕g5+ ♔h7 41.♕f6 ♔g8 42.♕d8+ ♔g7 43.g3 ♕b4 44.♕f6+ ♔g8 45.♕d8+ ♔g7 46.♕f6+ ♔g8 ½-½ Efimenko-Vovk, Kyiv 2012.

7.♘gf3 ♗xc5

7...♘b4!? deserves attention. Black immediately exchanges the important bishop. There can follow 8.0-0 (8.♘b3 ♘xd3+ 9.cxd3 a5 10.♗g5 a4 11.♘bd2 h6 12.♗xf6 ♗xf6 13.e5 ♗e7 14.♖c1 ♖a5 15.♕e3 0-0 16.0-0 ♗d7 17.♖c2 ♕a8 18.♖fc1 ♖c8 19.♘f1 ♕a7 20.d4 ♕a6 21.♘g3 b6 22.c6 ♗e8 23.♘h5 ♕b5 24.g4 ♖a7 25.g5 hxg5 26.♘xg5 ♖ac7 27.♔h1 ♖xc6 28.♖xc6 ♖xc6 29.♖g1 ♕xb2 30.♘xg7 ♕c3 31.♘xe8 1-0 Adams-Morozevich, Sarajevo 2000) 8...♘xd3 9.cxd3 ♗xc5 10.♘b3 ♗e7 11.♗g5 h6 12.♗h4 0-0 13.e5 ♘h7 14.♗xe7 ♕xe7 15.♖ac1 ♗d7 16.♘c5 ♖fb8 17.♕e3±.

8.0-0 ♕c7!?

Black improves the queen and does not rush to castle. He takes control of the e5-square. If 8...0-0 9.e5 ♘d7 10.♘b3 ♗e7 11.c3 a5 12.♗f4 a4 13.♘bd4 ♘c5 14.♗c2 ♗d7 15.♖fd1±.

9.c4!?

Here I thought for a long time and pondered over various continuations. After some calculating, I came to the conclusion that an immediate breakthrough in the centre gives White the initiative!

A) 9.exd5 ♘xd5 10.♘e4 ♗e7
11.c4 ♘f4 12.♗xf4 ♕xf4 13.g3 ♕c7
14.♖ac1 0-0 15.♘c3 ♗d7=;

B) 9.e5 ♘g4 10.♘b3 ♗b6 11.♗b5
(11.♗f4 f6 12.♖ae1 0-0=) 11...f6
12.c4 dxc4 13.♕xc4 ♘gxe5 14.♘xe5
fxe5 15.♗e3 0-0 16.♕e4 with
compensation.

9...dxc4

A) 9...0-0!? is a logical and solid
continuation for Black, for example:

A1) 10.♘b3 dxe4 11.♗xc4 ♗e7
12.♗c2 b6⇄;

A2) 10.cxd5 exd5 11.exd5 ♖e8
(11...♘xd5 12.♗xh7+ ♔xh7 13.♕e4+
♔g8 14.♕xd5 ♗e7 15.♘e4 ♗g4
16.♘g3 ♕d6 17.♕xd6 ♗xd6
18.♗e3±) 12.♗xh7+ ♔xh7 13.♕d3+
♔g8 14.dxc6 ♕xc6 15.♘b3 ♗b6
16.♗g5 ♗g4 with mutual chances;

A3) 10.e5!? ♘g4 11.♘b3 dxc4 12.♘xc5
cxd3 13.♘xd3 b6 14.♗f4 ♗a6 15.♖fc1
♕b7 16.♕e4 ♘e7 17.♕xb7 ♗xb7
18.♖c7 ♗xf3 19.♖xe7 ♗e4 20.♘e1±.

B) 9...dxe4 10.♘xe4 ♗e7 11.b3 b6
12.♗b2 ♗b7 13.♖ad1± ♖d8 14.♗b1
♘xe4 15.♖xd8+ ♗xd8 16.♗xe4
♗f6 17.♗xf6 gxf6 18.♖d1 ♔e7 19.h3
♘a5 20.♗xb7 ♘xb7 21.♘d4 ♘d6
22.♕g4 ♖d8 23.♕f3 ♖g8 24.♘c6+
♔f8 25.♘xa7 ♕xa7 26.♖xd6 ♔e7

27.♕c6 ♖b8 28.♖d4 ♖d8 29.♖xd8
♔xd8 30.b4 f5 31.a4 ♔e7 32.c5 bxc5
33.♕xc5+ ♕xc5 34.bxc5 f4 35.a5
♔d7 36.a6 ♘c7 37.g4 fxg3 38.fxg3 h5
39.g4 h4 40.g5 1-0 Bulski-Hausner,
Slovakia tt 2013/14.

10.♗xc4

Now, after ...e6-e5, Black cannot
develop his bishop to e6 without
obstacles.
10.♘xc4!? e5 (10...0-0? 11.e5 ♘d5
12.♗xh7+! ♔xh7 13.♘g5+ ♔g8
(13...♔g6 14.h4 (14.♖d1 with an
attack) 14...♖h8 15.♕e4+ f5 16.exf6+
♔xf6 17.♗e3 ♗b6 18.♖ac1+−)
14.♕h5 ♖e8 15.♕h7+ ♔f8 16.♕h8+
♔e7 17.♕xg7 ♖f8 18.♘h7+−) 11.♗e3
(11.h3 0-0 (11...♘h5 12.♗e3 ♘f4
13.♗xf4 exf4 14.e5 ♗e6 15.♖ac1±)
12.♗e3 ♗xe3 13.♕xe3 ♗e6
14.♖ac1±) 11...♗xe3 12.♘xe3 0-0
13.♖ac1±.

10...♘g4?!

A dubious decision! Black violates
the main principles of chess and
forgets about the development of
his pieces. First you need to provide
security for the king, and only
then you start active operations.
Therefore, in this position, the
most logical continuation was to
castle. Morozevich has always been
an extraordinary chess player, so
he tried to make non-standard
decisions.
10...0-0!? 11.♘b3 ♗b6 (11...♗d6
12.♖d1 ♘g4 13.g3 e5 14.♘h4 ♗e7
15.♘f5 ♗xf5 16.exf5 ♘f6 17.♗g5±)
12.e5! (12.♗g5 ♘e5 13.♖ac1 ♘xf3+
14.♕xf3 ♕e5 15.♗xf6 ♕xf6 16.♕xf6
gxf6 17.♖fd1=) 12...♘g4 13.♗f4 f6

14.♖ac1 ♘gxe5 15.♘xe5 fxe5 16.♗e3
♗xe3 17.♕xe3 with compensation.

11.h3 h5

A) 11...♘d4 12.♕d3 (12.♘xd4??
♕h2#) 12...♘e5 13.♘xe5 ♕xe5
14.b4! ♗b6 (14...♗xb4? 15.♖b1 ♗c5
16.♗b2 0-0 17.♘b3 ♖d8 18.♖fd1+−)
15.♗b2 0-0 16.♖ab1±;

B) 11...♘ge5 12.♘xe5 ♘xe5
13.♗b5+ ♗d7 14.♘b3 0-0 15.♘xc5
♕xc5 16.♗xd7 ♘xd7 17.♗e3 ♕e5
18.f3±.

12.b4!

Here I thought for a long time
and found the best move in the
game! I remember that 14 years
ago the computer did not show
this solution. Now, of course, this
is the first Stockfish line! White
sacrifices a pawn for the initiative
and at the same time makes room
for the development of the bishop
to b2. Also, this move introduces
disharmony into the position of the
black pieces.

12.hxg4 hxg4 is out of the question.

12...♗d4

A) 12...♗xb4 13.♗b2 ♘f6 (13...0-0
14.hxg4 hxg4 15.♘e1+−; 13...♔f8 14.e5
♘h6 15.♘e4 ♘f5 16.♖fd1±) 14.e5 ♘d5
15.♘e4 with compensation;

B) 12...♘xb4 13.♗b2 ♗d7 14.♖ac1±.

13.♖b1 ♗d7 14.b5 ♘e7

A) 14...♘ce5 15.♘xd4 ♘xc4 16.hxg4
(16.♘4f3±) 16...hxg4 17.f4+−;

B) 14...♘a5 15.♗d3+−.

15.e5!

Another very important move!
White breaks off the communica-
tion between Black's pieces. They
are in hanging positions, and his
king is still stuck in the centre.

15...♗b6

A) 15...♗xe5 16.hxg4 ♗d6
(16...hxg4 17.♘xe5+−) 17.g5+−;

B) 15...♘xe5 16.♘xd4+−.

16.♗a3

16.hxg4 hxg4 17.♘g5 ♘f5 18.♖b3 g3
was unclear.

16...♘f5 17.♘e4

Now the white pieces are fully
mobilized and ready for action.
There is complete disharmony in
the enemy camp, where the rooks
still do not take part in the struggle.

17...f6

It is very difficult to give any good
advice to Black. His position is
close to lost, for example:

A) 17...♖c8 18.♖bc1 ♕d8 19.♖fd1
♖h6 20.♗d3+−;

B) 17...♘xe5?? 18.♘xe5 ♕xe5
19.♘d6+ ♗xd6 (19...♕xd6
20.♗xd6+−) 20.♕xe5+−.

18.♘d6+!
Now Black's king is completely
vulnerable. White exchanges
knights with tempo and opens lines
for an invasion.
**18...♘xd6 19.exd6 ♕d8 20.♗xe6
♔f8 21.♗xd7**
21.♖be1+−.
21...♕xd7 22.♕e7+!
The most technical solution. After
the exchange of queens, Black loses
a piece.
22...♕xe7 23.dxe7+ ♔f7 24.hxg4
Now it's time to destroy this nasty
knight.
24...hxg4 25.♘d2

25...g3
A) 25...♖h5 26.♘e4 ♖ah8
27.♘g3+−;
B) 25...♖h7 26.♖fd1 ♖ah8
27.♔f1+−.
26.♘c4
White's position is absolutely
winning! Black does not have
enough compensation for the piece.
26...♖h5
26...gxf2+ 27.♖xf2 ♗xf2+ 28.♔xf2
♖h5 29.♖e1+−.
**27.♘xb6 axb6 28.♖b3 gxf2+ 29.♔xf2
♖d5 30.♖e1 ♔e8 31.♖c3 ♔f7**
Here my opponent made his move
and immediately resigned. He
realized that after 32.e8♕ followed
by a check with 33.♖c7, Black also
loses the rook.

NOTES BY
Zahar Efimenko

Game 17   Ruy Lopez

Zahar Efimenko   2783

Vladimir Malakhov   2725

Khanty-Mansiysk Olympiad 2010 (8)

1.e4 e5 2.♘f3 ♘c6 3.♗b5 ♘f6 4.0-0 ♘xe4 5.d4 ♘d6

So! The Berlin version of the Ruy Lopez is very popular lately! Of course, I was mainly preparing for the Rio de Janeiro Variation, which Vladimir had been using regularly lately! But I also spent a bit of time on the Berlin Wall! 5...♗e7!? 6.♕e2 ♘d6 7.♗xc6 bxc6 8.dxe5 ♘b7 9.♖d1 with mutual chances.

6.♗xc6 dxc6

6...bxc6 7.dxe5.

7.dxe5 ♘f5 8.♕xd8+ ♔xd8 9.♘c3 ♔e8 10.♘e2!?

I decided to choose this rare continuation. Twelve years ago, this idea was practically not used in tournaments. In our time, many games have already been played in this direction. In the main variation after 10.h3, Black has achieved good results! This is shown by the game Caruana-Kramnik, Khanty-Mansiysk ol 2010.

10...♘e7

10...b6!? 11.♖d1 ♗b7 12.b3 ♖c8 13.♗b2 ♗e7 14.♘ed4 ♘xd4 15.♘xd4 ♖g8 16.♘f5 c5 17.c4 ♗e4 18.♘g3 ♗g6 19.f4 h5 20.f5 h4 21.fxg6 hxg3 22.gxf7+ ♔xf7 23.hxg3 ♔e6 24.♔f2 ♖cd8 25.♔e2 ♖xd1 26.♖xd1 ♖h8

27.♗c3 c6 28.♗d2 ♖e8 29.♖h1 ♔xe5 30.♗c3+ ♔f5 31.♔f3 ♔g6 32.♖d1 ♖d8 33.♖xd8 ♗xd8 34.♗e5 ♔f7 35.♔f4 a6 36.♗b8 ♔e6 37.g4 b5 38.♗e5 g6 39.♔e4 ♗e7 40.♗f4 ♗f8 41.♗e3 ♗d6 42.♗f4 ♗f8 43.♗e3 ♗d6 44.♗f4 ♗f8 ½-½ Caruana-Giri, London 2014.

11.h3 ♘g6

11...a5!? 12.♖e1 ♘d5 13.♗d2 h6 14.♘fd4 a4 15.e6 fxe6 16.♘xe6 ♗xe6 17.♘d4 ♔f7 18.♘xe6 a3 19.bxa3 ♗xa3 20.c4 ♘b4 21.♘xc7 ♖ac8 22.♖e3 ♘c2 23.♖f3+ ♔e7 24.♖d1 ♖xc7 25.♖c3 ♗b4 26.♖xc2 ♗xd2 27.♖cxd2 ♖a8 28.♖e2+ ♔f7 29.♖b2 ♖a4 30.♖db1 ♖xc4 31.♖xb7 ♖xb7 32.♖xb7+ ♔f6 33.♖a7 ♖c1+ 34.♔h2 c5 35.a4 c4 36.♖c7 c3 37.a5 ♔e5 38.a6 ♔d4 39.a7 ♖a1 40.♖xg7 c2 41.♖c7 ♔d3 42.♖d7+ ♔e2 43.♖c7 ♔d2 44.♖d7+ ♔e2 ½-½ Gashimov-Efimenko, Poikovsky 2009.

12.b3!?

A typical idea! White fianchettoes the bishop on the long diagonal. Here he will create powerful pressure. 12.♖e1 ♗d7 13.♘f4 ♘xf4 14.♗xf4 c5 15.e6 ♗xe6 16.♘g5 ♗e7 17.♘xe6 fxe6 18.♖xe6 ♔d7 19.♖ae1 ♗f6 20.c3 ♖ad8 21.g4 h6 22.♔g2 c6

23.♗d6 c4 24.f4 ♖he8 25.♖xe8 ♖xe8
26.♖xe8 ♔xe8 27.♔f3 ♔d7 28.♗b8
a6 29.♔e4 ♔e6 30.f5+ ♔f7 31.♗e5
♗e7 32.♔d4 b5 33.♗g3 a5 34.a4 bxa4
35.♗c7 a3 36.bxa3 a4 37.♔xc4 ♗xa3
38.h4 g6 39.fxg6+ ♔xg6 40.♗f4
h5 41.gxh5+ ♔xh5 42.♗g5 ½-½
Maghsoodloo-Goryachkina, Europe
Échecs online 2020.

12...h6

12...♗e7 13.♗b2 a5 14.a4 c5 15.♘c3
♗e6 16.♖ad1±.

13.♗b2 c5 14.♖ad1 ♗e6

15.♘c3!?

The knight immediately goes to the
excellent d5-square. Here it will
limit the enemy's opportunities.

  A) 15.♘h2!? ♗e7 (15...h5 16.f4 ♘h4
17.c4 ♖d8 18.♘g3 ♘f5 19.♖xd8+
♔xd8 20.♖d1+ ♔c8 21.♘e4 ♗e7
22.♘f3=) 16.f4 ♘h4 (16...♗f5 17.♘g3
♘h4 18.♘xf5 ♘xf5 19.♖fe1 ♖d8
20.♘f3±) 17.g4 g6 18.♘c3±;

  B) 15.♘d2!? ♖d8 16.♘e4 ♖xd1
17.♖xd1 c4 18.♘d4 cxb3 19.♘xc6
fxe6 20.axb3±.

15...♗e7

  A) 15...c6 16.♘e4 ♖d8 17.♘fd2 ♗e7
18.f4 ♘h4 19.g4±;

  B) 15...♖d8 16.♘d2 a6 17.♘c4±.

16.♘d5

White has achieved his goal. He
also has a spatial advantage.

16...♗d8

16...♗xd5 17.♖xd5 ♘f4 18.♖dd1 ♖d8
19.♔h2 ♘e6 20.♖fe1±.

17.c4 a5 18.a4!

Preventing the activation of the
black rook.

18...c6

19.♘e3!

Here the knight is much stronger!

19...♗e7

19...♗c7 20.♘d2! – when calculating
the variation with 19.♘e3, I did not
see this strong manoeuvre with
the knight to d2! White sacrifices a
pawn but obtains sufficient compensation, e.g. 20...♘xe5 (20...♖d8
21.♘e4 ♖xd1 22.♖xd1 b6 23.♘d6+
♔e7 24.♘ef5+ ♔f8 25.f3 h5 26.♔f2
h4 27.♔e3±; 20...♗xe5 21.♗xe5 ♘xe5
22.f4 ♘d3 23.f5 ♗c8 24.♘e4 ♘b4
25.♖fe1+−) 21.♘e4 f6 22.♘xc5±.

20.♘e4 ♖d8 21.♖fc1

White improves the position of the
rook, and at the same time prepares
for the knight's invasion on d6.
21.♔h2!? ♗f5 22.♘fd2 with mutual
chances.

21...♖xd1

21...b6 22.♘d6+ ♔f8 23.♖d3 ♘f4
24.♖d2 g5 25.♔h2 h5 26.♘f1±.

22.♖xd1 ♘f4
22...♗f5!? 23.♘d6+ (23.♖e1 ♔d8
24.e6 f6 25.♘g3 ♗c2 26.♖e3)
23...♗xd6 24.♖xd6 ♘f4 25.♘e1 ♔e7
26.♗a3 b6 27.♖xc6 ♖d8 28.♖xb6
♖d1 29.♖b7+ ♔e6 30.♖b6+ ♔e7=.

23.♗a3!?
Here I thought for a long time! I
studied many interesting continuations, which I will give below! Also
at that moment it became clear
that Pavel Eljanov's position was
practically lost after an opening
disaster, and the prospects of our
team at that moment were not
good. Therefore, I understood that
I had to fight and do my best to
save this tough match against the
Russian team!
23.♔h2! b6 24.♘d6+ ♔f8 25.♘g1! (a
very strong move; White defends
the h3-pawn and wants to drive
the black knight out of its active
position) 25...g5 26.g3 ♘g6 27.♘e2
h5 28.f3±.

23...b6
23...♗f5!? I spent most of my time
on this sequel! For example:
  A) 24.♘xc5?! ♘e2+! (24...b6?
25.♘b7! ♗xa3 26.♖d8++−) 25.♔f1
(25.♔h2 ♘c3 26.♖g1 ♘b1 27.♘d4

♗h7 28.♖d1 ♘xa3 29.♘xb7 c5
30.♘b5 ♘xb5 31.axb5 ♗e4 32.♘xa5
♗d8∓) 25...♘c3 26.♖c1 ♘b1∓;
  B) 24.♘d6+!? ♗xd6 25.exd6 ♘d3
26.g4 ♗h7 27.♖d2 b6 28.♖e2+ ♔d7
29.♖e7+ ♔xd6 30.♖xf7 ♖g8 31.♘d2
♘e5 32.♖b7 ♘d7 33.f4 with chances
for both sides.

24.♘d6+ ♔f8
24...♗xd6? 25.♖xd6 ♗d7 26.e6!
♘xe6 27.♘e5 ♗c8 28.♖xc6+−.

25.♔f1
White improves the position of the
king and at the same time takes
control of the important e2-square.
25.♔h2!? g5 26.♗c1 ♘g6 27.g4 ♗d8
(27...h5? 28.♔g3+−) 28.♗b2 would
give Black counterplay.

25...g5!?
A typical move for the Berlin
system. Black is fighting for space
and at the same time making room
for his king. If 25...♘g6 26.♗b2 ♔g8
27.♘d2 ♔h7 28.♘2e4 ♖f8 29.♖d2±.

26.♗c1 ♔g7
26...♘g6 27.g4 ♗d8 28.♔g2 ♗c7
29.♔g3 with mutual chances.

27.♗xf4!?
I thought about 27.♘h4! for a long
time, but in the end decided against
it − although it was the best plan in

this position! 27...♗xd6 (27...gxh4
28.♗xf4 ♖d8 29.♔e2 ♔g6 30.♖d3±)
28.♖xd6 ♘xh3 29.♘f3 g4 30.♘h4
♘g5 31.♖xc6 ♖d8 32.♔e2 ♖b8
33.♔e3±.

27...gxf4

An interesting position has arisen
in which the two knights are not
inferior to the black bishops.

28.♘d2!?

28.♔e2 ♖d8 29.♖d2 ♗xd6 30.♖xd6
♖xd6 31.exd6 ♔f6 32.♔d2 ♗f5
33.♘e1 ♔e6 34.♘d3 ♗xd3 35.♔xd3
f5 36.d7 ♔xd7 37.♔e2 ♔d6 38.♔d2
♔e5 39.♔d3=.

28...♗xd6!

Black destroys the strong knight
in time; 28...f6!? 29.exf6+ ♗xf6
30.♖e1 ♗d7 31.♘f3 ♔g6 32.♖e4 ♗f5
33.♖xf4 ♗c2 34.♘e4 ♗g7 35.♘fd2
♖d8 with compensation.

29.exd6 ♖d8 30.♘e4

30...f5?

In mutual time trouble, Vladimir
makes a serious strategic mistake!
After 30...♗f5! 31.f3 f6 32.♔f2 ♔f7,
neither opponent has the potential
to strengthen the position!
Therefore, it is completely equal.

31.♘c3 ♔f6 32.♔e2 ♗f7

32...♔e5 33.f3 ♖xd6 34.♖xd6 ♔xd6
35.♔d3 ♔e5 36.♘e2 ♗d7 37.♔d2
♗e8 38.h4 ♗d7 39.♔c3 ♗e8 40.♘c1!
♗d7 41.♘d3+ ♔d6 42.♘xf4±.

33.d7 ♗h5+?

Black loses important tempi and
does not feel the danger.
33...♔e6 34.f3 ♖xd7 35.♖xd7 ♔xd7
36.♔d3 ♔d6 37.♘e2 ♔e5 38.♔c3
♗e8 39.h4 ♗f7 40.♘c1± with good
chances of winning!

34.f3 ♔e6

35.♔e1!

It was this resource that my
opponent had not noticed! This was
clearly visible in his reaction, and
because he spent his last minutes
thinking here. White vacates the
e2-square for the knight. One of
the hardest-to-find motifs in chess
is the backward move! Usually you
look only forward.

35...♗f7

35...♖xd7 36.♖xd7 ♔xd7 37.♘e2
♗f7 38.♔d2 h5 39.h4 ♔d6 40.♘xf4
clearly favours White.
36.♘e2 ♔e5

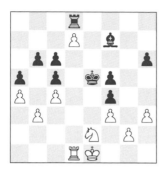

37.♘c1!
The white knight slowly starts
attacking Black's fixed pawn
weaknesses. Black's position is
already close to losing!
**37...♗e6 38.♘d3+ ♔f6 39.♘xf4
♗xd7 40.♔f2 ♔e7 41.♘g6+ ♔e6
42.f4 ♖b8**

43.g4!

White is starting to use his pawn
majority on the kingside!
43...♗e8
43...fxg4 44.hxg4 ♗e8 45.♘e5+−.

44.♘h4!
An important move! The knight is
now heading to f5 with a further
invasion of the rook along the
sixth rank! White is dominating
completely.
**44...fxg4 45.hxg4 b5 46.♘f5 bxa4
47.bxa4 ♖b4 48.♖d6+ ♔f7 49.♖xh6**
It's time to collect material!
49...♖xa4 50.g5 ♔g8 51.♘d6
51.g6! ♖xc4 52.♔f3 ♖c1 (52...♗d7
53.♘e7+ ♔f8 54.♖h7 ♗e6 55.f5+−)
53.g7+−.
51...♗f7 52.♘xf7 ♔xf7 53.f5
Two passed pawns in a rook
endgame win easily! Such pawns are
usually unstoppable.
**53...♖xc4 54.♔f3 ♖b4 55.♖h7+ ♔g8
56.g6 1-0**

Viktor Moskalenko

Viktor Moskalenko (born 1960 in Odessa) became a Grandmaster in 1992. Three years earlier he had become Ukrainian Champion in Mikolayiv. From 1992 to 1994 he worked as Vasyl Ivanchuk's second. In 2000, Viktor and his wife Tatyana emigrated to a town near Barcelona, Spain. He has won many international tournaments in his long career, based on a dynamic opening repertoire. Moskalenko started writing books for New In Chess in 2007. His debut, *The Fabulous Budapest Gambit*, as well as several books on his pet opening, the French Defence, all written in colourful style, are acclaimed classics. Viktor's peak rating was 2591 (July 2011) and he remains a strong grandmaster to this day.

NOTES BY
Viktor Moskalenko

This old game ended in a complete strategic defeat for the future FIDE World Champion (1999-2000).
At the end of the tournament, Khalifman's coach Gennady Nesis admitted they had chosen a wrong opening and had clearly underestimated White's attacking resources in the resulting closed structure.

Game 18   Dutch Defence
Viktor Moskalenko   2460
Alexander Khalifman   2485
Lviv 1985 (12)

1.d4 e6 2.c4 f5 3.♘c3 ♘f6 4.g3 ♗b4
Black has opted for a fairly combative scheme, combining this 'Nimzo' move with the centre-strengthening advance ...f7-f5.

More common is the solid Stonewall set-up with 4...d5, or the Classical Dutch 4...♗e7.

5.♗g2 0-0 6.♘f3 ♗xc3+
Exchanging the bishop to double the pawns is part of Black's main plan.
6...♘e4 7.♗d2!?.
7.bxc3 d6 8.0-0 ♕e7
My opponent is too hasty with the ...e6-e5 advance, missing the typical counter-break in the centre.
More natural seems 8...♘c6 9.c5!?±.

9.c5!

With the clear goal of opening the a3-f8 diagonal for the white bishop.

9...♘c6 10.cxd6 cxd6 11.♗a3! ♕c7?

Black immediately withdraws his pieces from the weakened diagonal. However, moving the queen twice in the opening is already a serious mistake – or maybe just a sign of disappointment.

White is better anyway, after, for instance, 11...♘a5 12.♕a4 b6 13.c4±.

12.c4!

Creating a mobile pawn centre.

12...♖d8

11 years later, another failed attempt was 12...♘e4 13.♖c1 ♗d7 14.d5! and White won on move 30 in Najer-Tchernyi, Moscow 1996.

13.♖c1 ♘a5 14.♘d2! ♖b8 15.e4!

The punishment begins.

15...e5

Too late, this blocking plan is not destined to live long.

16.d5 b6

The issue is the bishop pair.

17.f4!

White's attack is unstoppable.

17...♘xe4

17...exf4 18.♖xf4+−.

18.♘xe4 fxe4 19.fxe5 dxe5 20.♗xe4 ♘b7

Black's pieces are very passively placed on the queenside and they can only look on while White fires the final shot.

21.d6! ♕d7

If 21...♘xd6 22.♕d5+ ♘f7 (22...♔h8 23.♗xd6) 23.♖xf7!, winning.

22.♕h5

Black resigned (with relief, it seemed to me).

Mikhail Golubev

Mikhail Golubev (1970) was born and lives in the Black Sea port city of Odessa. He won the Ukrainian Championship in 1996, which was the same year he earned the grandmaster title. He won a lot of tournaments throughout his career.

Mikhail has combined his career as a chess professional with that of a writer, publishing various books on the Sicilian and the King's Indian and, as a chess journalist, working as a prolific contributor for publications such as Chess Today, ChessPro and Chess-News.ru. From 1998-2003 he was the editor of the website Ukrainian Chess Online. Golubev has worked as an assistant for Ruslan Ponomariov and was a member of the Board of the Association of Chess Professionals in 2006/7.

NOTES BY
Mikhail Golubev

From the current, already quite long, period when I've no longer been playing chess professionally, I like the following effort most.

Game 19   French Defence
Mikhail Golubev   2479
Stefan Tomici   2319
Lviv 2019 (3)

1.e4 e6 2.d4 d5 3.♘c3 ♗b4 4.e5 b6
The main line is 4...c5; or 4...♘e7 5.a3 ♗xc3+ 6.bxc3 and now 6...c5.
5.a3
An important alternative is 5.♕g4 which can be answered by 5...♗f8!? as well.
5...♗f8
This retreat was used by such giants as Kortchnoi and Petrosian as

long ago as 1957. In this objectively dubious variation, Ivanchuk, playing Black, much later defeated Kasparov! All this suggests that things are not particularly simple. Less often Black goes for 5...♗xc3+ 6.bxc3 where White is surely somewhat better as well. In the mid-1990s I analysed, quite correctly, the variation 6...♕d7 7.♕g4 f5 8.♕g3! ♗a6 9.♗xa6 ♘xa6 10.♘e2 ♘b8 (10...0-0-0 11.a4!; 10...♔f7)

analysis diagram

11.♘f4! ♞c6? (a funny idea, which, however, does not work against precise play) 12.♘xe6! ♕xe6 13.♕xg7 0-0-0 14.♕xh8 ♕g6 15.0-0 ♖d7 (if 15...♖e8 16.h4! ♞d8 17.h5) 16.♖e1!! ♚b7 (or 16...h5 17.e6! ♖h7 18.e7! ♞cxe7 19.♕e5+−; 16...♖g7 17.g3 h5 18.e6, etc.) 17.h4 (after 17.♗f4 (Martin-J.Fernandez, Spain tt 1990) 17...♖g7! 18.g3 h5 19.e6! ♖h7 20.e7 ♞gxe7 21.♕f8 h4! White has to find 22.♖e2!!) 17...h5 18.e6! ♖h7 19.e7! ♞gxe7 20.♕f8+−. Later, this variation was seen in correspondence play.

6.♘f3

White has a large choice of plans and ideas, which does not make his practical task easier, however. In principle, he also can play 6.♗b5+!? immediately. After 6...c6 (the alternative is 6...♗d7 7.♗d3! c5 8.♘f3 ♞c6 9.0-0) 7.♗a4 ♕d7 8.♘ce2 ♞a6 (the passive plan) 9.c3 ♞c7 10.♘f3 ♗a6 11.0-0 0-0-0 12.♖e1 f5 13.♘f4 ♞h6 14.♗c2 ♞f7 15.♘h5 ♖g8 16.a4 ♗e7 17.a5 White was much better in Golubev-Nosenko, Odessa Open 2003.

6...♘e7

6...c5 is riskier:

A) 7.♗g5!? ♕d7?! 8.dxc5 bxc5 9.♗b5 ♞c6 10.0-0 a6?! 11.♗a4 h6? 12.♞xd5!! hxg5 13.♞b6 ♕b7 (V.Moskalenko-Gonzalez Rodriguez, Montcada 2006) 14.♞xg5!+−;

B) 7.♗d3 ♞c6 (after 7...♗a6 one curious strategic idea for White is 8.0-0 ♗xd3 9.cxd3, Al.Kovacevic-Dizdar, Murska Sobota 2007) 8.0-0 ♞ge7?! (8...a6 9.b3!?) 9.♞b5! ♞g6 and instead of the gamble 10.♗g5?! (Golubev-Nosenko, Klaipeda Wch jr prel 1985), 10.c4 or first 10.dxc5!? would have been clearly better for White.

7.♗b5+

7.h4!? h6 has occurred, in particular, in the games Kasparov-Ivanchuk, Horgen 1995 and Kryvoruchko-Yusupov, Swiss Team Championship 1997. Also of definite interest is 7...c5.

7...c6

In my view, this leads to a clearly dubious, difficult position for Black. Preferable, but still insufficient for equality, is 7...♗d7 8.♗d3!, etc.

8.♗a4! a5 9.♘e2

It was also possible to castle here or on the next move, with the same plan.

9...♗a6 10.c3 ♞d7

During the game I thought that maybe Black could try the strategically crazy 10...b5?! 11.♗c2 b4, while after the game I found in the database the encounter Benjamin-Jussupow, Dresden 2018: 10...h6 11.0-0 (other options include 11.h4!? and 11.♗c2) 11...♞d7 12.♖e1 g6 (12...♕c7 13.♞f4) 13.h4 ♖c8 14.h5!

with a clear advantage to White and with the idea of 14...g5 15.♘h2.

11.0-0 c5 12.♖e1

So, White is ready to develop the initiative, using his light-squared bishop, avoiding the exchange of which was the idea behind the ♗f1-b5-a4 manoeuvre.

12...b5?

12...♕c7± , after which White has a number of attractive continuations, has been tested in several games.

13.♗c2 ♘c6 14.♘f4 cxd4

A possible answer to 14...♗e7 is 15.dxc5!? ♘xc5 16.♘h5 g6 17.♘f6+ ♗xf6 18.exf6 and Black is in trouble.

15.♘xe6!

For a while before finding this surprisingly strong sacrifice, I couldn't decide between 15.♘xd4(?) ♘xd4 16.cxd4 g6 and 15.cxd4(?) ♗e7

and was not overly satisfied with these lines. But objectively, there was one more serious opportunity, 15.♘g5!? when capturing the knight with the queen is totally hopeless for Black after ♘xe6. Instead, Black's best practical chance is probably 15...♘b6!, still with a quite bad position. But the rest is even worse: 15...♘dxe5 16.♘fxe6!? fxe6 17.cxd4+− ; or 15...d3 16.♘xf7!? and now 16...♔xf7 17.♘xe6! ♔xe6 18.♕g4+ ♔e7 19.♗g5+ ♔e8 20.♗xd8+− or 16...dxc2 17.♕h5 g6 18.♕h3 with the idea 19...♔xf7 19.♕xe6+ ♔g7 20.♘h5+! gxh5 21.♗h6, a nice checkmate!

15...fxe6 16.♘xd4!

The point. Now Black's position is going to be destroyed inevitably.

16...♘cxe5

He obviously loses after 16...♘xd4? 17.♕h5+ ♔e7 18.♗g5+ ♘f6 19.cxd4. It's easier to evaluate the position over the board than to calculate everything to the end, but everything turns out to be hopeless for Black. If 16...♘dxe5 17.♘xc6 ♘xc6 18.♖xe6+ ♘e7, then, for example, 19.♕h5+ ♔d7 20.♕h3 ♔e8 21.♗f4, etc.

After 16...♘e7 17.♘xe6 ♕b6, any sensible move works for White. 18.♘g5 with ideas of e5-e6, ♕f3, ♗e3 is the most concrete.

17.♘xe6 ♕b6

18.♖xe5!?

Engines like 18.♗f5 even better, but during the game I was looking for more forcing ways.

18...♘xe5 19.♕xd5

For the time being White is a rook down (for two pawns) but Black is unable to solve his concrete problems properly.

19...♘c6?!

The most stubborn would have been 19...♗c8!. Following 20.♘xf8 ♖xf8 21.♕xe5+ ♕e6 22.♕xb5+!? ♗d7 23.♕f1 White has three pawns for the exchange and a strong initiative. After my opponent's move, White wins directly.

20.♗e3 ♕b7 21.♕h5+ g6
22.♗xg6+! hxg6 23.♕xg6+ ♔d7

Or 23...♕f7 24.♘c7+ ♔e7 25.♗c5+ and Black loses the queen.

24.♖d1+ ♗d6

If 24...♔c8 25.♕e8+.

25.♘c5+ ♔c8 26.♖xd6

Black resigned.

Vladimir Baklan

Vladimir Baklan (born 1978 in Kyiv) has been a grandmaster since 1998. He won the Ukrainian Championship twice in a row, in 1997 and 1998. In 2000, he was a member of the bronze-winning Ukrainian team at the Istanbul Olympiad, and also of the national team that won the World Team Championship one year later. He tied for first in the Balaguer Open in 2005 and the Reykjavik Open in 2011. His peak rating, in 2009, was 2655. In 2005, he was the fastest player in the Dutch Open Blitz Championship in 2005. Vladimir has worked as a chess coach with pupils like Illya Nyzhnyk and Kirill Shevchenko. He has also been the coach of the German national team and the Ukraine Women's team.

NOTES BY
Vladimir Baklan

This game was played in the European Club Championship, in the match between Medny Vsadnik (St Petersburg) and Danko-Donbass (Donetsk).

Game 20   Benoni Defence
Viktor Kortchnoi   2620
Vladimir Baklan   2599
Neum 2000 (6)

1.d4 ♘f6 2.c4 c5 3.d5 b5 4.cxb5 a6 5.bxa6 g6 6.♘c3 ♗xa6 7.g3 d6 8.♗g2 ♗g7 9.♘h3
An interesting move, the idea of which is to transfer the knight to f4. I am not convinced it is needed there, though, since one of White's main plans is e2-e4, f2-f4 and e4-e5, which the knight on

f4 interferes with. 9.♘f3 is a more popular move.
9...0-0 10.♖b1 ♘bd7 11.0-0 ♕a5 12.♗d2 ♖fb8 13.♕c2 ♘e8
A standard knight manoeuvre to b5, aiming to exchange the ♘c3 and then attack the queenside pawns.
14.b3

14...♕a3!N
This idea has become standard in such positions, but it was a novelty at the time. Black does not allow White to put the pawn on a4.

A) 14...♘e5;
B) 14...♘c7.

15.♘f4

15.♗c1 ♕a5 16.♗b2 (16.♗d2 ♕a3=)
16...c4 with mutual chances.

15...♘c7 16.♗h3?!

16.♗c1 ♕a5 17.♗b2 c4 18.♗a1∞.

16...♘e5 17.♘g2?

An artificial piece regrouping,
which leads to catastrophe. One
cannot afford to make so many
moves with the same piece in the
opening.

17.♗c1 ♕a5 18.♗d2 ♕a3=.

17...♗xe2!

Not a difficult move, yet not many
pupils have found it in my training
experience.

18.♘xe2 ♕xa2!

18...♘f3+? 19.♔h1 ♕xa2 gives
White chances to save himself
after 20.♕xa2 ♖xa2 21.♗c3 ♖xe2?

(admittedly, after 21...♘xd5 22.♗xg7
♔xg7 23.♘gf4 ♘xf4 24.♘xf4 e6
Black has the advantage, as the
pawn b3 will fall sooner or later)
22.♗xg7 ♔xg7 23.♗g4 ♘d4 24.♗xe2
♘xe2 25.♖be1 ♘c3 26.♖xe7 ♘7xd5
27.♖a7 ♖xb3 28.♘e3=.

19.♕xa2

19.♖bc1 ♘f3+ 20.♔h1 ♘xd2−+.

19...♖xa2 20.f4 ♖xd2 21.♔f2 ♘d3+

Other moves also win, but this is
the simplest.

**22.♔e3 ♖b2! 23.♖xb2 ♘xb2 24.♘c1
♘xd5+ 25.♔f3 c4 26.bxc4 ♘xc4
27.♖d1 ♘c3 28.♖e1**

28.♖d3 ♖b1.

28...e5 29.fxe5 dxe5 0-1

Black's two extra pawns and piece
activity make further resistance
pointless. Viktor Lvovich signed the
scoresheet and left, without shaking
hands. Such things happen!

Alexander Moiseenko

Although Alexander Moiseenko (1980) was born and took his first steps in chess in the Northern Russian naval base of Severomorsk, his Ukrainian family moved back to Kharkiv when he was 9. As a teenager he shared first place in the 1999 Ukrainian Championship. He also shared first place in the 2011 European Championship but was unlucky to miss out on the podium behind Judit Polgar, Radek Wojtaszek and Vladimir Potkin. He made up for it in 2013, when he topped a 10-player tie for first to become European Champion.

Alexander's greatest success arguably came in team events, where Ukraine claimed gold in both the 2004 and 2010 Olympiads. He won individual silver at the 2014 Olympiad, while he claimed individual gold as Ukraine took bronze at the 2011 World Team Championship. 2011 was also the year in which Alexander achieved his personal best 2726 rating, which placed him at world no. 22.

NOTES BY
Alexander Moiseenko

Game 21   Grünfeld Indian Defence
Alexander Moiseenko   2699
Maxime Vachier-Lagrave   2719
Biel 2013 (9)

This game was played in the 9th round in a tournament played according to the 'soccer system' (3 points for a win, 1 for a draw). At that moment, the leader was Etienne Bacrot with 12 points, Maxime Vachier-Lagrave and Ding Liren had 11 points and I had 10. So this game was very important!
1.d4 ♘f6 2.c4 g6 3.♘c3 d5 4.cxd5 ♘xd5 5.e4 ♘xc3 6.bxc3 ♗g7 7.♕a4+

I have played the variation 7.♘f3 c5 8.♗e2 0-0 9.♖b1 cxd4 10.cxd4 a few times.
7...♕d7
Or 7...♗d7 8.♕a3 0-0 9.♘f3.
8.♕b3 0-0

9.♗e3
9.♘f3 c5 (9...♕g4).
9...b6 10.♘f3 ♗b7 11.♗d3 c5

11...♕g4 12.h3 ♕xg2 13.♔e2.
12.0-0 cxd4 13.cxd4 ♘c6

14.♗b5!
A novelty! This is an idea I had
prepared with Ukrainian GM
Alexander Zubarev for this game.
The pin is annoying for Black, and
if he moves his pawns to a6 and
b5, it will be easy to attack them by
a2-a4!.
Here are two games that continued
with 14.♖ad1:
  A) 14...♖ac8 15.d5 ♘a5 16.♕b4 ♗c3
17.♕b1 ♕a4 18.♗g5 ♕b4 19.♕xb4
♗xb4 20.♖b1 ♗a3 21.♖fd1 e6
22.dxe6 fxe6 23.h4 ♗c5 and Black
had active counterplay in Milov-
Krasenkow, Antalya 2004, which
ended in a draw on move 41;
  B) Ragger-Vachier-Lagrave,
Schwetzingen 2013, saw the same
idea for White after 14...e6: 15.♗b5
♕d6 16.♗c1 ♖fd8 17.♗g5. Now
Vachier-Lagrave sacrificed the
exchange with 17...♘xd4 18.♗xd8
♖xd8 19.♕e3 ♕b4 20.♘xd4 ♗xd4
21.♕e2 e5 and with the extra pawn
and the strong bishop on d4 Black
never had any real problems (draw in
54 moves).
14...a6 15.♗e2

15.♗xc6 ♗xc6 16.d5 ♗b5.
15...b5
Impossible is 15...♘xd4? because of
16.♗xd4! ♗xd4 17.♖ad1 e5 18.♘xe5
♕e7 19.♘xf7 with a decisive
advantage. Likewise, if 15...♗xd4
16.♖fd1 e5 17.♘xe5.

16.d5!
This is the key moment in the
opening. White sacrifices the
exchange for a strong initiative.
16.♖ad1 ♖ac8 (or perhaps 16...♘a5
17.♕b4 ♘c4 18.♗xc4 bxc4 19.d5 a5)
17.d5 ♘a5 18.♕b1 ♘c4 gives Black
counterplay, as does 16.a4 ♘a5
17.♕b4 ♘c4.
16...♘e5
It was more principled to take the
exchange with 16...♘a5 17.♕b4 ♘c4
(17...♗xa1 18.♖xa1 ♘c4 19.♗xc4
bxc4 20.♘e5 (20.♗h6 ♖fc8 20.♖b1)
20...♕c7 21.♘xc4 a5 22.♘xa5 ♖xa5
23.♗b6) 18.♗xc4 ♗xa1, but it's
not easy for Black to play such
an unbalanced position against
a prepared opponent. There can
follow 19.♖xa1 bxc4 20.♖b1!? with
strong compensation.
17.♘d4
17.♘xe5 ♗xe5 18.♖ad1.
17...♖fc8

17...♘g4 18.♗xg4 ♕xg4 19.f3 ♕d7
20.a4 gives White a stable edge.

18.a4!

18.f4 ♘c4 19.♗xc4 ♖xc4 20.♖ad1 ♖ac8.

18...♘c4!

The natural 18...bxa4?! 19.♖xa4 ♖c7
20.h3 leads to a very unpleasant
position for Black. White will press
on the b-file (with ♖b1 and ♖b4)
and Black's pieces are not well
coordinated.

19.axb5 axb5

19...♘xe3 20.fxe3 (20.♕xe3 axb5
(20...♗xd4 21.♕xd4 axb5 22.♕b4)
21.♗xb5 ♗xd4 (21...♕d6) 22.♗xd7
♗xe3 23.♗xc8) 20...axb5 21.♗xb5
♕d6.

20.♖xa8 ♖xa8

I think better for Black was
20...♗xa8 21.♘xb5 (weaker is
21.♕xb5? ♕xb5 22.♘xb5 ♘xe3
23.fxe3 ♖c2 with positional
compensation) 21...♘xe3 22.♕xe3
but anyway White has a healthy
extra pawn, for example 22...♖b8
23.♖c1! ♖xb5 24.♗xb5 ♕xb5
25.♖c8+ ♗f8 26.h3 ♗b7 27.♖b8 ♕b2
28.♕f4 ♔g7 29.♕c7 ♕b1+ 30.♔h2
♕xe4 31.♖xb7 ♕xd5. White still has
an advantage here, though Black has
good drawing chances.

21.♗xc4 bxc4 22.♕xc4 ♖c8

White does not lose the exchange
now: 22...♗a6 23.♖a1 ♗xc4??
24.♖xa8+ ♗f8 25.♗h6 and mate.

23.♕a2±

Less strong was 23.♕b5 ♕xb5
24.♘xb5 f5 25.exf5 gxf5 26.d6 ♗a6
27.♘a7 ♖d8 28.♘c6 (28.dxe7 ♖e8
29.♖d1 ♖xe7 30.♘c6) 28...♖xd6
29.♘xe7+ ♔f7 30.♘xf5 ♖d5.

23...♗xd4!?

A very concrete defensive try!

24.♗xd4 e6 25.♗a1!

After the logical 25.♗f6 exd5
26.♕d2 ♕d6 27.e5 ♕f8 28.h4
h5, it is not easy to break Black's
defences.

If 25.♕d2 exd5 26.♕h6 f6 27.♗xf6
dxe4 28.h4 Black can defend with
28...♖f8, or also 28...♖c5 or 28...e3!?
with the idea ...♕c6.

25...exd5 26.♕b2

The careless 26.♖d1? is met
by 26...dxe4!.

26...d4 27.f3

My idea was to take the pawn on
d4 and keep the queens, rooks and
bishops on the board. Any exchange
will increase Black's drawing
chances.

27...♖d8

27...♖c3 28.♖d1 ♕c7 29.♕d2; or 27...
h5 28.♕xd4 ♕xd4+ 29.♗xd4.

28.♕b6!

This offers better winning chances
than 28.♖d1 h5 29.♖xd4 ♕xd4+
30.♕xd4 ♖xd4 31.♗xd4.

28...♕e7 29.♖d1 f5

The computer suggests 29...d3,
but after 30.♕b2 f6 31.♕xf6 ♕xf6
32.♗xf6 ♖d6 33.♗c3 ♗a6 (33...d2
34.♗xd2 ♗c6 35.♔f1 ♗a4 36.♖a1+−)
34.♗d2! the ending is winning. If
29...♖d6, 30.♕b4 ♖d7 31.♕b5 ♕d8
32.h3 with big pressure.

30.exf5

More complicated was 30.♖xd4
♖xd4 31.♕xd4 fxe4 32.♕h8+ ♔f7
33.♕xh7+ ♔f8 34.♕h6+ ♔f7 (in
the opposite-coloured bishops
ending after 34...♔e8 35.♕xg6+
♕f7 36.♕xf7+ ♔xf7, 37.fxe4 should
win for White – or also 37.f4 e3
38.♗d4 e2 39.♗c3 (39.♔f2? ♗xg2
draws) 39...♔g6 40.g4) 35.♕g7+ ♔e8
36.♕xg6+ ♔d7 37.♕b6.

30...♖d6

The sacrifice 30...♗xf3 does not
work because after 31.gxf3 ♕e3+
32.♔g2 ♕e2+ 33.♔g3 ♕e5+ 34.♔h3
♕xf5+ 35.♔g2 ♕c2+ 36.♔g3 Black
has no more checks.

31.♕b3+ ♗d5 32.♕b8+ ♖d8
33.♕g3 ♗f7

34.♕f2!

34.fxg6 ♗xg6 35.h4 d3 was less
clear, but also a big advantage.

34...♗b3?!

More stubborn was 34...gxf5, but I
think the position after 35.♗xd4
should be winning because Black's
king is very weak.

35.♖e1 ♕d6 36.fxg6 hxg6 37.h3 ♕f4

In a blitz game, Black could try
37...d3!? with the idea 38.♕b2??
♕d4+! 39.♕xd4 ♖xd4 40.♗xd4 d2
41.♖a1 d1♕+ 42.♖xd1 ♗xd1 and
despite White's two extra pawns,
the ending is drawish. But of course
38.♕h4 is just mate!

38.♖e4 ♕c1+ 39.♖e1

I repeated the moves because I was
in slight time pressure.

39...♕f4 40.♗b2 d3 41.♕b6 ♖b8
42.♕xg6+ ♔f8 43.♕g7#

I was very happy to win such a
good game against a very strong
opponent. Despite this loss, on the
next day Maxime showed great
fighting skills in the final round,
beating Ding Liren in a long and
instructive ending. And finally he
won the tournament after a rapid +
blitz knock-out.

CHAPTER IV

Heroic Ivanchuk leads Ukraine to victory at the Calvia Olympiad in 2004

Ukraine won the 36th Olympiad, played in 2004 in Calvia on the Spanish island of Mallorca. In this interview, published in *New In Chess* magazine, the happy team captain **Vladimir Tukmakov** explained to Dirk Jan ten Geuzendam what was behind this huge success.

The Calvia Olympiad, 2004.

Some sports successes are so impressive and astounding that they seem almost unrepeatable. Everything goes your way, everything falls into place and in the end you can only marvel at what you've achieved. In Calvia, Ukraine was an unstoppable, well-oiled machine. The men's team started with three clean sweeps, beat arch-rivals Russia in Round 4 and never looked back. A proud coach tells us when the oiling started and how they kept the machinery greased.

'For me, everything started in the beginning of January, when I became the official trainer of the Ukrainian team. At first nothing much was happening; there were no sessions with the best players or anything. But I did have problems with the selection of the team. The main problem was the first board. I thought that it was very important to have Ivanchuk on first board. Ponomariov had a higher rating and was still the reigning World Champion, but he hadn't been playing at all for more than one year. Ivanchuk feels much better when he plays as a leader on the first

Ukraine's captain Vladimir Tukmakov:
'We had one great goal, we knew the
direction and we moved.'

board against really strong opposition.
Obviously I had to convince Ponomariov.
This was not an easy task, but I managed
to convince him.

Another complication was that I have
not taken part in Ukrainian chess life for
many years, because of my opposition
against the federation and its President,
and that most of the candidates were
very young people whom I didn't know
personally. So I was hoping to organize
at least one or two sessions to meet and
watch them. This didn't work out and in
the end the only possibility was to have
a training session during the Ukrainian
Championship. It was a knockout
championship and I could start working with the losers. Ironically this
proved to be a very fruitful solution for me, as almost all candidates lost
in the first or second round! After the first round I could already work
with Ponomariov, Karjakin, Eingorn and Eljanov. And in the second round
Ivanchuk was eliminated. I don't know what these meetings meant to
them, but for me they were very useful.

Right before the Olympiad, the situation was not ideal either. Ivanchuk
competed in the European Club Cup but he played badly, three out of
seven. And it was not only his form I was worried about. I believe that
the worst possible preparation one could imagine for Karjakin and
Ponomariov was what they actually did: playing against computers in
Bilbao.

First of all, Ivanchuk should be mentioned, he was the real hero of
our team. My expectation was that he would 'close' the first board and
score plus three, which would have been a very good result. But he scored
plus six and played games of such quality... and he remained focused and
ambitious till the very last day. I participated in the preparation for his
game against Lautier in the last round. I would have preferred a quieter
opening, but he opted for the King's Indian. We looked at a number of
variations and each time his choice was for the most complicated and most
unbalanced position. That is a man in form and in the right mood.

Ivanchuk's position in the team was a very special one. We had team
meetings every evening after dinner, but only six people would be there:
me and five players – no Ivanchuk. He was so wrapped up in his own
world of chess and his preparation that I didn't disturb him. He was much

more important for the team during the playing sessions.

Likewise, I did expect a good result from Karjakin, but I had not foreseen that he would crush his opponents so easily and quickly. His result was great, but it was not just the result. He plays just natural and simple-looking moves and somehow he wins almost effortlessly.

On the other hand, the plus five of Volokitin was just what I had expected from him. I have a very high opinion of his level of chess and his approach. He is a very strong player and I am

> In 2004 Karjakin, who was born in Crimea, still played for Ukraine. In 2009 he emigrated to Russia. In 2022 he was banned by FIDE for six months because of his public support of Putin's choice to invade Ukraine. (Editor)

sure that he will progress further. Eljanov is very stable, both as a person and as a chess player. These are very important members to have in a team, because it was clear that it was better to let Volokitin play with the white pieces as often as possible. At one moment he even played four white games in a row.

The division of the colours was my responsibility and my decision, but I am also a chess player and I understand how they feel about this. There are also personal ambitions, thoughts about rating and performance. But luckily we had such a splendid start and after the win over Russia, we no longer considered second place a success. Our only goal was first place. In this situation the team was much more important than personal ambitions and my boys understood this very well. We had not one conflict or quarrel about who would play or with which colour or whatever. This was the team spirit. And in our case this was not just empty words. We had one great goal, we knew the direction and we moved.

Finally, a few words about Moiseenko, who is a very good and strong player. He made huge progress after the Bled Olympiad and his rating now is 2653. The first half of the Olympiad he played very well. Then he overestimated his chances with White and after this he lost his balance. He only made plus two, which nevertheless corresponded with his rating, and he too was an important part of the team.

To lead from the very first round to the very end and to keep your concentration is hard. I believe we saved a lot of team energy by not discussing who would play. My only question was: who doesn't want to play? Usually everybody wanted to play. If someone didn't, he was automatically not playing. This never caused any problem, except for the last round. Now it was not a matter of not wanting, but they preferred not to play. But they all said, if you need me, okay. After that I named the people and that was it.

Vasyl Ivanchuk in Bilbao in 2011.

Here, too, Ivanchuk held a different position. At the last Olympiad in Bled he played all 14 games. This is very tough, particularly in 15 days, as here the second free day was canceled. My original idea was for Ivanchuk to play twelve games and to give him two rest days. My first attempt was before the third round, before the match with the Czech Republic and after he had won his first two games. I told him: 'Vasya, it's a long distance and if we win this match convincingly, most probably we will play against Russia. Maybe it's a good idea to take a rest.' He told me: 'It's your choice, it is your final decision, but I feel that I am in good shape and I would like to play.' And he played a very good game against Navara and won. Then he won a fantastic game against Morozevich and I didn't raise the issue again. But it emerged one more time, before the match with Azerbaijan. We were White on Board 1 and our second board, Ponomariov, who was not playing well, had asked me for a rest. So I put Ivanchuk on first board and Volokitin on second. But because Vasyl wasn't present at the team meeting, he didn't know how this had gone. At four in the morning my telephone rang. A call from Ivanchuk. He couldn't sleep and of course he didn't know what time it was... he asked me why I didn't put Ponomariov into the team. Because of the black pieces? And he said that if this was the reason, he could take a rest and Ponomariov could play on first board with White. And I said: 'Vasya, think about your game and forget about this.' And he immediately answered: 'Okay, I understand.' That was it. And he played a fantastic game against Radjabov. The only time he didn't play was against Georgia, but that was something else.

Our victory in Calvia was a historic win, not only for chess but for Ukrainian sport in general. This was a magnificent achievement, not just because we won, but also because of the way we won. Typical was the way we also won the last match very convincingly. During the match Lautier offered me a draw, four draws, but I rejected. Our only goal was to win the gold medals. If there had been any risk, I would have accepted, but in this case there was no reason. I am very satisfied with the job we did in Calvia. I can even say that I am happy.

The prospects for Ukrainian chess are excellent. Our team is very young and more youngsters are waiting in the wings. The only problem is that our success is not the confirmation of a good chess organization. Just the contrary. Therefore it must be hoped that this win has a positive impact on the organization and the development of chess in Ukraine.'

NOTES BY
Vasyl Ivanchuk

Game 22 Caro-Kann Defence
Alexander Morozevich 2758
Vasyl Ivanchuk 2705
Calvia Olympiad 2004 (4)

1.e4 c6 2.d4 d5 3.e5 ♗f5 4.f4!?
I find it hard to understand why this quite logical move occurs so rarely. However, fashion in opening variations is very changeable. For example, a couple of years ago the currently popular move 4.♗e3 hardly ever occurred in top grandmaster events.

4...e6 5.♘f3 c5
This thematic undermining of the centre by Black could well have been delayed. Moves such as 5...♘e7 or 5...♘d7 were perfectly possible. But in general Black cannot get by without playing ...c6-c5, since here the plan with ...f7-f6 looks very dubious, as White's e5-pawn is better supported than in many other branches of the 3.e5 ♗f5 variation.

6.♗e3

6...cxd4

Black takes a pawn! What could be more natural? But in fact this capture is a novelty, with which the independent play in this game essentially begins. I did not want to play 6...♘c6 in view of 7.dxc5, when it is not so easy to regain the pawn, since after 7...♕a5+ 8.c3 ♗xc5 9.b4 Black has to sacrifice a piece for rather dubious compensation.

7.♘xd4 ♘e7
Even the most unfamiliar position in chess always reminds one of something. In the given case one very much wants to compare this situation with the variation 1.e4 c6 2.d4 d5 3.e5 ♗f5 4.♘f3 e6 5.♗e2 c5 6.♗e3 cxd4 7.♘xd4 ♘e7.
Here White tries to fight for the initiative by playing either 8.c4 or 8.♗g5!?. In fact, the difference between these two positions is not so great. Instead of ♗f1-e2, in the game White has played f2-f4. Whom does this favour? It is hard to give a straightforward answer to this question. On the one hand, White's e5-pawn is better defended and after the retreat of the bishop from f5 to g6 Black constantly has to reckon with the possibility of f4-f5. In addition, the bishop at f1 can be developed on a more active square than e2. On the other hand, now White does not have the bishop sortie to g5, in some variations the bishop at e3 may be hanging, and the slight weakening of the g1-a7 diagonal may tell after he has castled kingside, which in addition still has to be prepared...

8.♗b5+

This move, made on the principle of 'development first and foremost', is one that I somehow did not expect. 8.c4!? looks very logical, especially taking into account the fact that it is extremely dangerous for Black to play 8...♘bc6?!, in analogy with the variation where instead of f2-f4 the white bishop is at e2, in view of 9.♘b5! (the e5-pawn is defended!).

Apparently he has to fight for equality with 8...dxc4 (8...a6!?) 9.♘c3 (9.♗xc4 ♘bc6) 9...♘bc6 (9...a6!?) 10.♕a4 (10.♘db5 ♘d5 11.♘xd5 exd5 12.♕xd5 is also possible, with very unclear complications) 10...a6 11.♖d1 (11.0-0-0) 11...♗d3! (11...♕a5?! 12.♘xf5 ♘xf5 13.♕xa5 ♘xa5 14.♗b6 ♘c6 15.♗xc4, or 14...♗b4 15.a3 ♗xc3+ 16.bxc3 ♘c6 17.♗xc4, with some advantage for White in both cases) 12.♗xd3 cxd3 13.♖xd3 b5 or 13...♕a5. Even 13...♘f5!? may be possible (the bishop at e3 is hanging!).

8...♘d7!?

I did not want to play either 8...♘bc6 9.0-0 a6 10.♗xc6+ bxc6 in view of Black's retarded development, or 10...♘xc6 11.♘xf5 exf5, since I did not like Black's resulting pawn structure. But 8...♘bc6 9.0-0 ♗g6!? was a reasonable alternative to the move in the game.

9.0-0 a6 10.♗e2

It is clear that White could not fight for an advantage by exchanging on d7. But instead of the move in the game, 10.♗a4!? b5 11.♗b3 was quite possible, switching the bishop to a more active position (especially if at some point he is able to play f4-f5!) and forcing Black to forget about the possibility of queenside castling.

However, I am not convinced that Black has to play 10...b5. True, it is dangerous for him to play 10...♗g6?! 11.f5! ♘xf5 12.♘xf5 ♗xf5 13.♖xf5 exf5 14.♕xd5 with a very strong attack for White, but 10...♕c7 or 10...♖c8 deserves serious consideration. After 10...♕c7 11.♘c3 0-0-0 Black does not stand badly, since 12.♘db5? axb5 13.♘xb5 does not work in view of 13...♕a5!. For White it would be interesting to play 11.♘d2, in order after queenside castling to have the possibility of attacking the centre with c2-c4. If 11...b5, White can, of course, modestly retreat his bishop to b3, but 12.♗xb5! is also quite possible (for certain tactical reasons the black queen is not so well placed on c7!), 12...axb5 13.♘xb5 and the white knight will then pick up the black rook at h8. Therefore, instead of 11...b5 Black does better to confine himself to the modest retreat of his bishop to g6, although even then, among other things, he has to reckon with 12.g4.

Whereas 10...♕c7 has the aim of preparing queenside castling, 10...♖c8 has an altogether different idea. Black prepares play with 11...b5 12.♗b3 ♘c5 (the immediate 10...b5 11.♗b3 ♘c5? is not possible in view of the knight sacrifice on b5, with which, exploiting the fact that the knight at c5 is undefended, White would win a pawn). After 10...♖c8 11.♘c3, apart from the afore-mentioned 11...b5 12.♗b3 ♘c5, Black can also play 11...h5, forcing White to forget forever about a possible g2-g4. Instead of 11.♘c3 White can play 11.♘d2, and if 11...♗g6, then 12.g4. But apart from 11...♗g6 Black can play either 11...h5 or 11...b5 12.♗b3 ♘c5 13.g4 ♗e4 with an unclear game. Also, he can even begin with 10...h5!?.

10...g5!?

Of course, it was possible to play more quietly (for example, 10...♗g6) but then the position would have been somewhat better for White in view of the rather unfortunate position of the black knight at d7. I did not want to reconcile myself to going onto the defensive, and I decided to take a risk, attempting to simultaneously bring two passive pieces into play: the knight at d7 and the bishop at f8.

11.g4?!

This move leads to interesting complications, which were not possible to calculate fully during the game, nor even to exhaust by detailed home analysis. But to a certain extent it resembles an attempt to put out a fire by pouring petrol on it. White wants to attack, but, with his rook at a1 and knight at b1 undeveloped, he seriously weakens the position of his own king and, what is also important, the black rook, which hitherto was standing peacefully in the corner at h8, now becomes very active.

The simple capture on g5 was a safer alternative for White. In this case I was afraid of allowing the exchange sacrifice on f5 both after 11.fxg5 ♗g7 12.♘xf5 ♘xf5 13.♖xf5 exf5 14.♘c3 and in the event of 11...♘xe5 12.♘xf5 ♘xf5 13.♖xf5 exf5 14.♘c3.

Therefore, in reply to 11.fxg5 I was planning 11...♗g6, when I considered the resulting position to be double-edged. In the centre, after the fall of the e5-pawn, Black will have some advantage, but White is well developed and has the possibility of play involving both c2-c4, and in some cases h2-h4-h5. It now seems to me that 11...♗g6, which is good in general, is not strictly the only move.

11...♕c7 is also possible, after which 12.♘xf5 ♘xf5 13.♖xf5 exf5 is not so dangerous for Black, as in the variations examined earlier, since after 14.♘c3 or 14.♕xd5 there follows the advantageous exchange of the dark-squared bishops after 14...♗c5! (the weakening of the g1-a7 diagonal is felt!).

Interesting complications can arise after 11...♕c7 12.♘c3 ♗g6 (otherwise White will be unable to refrain from sacrificing the exchange on f5 in favourable circumstances) 13.♘db5!? axb5 14.♘xb5 ♕b8! (after 14...♕xe5? 15.♗f4?! ♕xb2 16.♘c7+? ♔d8 17.♘xa8 e5 things are not so bad for Black, but, firstly, instead of 16.♘c7+? much stronger is 16.♖b1! followed by 17.♘d6 ♔d8 18.♘b7, and secondly, instead of 15.♗f4?! White wins altogether simply by 15.♗d4!) 15.♘d6+ ♔d8 16.♘xf7+ ♗xf7 17.♖xf7 ♘f5 (17...♘xe5 18.♖f6 gives White a strong attack) 18.♖xf5! (after the tempting 18.♗b5 ♘xe3 19.♖xd7+ ♔c8 Black does not stand badly, in my opinion) 18...exf5 19.♗f4!. How should this position be evaluated? I don't know! Black is a rook up, but he has many weaknesses and his king is insecure.

Of course, all these variations are not obligatory. For example, after 11...♕c7, apart from 12.♘c3, 12.♘d2 is also possible, in order to play c2-c4...

11...gxf4

It is obvious that after 11...♗e4 12.f5 exf5 13.e6 or 12...♘xe5 13.fxe6 the initiative is with White, and since this is so, the move made by Black must to some extent be considered forced.

12.gxf5

12...♘xf5!

Possibly it was this largely intuitive piece sacrifice that my opponent underestimated when he played 11.g4. In other variations, things would have been significantly better for White. For example, 12...fxe3 13.fxe6 fxe6 (or 13...♘xe5!? 14.exf7+ ♘xf7 15.♘c3 with the initiative for White) 14.♗h5+! (14.♘xe6 ♕b6! is less convincing) 14...g6 15.♕g4 ♘xe5 (15...♕e7 16.♗xg6+ hxg6 17.♕xg6+ ♔d8 18.♘xe6+ ♔c8 19.♘c3) 16.♕xe6+ ♕e7 17.♘c3 ♕xe6 18.♘xe6 ♔d7 (18...♗d6 19.♘xd5 ♔d7 20.♖f6) 19.♘xf8+ ♖axf8 20.♘xd5 ♔e6 21.♘xe3 ♘f4 22.♗f3! (22.♗d1 ♖hg8+ 23.♔h1 ♘h3!) 22...♘h3+ 23.♔g2 ♖hg8+ 24.♗g4+ ♘xg4 25.♘xg4 and White is a pawn up in the endgame.

13.♘xf5

13.♗f2, which is desirable from the positional point of view, runs

into the strong tactical rejoinder
13...♖g8+ (13...♕g5+ 14.♔h1 ♘g3+
is weaker in view of 15.♗xg3 fxg3
16.♖g1!) 14.♔h1 ♘g3+! 15.♗xg3 fxg3
16.♖g1 and here Black has a pleasant
choice between 16...♕b6, 16...♘xe5,
16...♕h4 and 16...♗c5.

13...fxe3

14.♘c3!?

White is ready to return the piece,
but Black does not want to take it...
I have to admit that I overlooked
this possibility in my preliminary
calculations. If 14.♘d6+ ♗xd6
15.exd6 I was intending to play
15...♕h4, although I was not
convinced that this really was the
strongest move. After 14.♘g3 Black
can play, for example, 14...♖g8 or
14...♕b6.

14...♖g8+ 15.♔h1 ♕g5 16.♗f3?!

A fresh surprise for me, but from
the purely chess viewpoint 16.♘g3
was perhaps better, a move which
I considered to be strictly forced
on White's part. I remember that
then 16...♕h4 did not seem very
convincing to me in view of 17.♘h5,
and therefore I was planning to
play either 16...♕xe5 or 16...0-0-0
17.♖xf7 h5 18.♗xh5 ♘xe5.

During the game the resulting
positions appeared completely
unclear to me, but my intuition
suggested that they should be good
for Black!

16...♘xe5

Of course, not 16...♕xf5? in view of
the reply 17.♗h5!, while I rejected
the move 16...0-0-0 because of
17.♘d6+ ♗xd6 18.exd6, with an
unclear game.

17.♕e2

If 17.♗xd5 or 17.♘xd5 I was
intending to castle long, and then
see what would happen next.

17...♕xf5

Of course, 17...0-0-0 18.♘xe3 ♗c5
(18...d4 19.♖g1 ♕xe3 20.♕xe3 dxe3
21.♗xb7+ ♔xb7 22.♖xg8) was also
interesting, but with the move in
the game Black finally regains the
piece, retaining an advantage.

18.♗xd5 ♕h3

If 18...♕g4, White had the reply
19.♕xe3, and after 19...0-0-0
(19...♘c4? 20.♕f2!) 20.♖g1
(20.♗xb7+? ♔xb7 21.♖g1 ♗c5!
or 21...♗h6!) 20...exd5 21.♖xg4
♘xg4 Black merely has sufficient
compensation for the queen.

19.♗xb7 ♖a7

I did not have very much time left and I wanted to play as safely as possible. 19...♖d8 may have been stronger. I was afraid of the queen capture on a6, but it would appear that in this case 20.♕xa6 ♗d6! gives Black a decisive attack. For example: 21.♘b5 (21.♖ad1 ♘f3!) 21...♗b8 22.♗c6+?! ♘xc6 23.♕xc6+ ♖d7 24.♕c8+ ♔e7 25.♖xf7+ (25.♕c5+ ♗d6) 25...♔xf7 26.♕xd7+ ♔f6 27.♕d4+ ♗e5. Instead of 20.♕xa6 White can play 20.♖ad1, but then too after 20...♖xd1 21.♖xd1 f5!? 22.♕xa6 ♔f7 it is extremely difficult, if at all possible, for White to defend his position.

20.♗f3

Of course, not 20.♗g2 ♕g4! and Black transposes into a won endgame.

20...♗h6

Of course, I very much wanted to defend my e3-pawn, but other moves were also perfectly possible: 20...♘xf3 21.♖xf3 ♕g4; 20...♗c7 21.♕xe3 ♘xf3 22.♕xf3 ♕xf3+ 23.♖xf3 ♖c7; or 20...♗c5 21.♘e4 ♗e7 22.♕xe3 ♘xf3 23.♕xf3 ♕xf3+ 24.♖xf3 f5. In the endgame Black has the advantage.

21.♘e4

21...♔e7?!

This would appear to be a mistake, after which White could have saved the game.

Stronger was 21...♖g6! 22.♗h5 (22.♖ad1 f5 23.♘d6+ ♔f8 or 22.♘d6+ ♔f8) 22...♖g7 23.♖ad1 (23.♖f6 ♗g5) 23...♔e7 24.♖f6 (24.♘f6 ♕h4!?) 24...♕h4! (on no account 24...♘g4? 25.♖xf7+! ♖xf7 26.♗xg4, while if 24...♗g5, then 25.♕e1 is possible) 25.♖d4 ♗f4, retaining the advantage.

22.♕e1 f5

There is no particular choice. After 22...f6 (RR: after both 22...♖b7 and 22...a5 23.♕c3 ♘d7 24.♕a3+ ♔d8 Black is still winning) it is bad to play 23.♘xf6? ♖g1+! 24.♔xg1 ♘xf3+ 25.♖xf3 ♕xf3 and Black wins, but after 23.♕b4+ ♔f7 24.♗h5+! White has a very dangerous attack.

23.♕b4+ ♔f7

24.♕d4?

After the correct 24.♘d6+! ♔f6 25.♘e4+ Black has nothing better than to agree to a repetition of moves after 25...♔f7. It is extremely dangerous for the king to step onto the g-file, not only in view of the rook check from g1, but also on account of the possible bishop retreat to g2.

24...♘xf3

25.♕f6+

It appears that White can gain a draw after 25.♕xa7+ ♔g6 26.♖g1+ ♗g5 (26...♔h5!?) 27.♖xg5+ ♘xg5 28.♘xg5 ♔xg5 29.♖g1+ ♔h6 30.♖xg8 ♕f1+ 31.♖g1 ♕f3+ 32.♖g2, but this is not so. In fact, Black wins by playing 27...♔h6! (instead of

27...♘xg5) 28.♖h5+ (28.♕c7 ♘xg5) 28...♕xh5 29.♕xe3+ ♖g5!.

25...♔e8 26.♕xe6+ ♔f8 27.♕f6+

RR: 27.♕c8+! ♔g7 28.♕c3+ ♔g6 29.♕c6+ ♔h5 30.♘f6+ ♔h4 31.♕xf3=.

27...♖f7 28.♕d6+

If 28.♕d8+ ♔g7 29.♖g1+ Black has 29...♗g5.

28...♔g7 29.♖g1+ ♔h8 30.♘f6

And White resigned.

NOTES BY

Vasyl Ivanchuk

Game 23   Sicilian Defence

Vasyl Ivanchuk   2705
Teimour Radjabov   2663

Calvia Olympiad 2004 (6)

1.e4 c5 2.♘f3 ♘c6 3.d4 cxd4 4.♘xd4 e5 5.♘b5 d6 6.♘1c3 a6 7.♘a3 b5 8.♘d5 ♘ce7 9.♘b4!?

This new and slightly unusual reply is partly justified by the somewhat artificial move 8...♘ce7. It was advised by Mark Dvoretsky that you should not exchange knights which are contending for one and the same square. In the given instance it is not only a question of the e7-square, but the entire plan of Black's kingside development.

9...♗d7?!

This is not the way for Black to solve his opening problems! Possibly he should go in for 9...♘f6 10.c4 ♘xe4 (10...bxc4 11.♘xc4 ♘xe4? 12.f3 or 12.♗d3) 11.cxb5 a5 (11...♕a5 12.♗d2) 12.♘a6.

10.c4!

Perhaps Radjabov was expecting 10.♕xd6?! ♘g6! (10...♘c6 11.♘xc6

♗xd6 12.♘xd8 would suit White perfectly well) 11.♕d2 ♘f6, when due to the terrible placing of the white pieces Black has more than sufficient compensation for the pawn.

10...a5 11.♘bc2

The piece sacrifice 11.♘xb5? ♗xb5 12.cxb5 axb4 13.♗e3 would have been senseless, since by playing 13...g6 14.b6 ♗h6!? Black easily parries the unprepared 'attack'.

11...♘f6

I was expecting 11...b4 12.♘b5 ♗xb5 13.cxb5 ♘f6 and here I was intending to choose between 14.a3 b3 15.♘e3 a4 16.b6 and 14.♘e3 ♘xe4 15.b6 ♕xb6? 16.f3!. Of course, the two sides' possibilities are not exhausted by these two variations.

12.♘xb5 ♗xb5

It is quite possible that in his preliminary calculations Radjabov had been intending to play 12...♘xe4 13.♘xd6+ ♘xd6 14.♕xd6 ♘c6 with compensation for the pawn, but now he noticed that White can play a move that is not only prettier, but also significantly stronger. Instead of 13.♘xd6+ he has 13.♕xd6!, which leads to an enormous advantage.

13.cxb5 ♘xe4

One feels that White stands better here, but how should he continue? Apart from the move in the game, I mainly considered 14.g3 and 14.♗d3. The continuation 14.g3 d5 15.♗g2 ♘f5 16.0-0 ♗c5 or 16.♕e2 ♗b4+ 17.♘xb4 axb4 18.♗xe4 ♘d4 did not appear altogether clear to me, although in fact this does not work in view of 19.♕h5!. In addition, instead of 16.♕e2, 16.♕d3 is also possible, comfortably winning a pawn. However, 15...♘f5 is clearly a bad move. Black should choose between 15...f5 and 15...g6, maintaining an inferior, but still defensible position. 14.♗d3 ♘c5 15.♗e3 looks good, but 14...d5 is also possible, and I was not sure that the exchange on e4 would increase White's advantage.

14.♗e3

The idea of this move is extremely simple. White wants to advance his pawn to b6 and create tactical threats. On the other hand, this plan looks rather risky, since if Black succeeds in defending himself, the far-advanced b6-pawn may well become a weakness in White's position.

14...d5

White stands clearly better after 14...g6 15.b6 ♗g7 16.♗b5+ ♔f8 17.b7 ♖b8 18.♗a6.

15.b6 f5!?

I have to admit that I somewhat underestimated this move and was mainly reckoning with the continuation 15...♕d7 16.a4 ♘d6 17.♘a3! d4 18.♘b5.

16.♕e2!?

Again, a highly questionable decision. After all, 16.b7 ♖b8 17.♗a6 was quite possible, creating the threat of 18.♗a7. If 17...d4 there is the promising-looking piece sacrifice 18.♘xd4 exd4 19.♕a4+ (19.♗xd4 or 19.♗f4!? is also quite possible) 19...♔f7 20.♗xd4 (and here there is also 20.♗f4 or 20.♖d1!?) 20...♕d6 21.♕c4+ ♔g6 22.0-0 ♘c6, although here Black has quite good chances of defending himself. In addition, Black is not obliged to play 17...d4. During the game I considered the variation 17...♘d6 18.♗a7 ♖xb7 19.♗xb7 ♘xb7 and although the position seemed to me to be better for White, it was not altogether clear what to do next. However, 18.♗a7 is not obligatory. There is the interesting-looking variation 18.♕e2 ♘xb7 (18...d4 19.♘xd4! exd4 20.♗xd4 gives White a very strong attack) 19.♗a7 ♖a8 20.♗d4! (but not 20.♕b5+? ♕d7), retaining the advantage, since Black's centre collapses and in the position with opposite-coloured bishops White will have excellent attacking prospects. Black can try another version of the exchange sacrifice with 17...♕d7!? 18.♗a7? ♖xb7 19.♗xb7 ♕xb7, but after the correct 20.♕e2 (20.♕d3!?) he again feels rather uncomfortable.

16...♔f7?!

16...d4 17.♕b5+ ♔f7 (17...♕d7? 18.♕xe5!) 18.♖d1 (or even 18.0-0-0) is extremely dangerous for Black, as is 16...f4 17.f3! fxe3 18.fxe4 ♕xb6 19.♕b5+ ♕xb5 20.♗xb5+ ♔d8 21.♘xe3 and the resulting endings do not promise Black any joy.

But perhaps he should have considered 16...g6!?.

analysis diagram

Then 17.♕b5+ ♔f7 (17...♕d7 18.♖c1 ♗g7 19.♘a3 is also possible, with some advantage to White) 18.b7 (if 18.♖d1 there is the reply 18...♘d6) 18...♖b8 19.♗a7 ♘d6 (also possible is 19...♗h6 20.♗xb8 ♕xb8 or even 20...♗d2+!?) 20.♗xb8 ♘xb5 21.♗xe5 ♘d6 (or 21...♘c6 22.♗xh8 ♕b6) 22.♗xh8 ♘xb7 leads to a completely unclear game. It has to be admitted that after 16...g6 one cannot talk about any particular advantage for White, and, if this is so, it means that my play between moves 14

and 16 causes serious doubts and requires correcting.

17.0-0-0

17...♕d7

If 17...d4 I was planning 18.♘xd4! exd4 19.♖xd4, when it is unlikely that Black can hold the position. And after 17...f4? it is even possible to play 18.b7 (18.f3! ♘c3 19.bxc3 fxe3 20.♕xe3 ♖b8 21.♗c4!? is also clearly to White's advantage) 18...♖b8 19.♗a7 ♖xb7 20.♕xe4.

Thus, for the moment Black's pawn centre is immobile. But I don't greatly like the move made by Teimour in the game. 17...g6 looks more natural, aiming for the development of the kingside. Then I would probably have played 18.g4 f4 (perhaps here 18...♕d7 should be played, although I am not altogether convinced about how useful this move is) 19.♗g2 (19. b7 ♖b8 20.♗a7 ♖xb7 21.♕xe4 dxe4 22.♖xd8 ♖xa7 does not present any danger to Black, while if 19.f3, then 19...fxe3 (19...♕c8 20.♕b5!) 20.fxe4 ♕xb6 is possible) 19...fxe3 20.♗xe4 ♕xb6 (note that 17...♕d7 removed the attack on the white b6-pawn) 21.♖xd5 (21.♗xd5+ ♘xd5

22.♖xd5 is possibly simpler and stronger) 21...♖b8! 22.♘xe3 ♘xd5 23.♘xd5 with compensation for the exchange.

18.♔b1

Here too, 18.g4 was possible, but I thought it was more useful to move the king off the open c-file.

18...♕e6?!

If 18...g6, I would now most probably have played 19.g4.

19.f3 ♘d6 20.f4

Now Black's queen is extremely badly placed, and he does not in fact manage to develop his king's bishop...

20...♘c4 21.fxe5

The game is effectively decided and White only needs to display accuracy in the conversion of his advantage.

21...♖b8 22.g4 f4

If 22...♕xe5 there would of course have followed 23.♗d4, and the exchange of queens would not have improved Black's position.

23.♕f3 g5 24.♗xc4 dxc4 25.h4 ♕c6 26.e6+

The immediate 26.♕f2 was perhaps slightly more accurate.

26...♔g6

If 26...♔e8 my reply would have been the same.

27.♕f2 ♕xe6 28.♗d4 ♗g7 29.hxg5 ♖bd8 30.♖de1 ♕d6 31.♗c5 ♕d2

32.♖e6+

This rook can leave the back rank only with check! After 32.♖xe7?? or 32.♖e2?? Black would have given mate in two moves! But now he resigned!

NOTES BY
Andrei Volokitin

With sparkling games and a fantastic 8½ out of 12 score, Ukrainian Champion Andrey Volokitin once again demonstrated his unique attacking skills.

Game 24   Sicilian Defence

Andrei Volokitin   2652
Alexander Delchev   2601

Calvia Olympiad 2004 (8)

1.e4 c5 2.♘f3 e6 3.d4 cxd4 4.♘xd4 ♘c6 5.♘c3 ♕c7 6.♗e2 a6 7.0-0 ♘f6 8.♔h1 h5

I studied this particular move before the Olympiad, but for Black. It is not so easy for White to gain an advantage here.

9.♘xc6!
The critical move. Nothing is achieved by 9.f4 ♘xd4 10.♕xd4 ♗c5, when Black has no problems.
9...bxc6
9...dxc6 comes into consideration: 10.f4 e5 11.♕e1! with an edge.
10.f4 d5

11.exd5!
A strong improvement. Black's play is justified after 11.e5?! ♘g4, when the white h-pawn plays no role, while Black has a solid centre and a clear plan of development. Only White would be likely to have problems.
11...cxd5
After 11...exd5 12.♗e3 ♗d6 13.♕d2 White has the advantage [eighteen years later, artificial intelligence disagrees and argues that Black is slightly better – ed.].
12.f5

Naturally, White's previous move was associated with this idea of opening the centre, when the 8...h5 move proves to be a serious weakening. Now the black king can hardly castle on the short side.

12...♗b7

The dangers of Black's position are illustrated by the variation 12...♗d6 13.fxe6 fxe6 (if 13...♗xe6 there is the strong 14.♖xf6! gxf6 15.♘xd5 ♗xd5 (or 15...♕d8 16.♘xf6+ ♔f8 17.♗g5 ♗e7 18.♕f1 and wins [Stockfish 14 prefers Black – ed.]) 16.♕xd5 ♖d8 17.♗e3 and White wins) 14.♗g5 ♗xh2? 15.♗xf6 gxf6 16.♘xd5! exd5 17.♕xd5 ♖a7 18.♗xh5+ with an easy win for White.

13.fxe6 fxe6 14.♗d3 0-0-0 15.♕e2 ♕c6

At home I also examined the aggressive move 15...♘g4, but after 16.♕xe6+ ♔b8 17.♗f4 ♗d6 18.♕f7! ♗xf4 19.♕xf4 White is a pawn up.

16.♗g5 h4

Black is unable to defend his numerous weaknesses, and so he seeks active counterplay. Here the optimistic 16...d4? does not work on account of 17.♗xf6 gxf6 18.♗e4 ♕b6 19.♗xb7+ ♔xb7 20.♘e4 with a winning position.

17.♖ae1!?

I wanted to win a pawn, while allowing my opponent the least counterplay.

Apart from the text move, White had two other tempting continuations:

A) 17.♗xf6?! gxf6 18.♖xf6 h3!. It was because of this move that I avoided 17.♗xf6. Now the rook capture on e6 is too dangerous for White: 19.♖xe6? hxg2+ 20.♔xg2 ♗d6! with a strong attack. 19.g3? also looks bad, for example 19...♖h6 20.♖af1 ♗g7! 21.♖xh6 ♗xh6 22.♖f6 ♗e3! with a strong initiative for Black. Thus, after 23.♕xe3?? d4+ 24.♗e4 dxe3 25.♗xc6 ♖d1+!! 26.♘xd1 e2 he wins prettily. That only leaves the capture with the queen on e6 – 19.♕xe6+ ♕xe6 20.♖xe6 hxg2+ 21.♔xg2 ♗d6. Here, compared with the game, the white pieces completely lack harmony. Thus, passive defence is dangerous: 22.♖h1 ♖h4 (with the idea of ...♔d7 and ...d5-d4) 23.♔f2 ♔d7 24.♖e2 ♖f4+ 25.♔e1 d4 26.♘e4 ♖e8! and it is only White who has problems;

B) 17.♖xf6! (a tempo-gaining move, and probably the strongest) 17...gxf6 18.♗xf6 ♗c5!. The best square for the bishop; now practically all White's logical moves lead to the same position: 19.♕e5, 19.♗xd8, or 19.♗xh8. The only incorrect one is 19.♖e1? h3! 20.♗xh8 hxg2+ 21.♔xg2 ♖g8+! (an important intermediate check), and if 22.♔h1? (22.♔f3! ♖f8+ is equal) 22...d4+! 23.♘e4 ♖xh8 and Black is a bit better. After 19.♗xd8 ♖xd8 20.♖e1 ♖e8 21.♕g4 ♔b8 22.♕xh4 e5 a position is reached where Black has some compensation, but after 23.♕h5! ♕e6 24.♘a4! White is better.

17...h3

Here 17...♖e8? is bad: 18.♗g6 ♖e7 19.♖xf6! gxf6 20.♗xf6 ♖h6 21.♗xe7 ♗xe7 22.♕g4!, winning.

18.♕xe6+ ♕xe6 19.♖xe6

19...d4?

Probably the decisive mistake; the knight should not have been allowed to go to e4. 19...♗d6! was correct, and now in the variation 20.♗xf6 hxg2+ 21.♔xg2 gxf6 22.♖fxf6 ♖xh2+ 23.♔g1 ♗c7 the knight is still at c3 and the pawn at d5, and after 24.♖f7 ♖g8+ 25.♖g6 ♖xg6+ 26.♗xg6 ♖d2 White is a pawn up, but it is very hard for him to convert it, and the position is probably drawn.

20.♘e4 hxg2+ 21.♔xg2 ♗d6

21...♖d6 does not change anything: 22.♖xd6 ♗xd6 23.♗xf6 gxf6 24.♖xf6 ♖xh2+ 25.♔g1, with roughly the same as occurred in the game.

22.♗xf6 gxf6 23.♖fxf6 ♖xh2+ 24.♔g1 ♗c7

Black had a dismal choice between the move in the game and a position with opposite-coloured bishops where he is two pawns down: 24...♗xe4 25.♗xe4 ♗c7 26.♖xa6 and White wins.

25.♘d6+ ♗xd6 26.♖xd6 ♖h1+ 27.♔f2

27...♖xd6

27...♖dh8 was hopeless: 28.♗f5+! (not 28.♖xd4?? ♖8h2+ 29.♔e3 ♖e1+ 30.♔f4 ♖f2+ 31.♔g5 ♖g1+ and Black wins) 28...♔b8 29.♖xd4 ♖8h2+ 30.♔e3 ♖e1+ 31.♔d3 and Black can resign.

28.♖xd6 ♖a1 29.a3 ♖a2

30.♖xd4!

An important moment: White had to find the most methodical way to convert his extra pawn, without allowing any counterplay. After

30.♖b6? ♚c7 31.♖b3 a5 he has great
difficulties, since the rook at b3
is passive and the black pieces are
active. With the move in the game
I forcibly transpose into a won
bishop ending, with a fixed black
pawn at a6. It is this pawn that
causes Black's downfall: had it been
at a7, the position would have been
drawn.

30...♖xb2 31.♖c4+ ♚b8

No better is 31...♚d7 32.♖b4 ♖xb4
33.axb4 ♚d6 34.♚e3 ♚e5 35.♗e2!
♗c8 36.c4 ♗f5 (otherwise ♚d3)
37.♗f3 ♗e6 38.♚d3!, transposing
into a position from the game.

**32.♖b4 ♖xb4 33.axb4 ♚c7 34.♚e3
♚b6 35.c4**

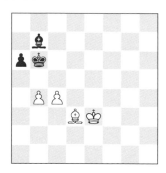

35...♗c6

The basic winning position of this
endgame is as follows: white king at
a5, pawns at b4 and c5, and bishop
on the f1-a6 diagonal; black king
at a7, bishop at c8, and pawn at a6.
White wins by c5-c6!.

After 35...♚c7 36.♚d4 ♗c8 37.c5
♚c6 38.♗e2! (zugzwang) 38...♚c7

39.♚d5! ♗b7+ 40.♚c4 ♗c6 41.♚c3!
♗b7 (41...♚b7 42.♚d4!, and 43.♚e5
and 44.♚d6+−) 42.♚b3, followed by
♚a4 and ♚a5 White wins.

36.♚d4 ♗a4 37.c5+ ♚b7 38.♚e5

The king breaks through to d6. It is
all over.

**38...♗d7 39.♚d6 ♗h3 40.♗c4 ♚a7
41.♗e6 ♗g2 42.♚c7 ♗f1 43.♗d7
♗g2 44.c6 ♗f3**

45.♗e6!

Avoiding the last trap: 45.♚d8??
♗xc6! 46.♗xc6 a5! with a draw.

**45...♗g2 46.♚d7 a5 47.c7 ♗b7
48.♗d5 ♗a6 49.bxa5 ♗b5+ 50.♚d8
♗a6 51.♗c6**

Black resigned.

NOTES BY
Andrei Volokitin

Game 25   French Defence
Andrei Volokitin   2652
Smbat Lputian   2634
Calvia Olympiad 2004 (9)

1.e4 e6 2.d4 d5 3.♘c3 ♗b4 4.e5 c5 5.a3 ♗a5

The day before the game, at a team meeting, our trainer Vladimir Tukmakov asked me whether I was ready to play against the fireproof variation of the French Defence with 5...♗a5, which had been played nearly all their lives by my prospective opponents Vaganian and Lputian. I said that I had a couple of ideas, and then he insistently recommended that I should take Seryozha Karjakin as a workmate and 'polish' this variation. Seryozha and I sat down and analysed for three and a half hours, and we found an advantage for White. This, naturally, improved my frame of mind and the following day I could hardly wait to employ our analysis.

6.b4 cxd4 7.♕g4!

In my view, this is stronger than the alternative 7.♘b5, when play is unclear.

7...♘e7 8.bxa5 dxc3 9.♕xg7 ♖g8 10.♕xh7 ♘bc6 11.♘f3!

This development of the knight is more logical than the reinforcement of the centre by 11.f4.

11...♕c7

Black has no time to take the a5-pawn - 11...♕xa5 12.♘g5! and if 12...♘xe5 13.f4 f6 14.fxe5 fxg5 15.♕h5+! and White wins.

12.♗f4 ♗d7

13.a6!

In the previous round, Grischuk had failed to gain any advantage against Vaganian after 13.♗d3 0-0-0 14.♗g3 ♕xa5 15.0-0 ♘f5 with counterplay. The move in the game is simple and logical; why give up the a-pawn without a fight?

13...0-0-0

The inclusion of the moves 13.a6 b6 in the variation 14.♗d3 0-0-0 15.♗g3 is clearly in White's favour.

14.axb7+ ♔b8

Black did not play 13...0-0-0 in order to capture on b7 – 14...♕xb7 15.♕d3 with a decisive advantage.

15.♕d3!

I had already reached this position in a blitz game against Vaganian, when I played the weaker 15.♗g3? and lost quickly after 15...♘f5!. There is nothing for the queen to do at h7!

15...♖g4

Bad here is 15...♘g6 16.♗g3 ♘cxe5 17.♘xe5 ♘xe5 18.♕d4 f6 19.♖b1. To those wishing to play this variation for Black, I recommend that they study 15...d4 with the idea of 16.♘xd4? ♘xd4 17.♕xd4 ♗b5 18.♕e4 ♗xf1 19.♔xf1 ♘f5 with the initiative.

16.g3

Weak here is 16.♗g3 ♖e4+ 17.♗e2 ♘f5 with counterplay.

16...♘g6 17.♕xc3 ♘xf4

18.h3!

At this point Smbat began thinking for a long time. Evidently he had ceased to like his position and my lightning replies.

18...♘xh3 19.♖xh3 ♘xe5

Smbat did not find anything better than to go into an endgame a pawn down. This position was known to me from the correspondence game Pletanek-Kohout, 1998, which went 19...♖e4 20.♗e2 ♗e8 (20...♘xe5 21.♕xc7+ ♔xc7 22.♘g5! ♖a4 23.f4 f6 24.♘h7, winning) 21.♖b1 ♘xe5 22.♕xc7+ ♔xc7 23.♘xe5 ♖xe5 24.b8+♕ ♖xb8 25.♖xb8 1-0. I also had an enormous time advantage: 1:36 against 0:26.

20.♕xc7+ ♔xc7 21.♘xe5 ♖e4+
22.♔d2 ♖xe5

23.♗d3!

Beginning the conversion of the extra pawn. Here I also considered 23.f4, but after 23...♖e4 (but not 23...♖f5? 24.♖h6!) 24.♖b1 ♔b8! 25.♖h7 ♖f8 the rook comes into play via a4 and creates counterplay.

23...♖g5

23...d4 also does not help on account of 24.♖b1 ♔b8 25.♖h7 f5 26.♖b4, and thanks to the b7-pawn White has a won position.

24.♖h7 ♗e8

The other defence 24...♖f8 has its drawbacks – 25.♖b1 ♔b8 26.♗a6! e5 27.♖bh1 ♗e6 (27...♖g6 28.♖xf7!) 28.♖1h5, winning.

25.♖e1!

After this move, White's position can be considered won. Subsequently I chose the strongest continuations and completed my best game in the Olympiad.

25...e5

25...♔d6 26.♖h8! ♔c7 27.♗b5 or 25...♔b8 26.♖h8 ♔xb7 27.♗b5 both win for White.

26.f4! exf4 27.♖h8! fxg3 28.♗a6 g2

The rest is all forced.

29.♖hxe8 ♖g8 30.♖xd8 ♖xd8 31.♖g1 ♖g8 32.♔e2 ♔b6 33.♗d3 ♔xb7 34.♔f3 ♔b6 35.♖xg2 ♖xg2 36.♔xg2 ♔a5 37.♔f3 ♔a4 38.♔e3 ♔xa3 39.♔d4 ♔b4 40.♔xd5 f5 1-0

NOTES BY
Pavel Eljanov

This was the final, 14th round of the Olympiad. We, the Ukrainian team, had already practically secured the gold medals, as our nearest rivals, the Russian lads, were three points behind. The mood in the Ukrainian team was excellent and we very much wanted to conclude this triumphal Olympiad on a high note!

'Eljanov is maybe not so bright as let's say Ivanchuk, Karjakin or Volokitin, but he is a very good player and at 21 he is still very young.'

Game 26   King's Indian Defence
Pavel Eljanov   2629
Igor Nataf   2565
Calvia Olympiad 2004 (14)

1.d4 ♘f6 2.c4 g6 3.♘c3 ♗g7 4.e4 d6 5.♘f3 0-0 6.♗e2 e5 7.0-0 ♘c6 8.d5 ♘e7 9.b4 ♘h5 10.♖e1 f5 11.♘g5 ♘f6

My opponent was also in a determined mood! He accompanied each move with a loud and confident pressing of the clock button. Nataf goes in for what is considered today to be the most critical line for Black in the 9.b4 variation. I also think that this is the strongest and most logical plan for Black, since he should play where he has the greatest resources for developing an initiative. The only drawback is the weakening of the e6-square.

12.♗f3
The alternative 12.f3 also comes into consideration.

12...c6

13.♕b3!?
A comparatively new and, in my view, logical move. Vasyl Ivanchuk, the leader of our team, who played brilliantly in the Olympiad, also

upheld the same position in this match against Lautier... only as Black! In their game Lautier decided to play for a win in an endgame with a microscopic plus: 13.b5 cxd5 14.cxd5 h6 15.♘e6 ♗xe6 16.dxe6 fxe4 17.♘xe4 ♘xe4 18.♗xe4 d5 19.♗a3 dxe4 20.♕xd8 ♖fxd8 21.♗xe7 ♖e8 22.♗c5 ♖xe6 23.♗e3 a6 24.b6, Lautier-Ivanchuk, Calvia 2004. Black gained a draw, although not without difficulty.

13...h6 14.♘e6 ♗xe6 15.dxe6 ♕c8

16.b5!?

A new move; earlier only 16.♖d1 was played. My idea is to place the other rook on d1, since in certain lines after the opening of the centre the rook at a1 may come under the X-ray attack of the bishop at g7.

16...♕xe6 17.♗a3

17...♔h7

The first critical moment in the game. At the board I saw an interesting resource for Black: 17...c5!? 18.exf5 (the pawn has to be taken, as otherwise after 18.♖ad1 f4 White's position is unpromising) 18...gxf5! (the right way – after 18...♘xf5 19.♗xb7 ♘d4 20.♕a4 ♖ab8 21.♗e4! ♘xe4 22.♘xe4 ♕g4 23.♔h1! White gains the advantage) 19.♗xb7 ♖ab8 20.♗f3 e4 21.♗e2 ♘c6! 22.♗b2 ♘d4 (by giving back the pawn, Black has achieved a great deal: he has set his centre in motion and transferred his knight to a dominating position) 23.♕d1 ♘d7 24.♗f1. This position is not easy to evaluate. Black has the initiative, but he must play actively, as otherwise in time his weaknesses (a7, d6 and the light square complex) may tell. 17...♔h8 also comes into consideration. As for the move in the game, it has its pluses and minuses.

18.♖ad1 ♖fd8

The alternative 18...♖ad8 19.bxc6 bxc6 20.♕a4 has the drawback that it slightly weakens Black's queenside. 18...c5 is no longer so good; after 19.exf5 gxf5 20.♗xb7 ♖ab8 21.♗d5 ♘exd5 22.♘xd5 White has a clear advantage.

19.bxc6

It is better not to delay this exchange. In the event of 19.♖d2 ♖d7 20.bxc6 ♘xc6! (the b7-pawn is defended!) 21.exf5 ♕xf5! (if 21...gxf5 22.♗d5 ♕e7 White has the very strong move 23.♕b1! when 23...

e4? fails to 24.♘xe4! fxe4 25.♗xe4+ ♘xe4 26.♖xe4) 22.♗xc6 bxc6 23.♖xd6 ♖xd6 24.♗xd6 ♖e8 25.c5 e4 Black gains counterplay.

19...bxc6

If 19...♘xc6, the difference in the placing of the white rooks becomes apparent – 20.exf5 ♕xf5 21.♕xb7 ♘d4. With the white rook on a1 Black would now be threatening 22...♘c2, and in some cases the ...e5-e4 thrust. But here after 22.♗xd6! ♖ac8 23.♖xe5! (after 23.♗xe5 Black has the fantastic 23...♖d7!! and White must sacrifice his queen: 24.♗xd4 (24.♕xc8? loses to 24...♘xf3+ 25.gxf3 ♖xd1 26.♕xf5 ♖xe1+) 24...♖xb7 25.♗xb7 ♖xc4 26.♗f3 with an unclear position) 23...♕c2 24.♖e7 ♘f5 25.♖xg7+! ♘xg7 26.♕b3 ♕xb3 27.axb3. With two pawns for the exchange and two strong bishops, White has the advantage here, for example: 27...♖d7 (27...♘f5? 28.♗b7) 28.g4! ♘e6 29.h4! (playing to restrict the knight) 29...♘e8 30.♗e5 ♖xd1+ 31.♗xd1.

20.♕a4 ♖ac8

Black could have considered 20...f4 21.♖e2 ♖d7 22.♖ed2 ♖ad8 23.♕a6, also with strong positional pressure for the pawn.

21.♕a6!

Beginning from this moment I found several strong prophylactic moves. Black wanted to play ...d6-d5. For example, after 21.♖d2 d5! 22.exd5 cxd5 23.♗xe7 ♕xe7 24.♘xd5 ♘xd5 25.♗xd5 e4 and Black's position is the more promising, since the c4-pawn is blocked and his hands are freed for an attack on the white king.

21...♘e8 22.♖c1!

Another less than obvious prophylactic move. Black was threatening to drive the queen from a6 and again play d5. Now in the event of 22...♘c7 I am ready to capture on a7, since the c4-pawn is indirectly defended.

Mark Dvoretsky, whose training sessions I attended a few years ago, would have been very happy! After all, one of the most important principles of chess playing – prophylactic thinking – was propagated very enthusiastically by him.

22...♕f7

The queen sacrifice after 22...♘c7 23.♕xa7 ♕xc4 is most probably insufficient. An approximate variation is 24.♘d5 cxd5 25.♗xc4 dxc4 26.h4! ♗f6 (with the idea of ...♘e6) 27.♕b6 ♘e6 28.h5 gxh5 29.exf5 ♘d4 30.♗e4 and White has a clear advantage.

23.♖ed1

23...fxe4?!

23...♖d7!? came into consideration, with the idea of playing the knight to e6 with gain of tempo. White must act resolutely: 24.h4! ♘c7 25.♕a5 ♘c6 26.♖xd6 ♖cd8 27.♖xd7 ♖xd7 28.♘e2. Black has given back the pawn, but activated his pieces. Even so, I prefer White's position.

24.♗xe4 ♘c7

My opponent decided to sacrifice a pawn in a different way. During the game I sensed that here the ...d6-d5 break was not so good. Therefore without much thought I played:

25.♕xa7

25.♕a5 ♘f5!? was also possible, but I sensed that I needed to choose the most critical move!

25...d5

The culminating point of the entire game! Here I thought for roughly fifteen minutes and made a seemingly modest move.

26.♕b7!!

This creates one concrete threat: to take on e7 and then on d5, when the queen at b7 will defend my light-squared bishop. At the same time I avoid a possible attack by the rook from a8. My opponent thought for 40 minutes over his next move, but was unable to find a defence. Here there isn't one. In all variations White has a great or decisive advantage!

Initially I considered 26.h4?!, but I noticed in time the reply 26...♘f5!? (26...♖f8!? is also not bad; in the event of 27.cxd5 ♖a8 28.♕c5 ♖xa3! 29.dxc6 Black wins prettily by 29...♘e6 30.♕xa3 ♕xf2+ 31.♔h2 ♖f4 32.♕xe7 ♘g5!! 33.♗xg6+ ♔xg6 34.♖d6+ ♔h5 35.♕e8+ ♘f7) 27.cxd5 ♖a8! (everything rests on this move; now White must play very resourcefully, so as not to lose immediately) 28.♕b7! ♖db8 29.♕xc6 ♖a6! (29...♖xa3 30.h5! with an attack) 30.♕c4 ♖xa3 31.h5!.

26.cxd5 was also not bad, but the drawback of the move is that Black can recapture with a knight: 26...♘exd5! (if 26...cxd5 White again has 27.♕b7!!), and now after 27.♗b2

♖d7!? 28.♕a4 ♖cd8 Black gains counterplay.

Other moves demonstrate that it is very dangerous to play 'by eye' in this position, for example: 26.♕a5? ♘f5! 27.♗xf5 gxf5 28.cxd5 ♖a8 29.♕b4 ♘xd5 30.♘xd5 cxd5, or 26.♗xe7? ♕xe7 27.cxd5 cxd5 with an attack.

26...♖f8

After 26...d4 White can gain a great advantage in various ways: 27.♘a4 [Very strong is 27.♘b5! cxb5 28.♗xe7 ♕xe7 29.cxb5 (threatening b5-b6) 29...♖b8 30.♕xc7 ♕xc7 31.♖xc7 ♖xb5 32.h4 – ed.] 27...♘g8 28.♘b6 ♖b8 29.♕xc6 ♘f6, when I like best of all 30.c5!? ♘xe4 [30...♘b5!∓ – ed.] 31.♕xe4 ♕xa2 32.♗b4. Also totally bad is 26...dxe4 27.♖xd8 ♖xd8 28.♕xc7 ♖f8 29.♘xe4. Apparently the most tenacious move was 26...♕e6, when White has a pleasant choice: 27.♗xe7 (or he can retain an advantage in the middlegame with 27.cxd5 ♘cxd5 28.♘xd5 ♘xd5 29.h3) 27...♕xe7 28.cxd5 ♘xd5 29.♕xe7 ♘xe7 30.♖xd8!? ♖xd8 31.♖d1 and Black has weak pawns at c6, e5 and g6 and a bad bishop, whereas White's

passed pawn is very dangerous. Therefore I think it unlikely that Black will be saved by the drawing tendencies of opposite-coloured bishops.

27.♗xe7 ♕xe7 28.cxd5 cxd5

The endgame is also completely bad: 28...♘xd5 29.♕xe7 ♘xe7 30.h4!?.

29.♘xd5 ♘xd5 30.♕xd5

Here we can take stock: White is a pawn up with the better position. His attack will soon decide the game.

30...♕a7

31.♕d2

I saw the possibility of 31.♗xg6+!?, but after 31...♔xg6 32.♕d3+ ♔f6 (White wins after 32...♔g5 33.♕g3+ ♔f6 34.♖d6+ ♔e7 35.♕xg7+ ♔xd6 36.♖d1+ ♕d4

37.♖xd4+ exd4 38.♕xd4+) I did not find a forced win, although I did not particularly look for one! In fact there is a win: 33.♖xc8 ♖xc8 34.♕f3+ ♔e7 35.♕g4! ♖g8 36.♕b4+! (I think it was this check that I missed during the game) 36...♔e8 37.♕c4 ♖f8 38.♕e6+ ♕e7 39.♕c6+ ♔f7 40.♖d7 and wins.
31...♖cd8 32.♕e2 ♖d4 33.♖xd4 ♕xd4 34.h4!

Launching the decisive offensive!
34...♖f1 35.♖e1 ♗f8
35...♖xh4 36.g3 ♖h3 37.♕g4.
36.g3 ♖f6 37.h5 ♗c5 38.♖f1 ♔g7
39.hxg6 ♖f8 40.♔g2 ♖f6 41.f3 ♖b6
42.♖d1

I think that transposing into the endgame is the simplest way to win.
42...♖b2 43.♖xd4 ♖xe2+ 44.♔f1 ♗xd4 45.♔xe2 h5 46.a4 ♗b6

47.♔f1!
Initially I was thinking of playing 47.♔d3 ♗a5 (if 47...♗f2 48.a5 ♗xg3 49.♔e2! ♗h2 50.♔f2 and the pawn queens) 48.♔c4 ♗e1 49.♔b5 ♗xg3, which also probably wins, but why choose this when it is not necessary?
47...♗c7 48.♔g2 ♔h6 49.♔h3 ♗d8 50.g4 h4 51.g5+! ♗xg5 52.a5 ♔g7 53.a6 ♗e3 54.♔xh4 ♔f6 55.♔g3 ♗a7 56.♔g2 1-0

CHAPTER V

Unstoppable Ukraine – The Women's Team wins the Turin Olympiad in 2006

By **Dirk Jan ten Geuzendam** (*New In Chess* magazine, issue 2006#5)

The men won the Olympiad in 2004, the women countered with a victory in 2006 in Turin. Led by Natalia Zhukova, Ukraine won their first ever Olympiad medals and making up for the long wait they immediately captured gold, winning their first twelve matches and coasting home with a draw on the final day. Top seeds Russia finished in second place, ahead of the old champions, China, who appeared with a rejuvenated team. Their new sensation, 12-year-old Hou Yifan, scored 11/13 on third board.

A proud coach Vereslav Eingorn and his girls: Inna Gaponenko, Natalia Zhukova, Kateryna Lahno and Anna Ushenina.

'No more China,' Natalia Zhukova had said to herself on the eve of the Olympiad. Her wish, silently expressed with an inaudible sigh, was understandable. At the Women's World Championship in Ekaterinburg last March she had met two opponents and they were both Chinese. Zhukova's

World Championship adventure ended as early as Round 2, when 12-year-old Hou Yifan brutally beat her 2-0.

Of course, it was not very likely that in Turin the Chinese women's team would repeat their recent Olympiad successes. Former World Champion Xie Jun rarely played, former World Champion Zhu Chen had chosen to represent Qatar, and current World Champion Xu Yuhua stayed at home because she was pregnant. The team that appeared in Turin was almost a junior team, whose main aim was to garner experience for the years ahead. The clear favourites in the women's competition were Russia, led by Alexandra Kosteniuk.

Ukraine were the second seeds, a statistic they only became aware of shortly before they left for Italy. A wondrous discovery for a team that has often been one of the top seeds, but never lived up to expectations. As Zhukova recalled while looking back on the greatest success in her career: 'During a two-day training session in Kyiv we suddenly realized that we were the second seeds and said to ourselves that if we were that strong we should go for it.'

To be honest, they would have been happy with any medal, but as the Olympiad got underway they began hoping for more. 'China was not so strong this time and we thought that Russia would be our main rivals. But they had other problems. Not chess problems, but certain psychological problems. They were the favourites and all of them wanted to make good results for themselves. That's not how it should be. You always have to think about the team and not about who will play with Black or with White. We were better as a team. Our coach would say, come on, it doesn't matter if you play Black six times. For example, Katya Lahno played four of her first five games with White. That's OK. If she is good with White let her do it with White!'

Extremely motivated and ambitious, Ukraine began winning their matches, but of course they knew that the crucial encounters would be the clashes with Russia and China. The match against China came in Round 4 and ended in a 2-1 victory thanks to Lahno's win against Wang Yu. The next day they were paired against Russia. Again they won 2-1, but in the decisive game on Board 1, Zhukova needed a helping hand of Lady Luck, when Kosteniuk misplayed a winning position and ended up losing.

All of them proved to be in great form and in the following rounds they became unstoppable. Zhukova scored plus 5 and even made her second (overall) grandmaster norm. Radiating happiness about this double success, she evaluated the performance of her team mates. 'Kateryna Lahno is a very active player. She had an excellent result on second board, plus 7. She just wants to win every game and if she is in good form she can do this. Of course we had our worries because she had played so badly in her last five tournaments. But here... our third board, Inna Gaponenko, is a very experienced player. She actually played first board at the 1996 Olympiad. Her individual results tend to be middling, but she is a great team player and she scored plus 5. Our reserve player Anna Ushenina is a new player, even for us. She made her Olympiad debut. She's only 20 years old and she doesn't believe in herself enough. But we told her, Anna, you play well! And she made plus 4 and that was enough for us.'

According to Zhukova, part of their achievement should be attributed to the Ukrainian chess federation's serious approach to the Olympiad. 'In the beginning of the year our federation said, girls please think about the Olympiad. Make your calendar accordingly. Don't come there tired. Which was what happened on previous occasions. We just played one tournament after the other and then there would be the Olympiad. Now we came well prepared.'

Her final words of praise are for their coach, Vereslav Eingorn. 'Our coach kept us sharp till the very end. Every day he'd tell us, you have to win! You have to win 2½-½! Before the last round, after we'd beaten India 2½-½, I said, now everything is decided and over. A draw in the last round, why not? It seems to me that... but he went, no, no, you have to play! And so we were ready to play. But, of course, when it became clear that our opponents didn't object to a draw either, the match was soon over.'

Natalia Zhukova in Turin in 2006.

Natalia Zhukova

Natalia Zhukova (born 1979 in Leipzig, GDR) was born into a military family serving abroad. Zhukova spent her childhood in Ukraine, in Kakhovka. She won both European and World Youth Championships and quickly afterwards moved to become Ukraine's foremost women's chess player.

In 1996 she tied for 1st-2nd places in the Ukranian Women's Championship at her debut at age 17.

She quickly entered the world elite with victories in supertournaments in Belgrade and Groningen in 1998 and was the first European Women's Champion in 2000, a feat she repeated in 2015 (both held in Georgia).

Zhukova headed the Ukranian Olympiad team since 1998 and was victorious in 2006 in Turin, taking both the team and the board gold medal. Subsequent successes include winning the Team World and the European Championships in 2013.

She was also part of the Agrouniversal women's super club which won multiple European Club Cups.

Zhukova is an honoured sports master of Ukraine and gained the male Grandmaster title in 2010.

Fun fact: there are two Olympic athletes who go by the same name: a volleyball player from Kazakhstan and a Russian cross-country ski star.

In 2019, after winning her second Ukranian women's championship, she made a career switch and is now actively involved in domestic politics as deputy of the Odessa city council. 'Odessa has become my home town and I love the sea.'

NOTES BY
Natalia Zhukova

Game 27   Queen's Indian Defence
Natalia Zhukova
Humpy Koneru
Turin Olympiad 2006 (12)

1.d4 ♘f6 2.c4 e6 3.♘f3 b6 4.g3 ♗a6 5.b3 ♗b4+ 6.♗d2 ♗e7 7.♘c3
More often White plays 7.♗g2 here, with the idea of 7...c6 8.♗c3 etc. But Humpy has ample experience with this sort of play, so I decided to go for another type of position.

7...d5
If 7...c6 then 8.e4 d5, and now either 9.♕c2 dxe4 10.♘xe4 ♗b7 (10...c5!? looks interesting too) 11.♘eg5 c5 12.d5, as in the game Topalov-Anand, Sofia 2005, or

9.e5 ♘e4 10.♗d3 ♘xc3 11.♗xc3 c5 etcetera.

Also possible is 7...0-0, and White has plenty of choice here: 8.♖c1 or 8.♕c2 or 8.e4, which has rarely been played in the two years since 8.♖c1 was introduced.

8.cxd5 exd5 9.♗g2 0-0 10.0-0 ♖e8
Usually Black starts with 10...♗b7 in order to possibly avoid playing ...♖e8, and now 11.♕c2 ♘a6 12.♖fd1 ♕c8 has been played in many games.

11.♕c2 ♗b7 12.♗f4 ♘a6 13.♖fd1

13...♗b4
Boris played the natural 13...c6 14.♘e5 h6 15.a3 ♘c7 16.e4 ♘e6 17.♗e3, and after 17...♗f8 18.b4 ♖c8 19.♕b3 got an unpleasant position.
14.♘e5 ♕e7 15.e3
Played analogously to the game Aronian-Khuzman, Warsaw 2005, where Levon just left his bishop to be taken by the g-pawn and won with a nice attack. I was not happy with the idea of presenting my bishop to Humpy (because I'm not so good in the attack as Levon is ☺) and hoped to have time to play g3-g4 quickly.

Unfortunately, 15.♘b5 is not good because of 15...c6 16.a3 (16.♘xc6? loses to 16...♗xc6 17.♕xc6 ♖ac8) 16...cxb5 17.axb4 ♘xb4, and Black is slightly better.

15...h6
Black could have exploited the move e2-e3 with 15...♗xc3!? 16.♕xc3 ♘e4 17.♗xe4 (forced) 17...dxe4 18.♘c6 ♕d7 19.♖ac1 ♕f5, with a nice position.

16.g4

My dream!
16...♗xc3 17.♕xc3 c5
Now after 17...♘e4 White will just play 18.♕b2.
18.a3 ♘c7
18...♖ac8 19.♕b2 ♘c7 was more precise.
19.h3
It was tempting to play 19.dxc5 bxc5 20.b4, trying to weaken Black's pawn structure, but after 20...♘e6! (20...d4? is bad because of 21.♕xc5; and after 20...c4 White is OK) 21.bxc5 d4 22.♕c4 ♗xg2 23.♔xg2 g5 24.♗g3 dxe3 25.fxe3 (Black wouldn't mind 25.c6 ♘f4+ 26.♗xf4 gxf4) 25...♘xc5 Black is fine.
19...♖ac8 20.♕b2

After 20.dxc5?! bxc5 21.b4 ♘e6
Black is clearly better.

20...♘d7?

A serious mistake. After 20...♘c6
21.♗h2 cxd4 22.cxd4 ♘e4 we would
have had a position with mutual
chances. A position in which it
would not be advisable for White
to look for a tactical solution:
23.♗xe4? dxe4 24.d5 ♘g5 25.d6 ♕f6
26.d7 ♘f3+ 27.♔g2 (27.♘xf3 loses to
the straightforward 27...♕xb2) 27...
e3, and Black is winning.

21.♘c4!

Humpy had only expected 21.♘xd7
♕xd7 22.dxc5 bxc5, with a position
that is hard to assess.

21...♘e6

22.♗g3

There's no need to rush to win
material. After 22.♘d6 ♘xf4

23.♘xc8 ♘xh3+ 24.♗xh3 ♖xc8
Black has compensation for the
exchange.
And after 22.dxc5 ♘xf4 23.exf4
dxc4 24.♗xb7 ♖xc5 Black is even
better.

22...dxc4 23.♗xb7 c3?!

In my opinion, a better way to
defend was giving up the exchange:
23...♘g5 24.h4 (if 24.♗xc8 ♖xc8,
with compensation for Black)
24...♘e4 25.♗xc8 ♖xc8 26.bxc4
♘xg3 27.fxg3 ♕xe3+ 28.♕f2 ♕c3
29.♖ac1 ♕xa3 30.g5, when White
has a clear advantage, but Black is
not entirely without chances.

24.♕xc3 cxd4 25.♕b4

Not so good was 25.♕xc8 ♖xc8 26.
♗xc8 ♘dc5.

**25...♖c2 26.♕xe7 ♖xe7 27.exd4 ♘f6
28.♗g2 ♖d7**

29.d5

Instead, much weaker was 29.♗e5
♘d5 30.♖ac1 ♖xc1 31.♖xc1 f6
32.♗b8 ♘xd4 33.♖c8+ ♔h7
34.♗xd5 ♖xd5 35.♗xa7 b5 (White
would have better chances after
35...♘e2+ 36.♔h2 ♖a5 37.♗xb6
♖xa3 38.b4) 36.♗xd4 ♖xd4 37.♖b8
♖d5, when White's advantage is
limited.

29...♘c5 30.b4?!
Better was 30.♖ac1 ♖xc1 31.♖xc1
♘xd5 32.b4 ♘e6 33.♖c8+ ♔h7
34.♗e4+ g6 35.♗e5 f6 36.♗xd5
♖xd5 37.♗xf6 g5 38.♖e8, with a
clearly better position for White.

30...♘ce4?!
She should have tried 30...♘b3
31.♖ab1 ♘d2 32.♖bc1 ♖xc1 33.
♖xc1 ♘xd5, when Black still has a
difficult position, but at least with
equal material.
31.♗e5
Now White is winning.
31...♘c3
If 31...♘xf2, then 32.♖d4, and Black
loses material.
**32.♖d3 ♘e2+ 33.♔f1 ♘c1 34.♖c3
♖xc3 35.♗xc3 ♘d3 36.♖d1 ♘f4
37.♗xf6 gxf6 38.d6 ♔g7 39.♗c6
♖d8 40.d7 f5 41.♖e1 ♔f6 42.♖e8
♘e6 43.f4 ♔g6 44.♗e4! ♖xd7
45.gxf5+ ♔f6 46.fxe6**
I believe that with a piece down
Humpy would resign in an
individual tournament. But for the
team she continued to play...
46...fxe6

47.♔f2
47.♔e2 was an easier win.
**47...♖d2+ 48.♔g3 ♖a2 49.♖h8
♖xa3+ 50.♔g4 ♖a4 51.♖xh6+ ♔e7
52.♖h7+**
More straightforward was 52.f5
exf5+ 53.♔xf5 ♖xb4 54.♖h7+ ♔d6
55.♖xa7, and wins.
52...♔f6 53.♔f3
A typical time-trouble move.
**53...♖xb4 54.h4 ♖b3+ 55.♔f2 ♖b4
56.♔e3 ♖b3+ 57.♗d3 a5 58.h5 ♖b2
59.♖b7 ♖h2 60.♗g6**
Black resigned.

With this victory, Katya's win
against Harika and Ushenina's
draw, we won our 12th match in
a row and had come very close to
becoming Olympic champions
(we only needed a draw in the last
round, which we duly made).
Many thanks to our coach
Vyacheslav Eingorn and all our
fans and friends who supported
us during the Olympiad. I hope
and believe this is not the last!!!
Bravissimo Ukraine!!!

NOTES BY
Inna Gaponenko

Inna Gaponenko once again proved to be a great team player.

Game 28   Sicilian Defence
Inna Gaponenko
Irina Krush

Turin Olympiad 2006 (9)

1.e4 c5 2.♘f3 d6 3.d4 cxd4 4.♘xd4 ♘f6 5.♘c3 ♘c6 6.f3

Normally, I prefer to play the main line with 6.♗g5, but before my game in Round 9 against Madl I had prepared this line. I won that game, so on the next day, when

I drew White again, I decided to repeat the variation.

6...e5
The principled answer. Other continuations are 6...e6 and 6...♕b6.
7.♘b3 ♗e7 8.♗e3 0-0
Another possibility is 8...♗e6, with the idea of playing ...d6-d5 and simplifying the position, with approximate equality. White can prevent this with 9.♘d5 or the more interesting plan 9.♕e2, and reach positions similar to the English Attack against the Najdorf Variation.
9.♕d2 a5 10.♗b5 ♘a7 11.♗e2
Another possibility was 11.♗d3.
11...♗e6 12.♖d1 ♘c8 13.♕c1

13...♘b6
A small surprise. My game from Round 9 saw 13...♕c7 14.♘b5 ♕c6 15.c4 a4 16.♘d2 ♗d8 17.♘f1 ♘e8 18.♘g3 ♗b6 19.♘f5 ♗xe3 20.♘xe3, but I think that the plan chosen by Irina is stronger.
14.0-0
I saw the game Bojkov-Rusev, in which play continued 14.♘c5 ♕c7 15.♘b5 ♕c6 16.♘xe6 fxe6 17.c4 ♘xe4 18.fxe4 ♕xe4, but unfortunately I hadn't analysed this

125

possibility for Black at home and I didn't want to take any risks.

14...♕c7

14...♘c4 15.♗xc4 ♗xc4 16.♖f2 was seen in Short-Stefansson, Reykjavik 2002 (½-½, 44).

15.♔h1 ♘c4 16.♗xc4 ♕xc4

16...♗xc4 looks stronger. After 17.♖fe1 b5 18.♘d2 b4 19.♘xc4 ♕xc4 20.♘d5 ♘xd5 21.b3 ♕c6 22.♖xd5 ♖fc8 the position should be equal.

17.♗g5

Fighting for the d5-point.

17...a4 18.♘d2 ♕c5 19.♘db1

After 19.a3 ♖fc8 20.♘db1 b5 Black is slightly better.

19...h6 20.♗xf6 ♗xf6 21.♕d2

In case of 21.♘a3 ♗g5 22.♕b1 ♖ab8 (if 22...b5, then 23.♘cxb5 ♖fb8 24.c4 ♗xc4 25.♘xc4 ♕xb5 26.♘xd6 ♕e2 27.b4 axb3 28.axb3 ♖a2 29.♖g1, with equality) 23.♘d5 b5 24.c3 f5 Black would have had an edge.

21...♖fd8

Here 21...♗c4!? looked like an interesting idea.

22.♘a3 b5 23.♘d5 ♗g5 24.♕d3 ♖ab8

At this point, I received the offer of a draw, but our coach told me to play on. I supposed that I ran no

risk of losing and might even be better, but that Black had several good possibilities to intensify the game.

25.c3 ♗xd5 26.♕xd5 ♕xd5

Also possible was the immediate 26...b4: 27.♕xc5 dxc5 28.♖xd8+ ♖xd8 29.cxb4 cxb4 30.♘c4 ♖d4 31.♘xe5 h5, with roughly equal chances.

27.♖xd5 b4 28.♘b5

28...bxc3

Stronger was 28...a3! 29.♖b1 (after 29.bxa3 ♖xb5 30.♖xb5 bxc3 31.g3 ♗e3 32.♖b3 ♖c8 Black also keeps a plus) 29...axb2 30.♖xb2 bxc3 31.♖c2 ♗d2 32.♔g1 ♖dc8 33.♔f2, and White has to be careful to make a draw.

29.bxc3 ♖dc8 30.♖fd1 ♗e3 31.g3 g6 32.♔g2 h5 33.♔f1

At this point I had 1 minute and 30 seconds left, so I played my next moves quickly, almost automatically. Irina had a little more time, but she followed my pace.

33...♔f8 34.♔e2 ♗c5 35.c4 ♔e7 36.f4 f6 37.f5?!

Better was 37.♔d3.

37...♖c6?!

Not accurate either. Better was 37...gxf5 38.exf5.

38.fxg6 ♖g8 39.♖5d3 ♖xg6 40.♘c3

40...♖g4?

A mistake that causes the black position to collapse. She should have played 40...♔e6 41.♖b1 f5! (after 41...♗d4 42.♘d5 ♖g4 43.♖xd4 exd4 44.♔d3 White clearly has the better chances) 42.exf5+ ♔xf5 43.♘d5 ♖g7 44.♖f1+ ♔g4 45.♘f6+ ♔g5 46.♘e4+ ♔h6, and the game would most likely end in a draw.

41.h3 ♖g6 42.♘d5+ ♔e6 43.♖b1 ♖g7

Black cannot allow the invasion of the white rook to b7, of course.

44.♖f3

And this loses the f-pawn.

44...♖f7 45.♖bf1 ♖c8 46.♖xf6+ ♖xf6 47.♖xf6+ ♔d7 48.♖f7+ ♔e8 49.♖h7

Black resigned.

CHAPTER VI

A fully deserved win by Ukraine at the Olympiad in 2010

By **Dirk Jan ten Geuzendam** (adapted from *New In Chess* magazine 2010#7)

The 39th Chess Olympiad of 2010 was played in Khanty-Mansiysk, Siberia. In the Ugra Tennis Centre, the fight for the gold medals was perhaps tenser than ever and was only decided at the very last moment. In spite of the prospect of a €50,000 bonus per player, the Russian favourites missed their goal by a hair's breadth and had to watch Ukraine, fired on by a brilliant Vasyl Ivanchuk, repeat their triumph of Calvia 2004.

Russia (silver), Ukraine (gold) and Israel (bronze), receive their medals at the closing ceremony in the icehockey stadium of Khanty-Mansiysk.

The chess in Khanty-Mansiysk, an oil town in Siberia, was great! Which might have been expected with virtually everyone of importance being present. In fact, the only grandmaster from the world's top 25 not to appear was World Champion Vishy Anand. The Olympiad has never been his favourite tournament and with other commitments ahead of him, Anand's absence had been expected. The world's number one, Magnus Carlsen, did come to Khanty-Mansiysk.

Russia were the clear favourites for gold. With Kramnik, Grischuk, Svidler, Karjakin and Malakhov their average rating was an astonishing 2755. On top of that, they were playing on home turf and could look forward to a bonus of €50,000 each if they finally repeated the success of Garry Kasparov and his men, who brought Russia the Hamilton Russell Cup in 2002 at the Olympiad in Bled. In that Olympiad, Russia won despite a loss in their match against Hungary. In Khanty-Mansiysk they also lost to Hungary, in Round 5 (Leko-Grischuk 1-0, and three draws), but this time they could not overcome this handicap. In the remaining rounds Russia 1 won their matches against the Czech Republic, Russia 2, reigning champions Armenia and third seed China, but they got no further than 2-2 in the crucial matches against Ukraine and Spain.

The match against Ukraine in Round 8 was a cliff-hanger that should have earned Zahar Efimenko a statue in bronze. Two games were drawn, Kramnik-Ivanchuk and Ponomariov-Svidler, while Sergey Karjakin gave his new country the lead against his old country with a wondrous win over Pavel Eljanov.

Game 29   Caro-Kann Defence
Sergey Karjakin
Pavel Eljanov
Khanty-Mansiysk Olympiad 2010 (8)

1.e4 c6 2.d4 d5 3.e5 ♗f5 4.♘f3
e6 5.♗e2 c5 6.♗e3 ♕b6 7.♘c3
♕xb2 8.♕b1 ♕xb1+ 9.♖xb1 c4
10.♖xb7 ♘c6 11.♘b5 ♘d8 12.♖c7
♖b8 13.♘d6+ ♗xd6 14.exd6 ♖b1+
15.♗d1 ♗xc2 16.♔d2 ♗xd1 17.♖xd1
♖b6 18.♗f4 ♘f6 19.♖e7+ ♔f8
20.♖xa7 ♘e4+ 21.♔c2 f6

This position Karjakin had studied in a training session with Alexander Motylev, Yury Dokhoian and the Kosintseva sisters Tatiana and Nadezhda. The previous moves had all been suggested by Tatiana. **22.h4!**

And this one was also her suggestion, a very important move preventing Black from playing 22...g5. As Karjakin said, 'The computer doesn't immediately understand that the situation is very bad for Black, but it soon becomes clear.' He thanked Tatiana for her help and was still wondering where exactly Eljanov had gone wrong.

22...♘xf2 23.♖b1 ♖xb1 24.♔xb1 ♘e4 25.a4 ♖g8 26.a5 ♘c6 27.♖a6

♘b8 28.♖a7 ♘c6 29.d7 ♘d8 30.♔c2 ♔e7 31.a6 e5 32.♗c1 ♔d6 33.♗a3+ ♔c6 34.♖a8

Black resigned.

Karjakin was in great form in Khanty-Mansiysk, and with 8 out of 10 and a performance rating of 2859 he won the gold medal on Board 4. The big question was whether his win would be enough to secure overall victory against his former fellow-countrymen. The Russians had high hopes, as Malakhov was only slightly worse against Efimenko, but in an admirable effort the young Ukrainian managed to win his game and keep the Ukrainian chances of winning the Olympiad alive. You can find the game against Malakhov, with Efimenko's notes, elsewhere in this book.

Standing behind Pavel Eljanov and Ruslan Ponomariov, captain Vladimir Tukmakov watches the first moves of the Ukrainian team in the last round. France's Laurent Fressinet is also interested.

Efimenko was one of the pillars of the Ukrainian team, and his score of 8½ out of 11 (TPR 2783) won him the silver medal on Board 4. Another pillar was Pavel Eljanov, who won silver on third board

(7/10, TPR 2737) and also annotated his best game from Khanty-Mansiysk for us.

But the undisputed star of the Ukrainian team was Vasyl Ivanchuk, who started with 6 wins in his first 6 games and won the gold medal on first board with 8/10 and a 2890 performance. Under his inspired leadership the Ukrainians managed to stay ahead of the Russians, with wins over Azerbaijan (2½-1½) and France (3½-½) in Rounds 9 and 10.

At the start of the last round, Ukraine had 18 match points, against 17 for Russia and 16 for Israel. The pairings were Russia-Spain and Israel-Ukraine. Although Ukraine was leading, Russia still had good chances, as in case of a tie in match points the tie-break would favour them. The Ukrainians knew that they had to win or have a result that was no less than Russia's to claim gold. At first things seemed to be going fine for Russia, as they quickly made draws in their two Black games, while in Israel-Ukraine the first two boards were also drawn. The key game proved to be the one on Board 3 between Svidler and Salgado. Before the match not only the Russians must have thought that this was a game in which the top-seeds should strike. Reality was different. Svidler got little or

nothing out of the opening, and once Black took over the initiative it was clear that White had to fight for his life. The end came remarkably quickly. After 36 moves White resigned and Russia's hopes were blown to pieces. A draw was the most they could get from their match (and that's what they did, as Kramnik beat Shirov).

This was the signal for Ukraine's captain Vladimir Tukmakov to propose draws on Boards 3 and 4. For Israel there was no reason to decline this proposal, either because of the positions on the boards or for any other reason, and so Ukraine won the gold medals. The Russians had to content

Still absorbed in thought after the game he has just finished, Vasyl Ivanchuk, the star of the Olympiad, patiently poses for a photo with a young fan.

themselves with silver and a bonus of € 25,000 each, still considerably more than the booty waiting for the winners.

Israel won the bronze medals. Their team had undergone several changes compared to the silver medallists from Dresden, but once again they finished among the very best, even if they were only seeded 11th. Their big man was Emil Sutovsky, who won the gold medal on Board 2 with 6½ out of 8 and the highest performance of the entire Olympiad, 2895.

Ukraine's victory was fully deserved. In 2004 the young Ukrainian team surprised each and everyone (including themselves) when they swept the field in Calvia. This time they could rely on many years of experience. In 2004, their captain Tukmakov felt that he still had a lot to learn; now he is like a father to the team members and understands every move that they make on and off the board. He follows them wherever they play and if he believes it is called for, he gets in touch with them. The departure of a player of Karjakin's level must have hurt, but instead of whining about his absence, his former team mates showed what they are worth themselves. And the Ukrainian chess federation seems to have changed too. The years of conflict appear to be over, as can be seen from Ponomariov's return to the team.

And then, of course, there was Vasyl Ivanchuk, who at 41 remains as devoted to chess as ever. Or in the words of Tukmakov: 'Saying that he loves chess is not the right word. He lives in chess. He lives in chess 24 hours per day, 365 days a year. He has chess dreams and he thinks about chess all the time. Outside of chess he is also a very interesting and unorthodox person, but in chess I believe he is a real genius.'

NOTES BY
Vasyl Ivanchuk

At this point, three teams were sharing first place: Georgia, Hungary and Armenia. Our team was a point behind. Therefore we needed to win.

Game 30   Slav Defence
Vasyl Ivanchuk
Peter Leko
Khanty-Mansiysk Olympiad 2010 (6)

1.♘f3 ♘f6 2.c4 e6 3.♘c3 d5 4.d4 c6 5.e3 ♘bd7 6.♕c2 ♗d6 7.♗d3 0-0 8.0-0 dxc4 9.♗xc4 a6 10.♖d1 b5 11.♗d3 ♕c7

12.♗d2
Also quite possible is 12.♘e4 ♘xe4 13.♗xe4 ♘f6 14.♗d3 h6 15.e4 ♗e7 16.e5 ♘d5 17.♕e2 with a white edge, as in Banikas-Nybäck, ICC 2009, but I think that Black's play can be improved.
12...c5 13.dxc5 ♕xc5
13...♘xc5 is bad in view of 14.♗xb5! White is looking for an opportunity to put pressure on Black's position.

14.a4
The game Jussupow-Stellwagen, Amsterdam 2008, lasted only two more moves: 14.♘e4 ♕xc2 15.♗xc2 and a draw was agreed.
14...bxa4 15.♖xa4
15.♕xa4 was also considered, but after 15...♗b7 16.♘e4 ♘xe4 17.♗xe4 ♘b6! 18.♕b4 ♕xb4 19.♗xb4 ♗xe4 too many pieces would have been exchanged.

15...♗b7
15...♘b6 would have been met by the unexpected 16.♖h4! h6 17.♖c1 ♗b7 (17...♗e7 18.e4!) 18.♕d1!, when the black queen is in danger! After 18...♘bd7 19.♘e4 White would have developed dangerous activity.
16.♖c4
The rook drives the black queen to an uncomfortable position.

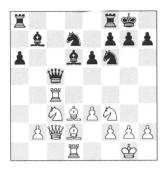

16...♕a7?!

The critical position would have arisen after 16...♗xf3!? 17.♖xc5 ♗xd1 18.♘xd1 ♘xc5 19.♗e2, when Black has two rooks for the queen. How should this position be assessed? I think that the chances are roughly equal. White has the two bishops and will try to break up the black king's position, while Black will press on the c- and b-files.

17.♘e4 ♘xe4 18.♗xc4 ♗xe4 19.♕xe4

Now White develops some definite pressure on Black's position.

19...♖ac8?!

A serious error; the queen on a7 should not have been left undefended.

Hardly an improvement is 19...♘f6 20.♕c2 ♕b7 (or 20...♕b8 21.♗a5 ♖e8 22.h3 h6 23.♘d4) 21.e4 with a clear advantage for White. However, 19...♖fc8! was correct: 20.♖dc1 ♖c5 21.♗c3 ♖xc4 22.♕xc4 ♕c5 23.♕e4 ♖d8, retaining a perfectly defensible position.

20.♕d4

Immediately exploiting Black's error. At the required time his pieces are uncoordinated.

20...♗c5

The alternative 20...♗b8 would have led to an inferior endgame after 21.♗b4 ♕xd4 22.♖cxd4 ♘c5 23.g3 (23.♖c4 ♘b7!) 23...♖fe8 24.♔g2 ♘b7 25.♖d7 ♘c5 26.♗xc5 ♖xc5 27.♖b7.

21.♕c3!

The series of unhurried moves by the white queen would appear to have dulled Black's vigilance. White imperceptibly improves the placing of his pieces, and unexpectedly Black finds himself in difficulties.

21...♖cd8

Nothing was given by 21...♖c7 22.♗e1 ♘f6 23.b4 ♗b6 24.♖xc7 ♕xc7 25.♕xc7 ♗xc7 26.♖c1.

22.♕c2

White is not in a hurry to create threats.

22...♖fe8

After 22...♗b6 23.♗c3 ♖fe8 24.b4 White retains the advantage. Weak was 22...h6 23.♗c3 ♗e7 24.♗xg7 ♔xg7 25.♖c7.

23.♘g5

With this move, additional weaknesses are created in Black's position.

23...g6

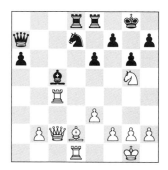

24.♗a5

Also strong was 24.♗e1! ♗b6 25.♘e4 ♔g7 26.♘d6 ♖f8 27.♗b4, when Black is helpless.

24...♗b6 25.♗c3 e5

It did not help to play 25...f6 26.♘e4 f5 27.♘d6 ♖f8 28.♕b3 ♘c5 29.♖xc5 ♗xc5 30.♕xe6+ ♖f7 31.♕e5 and Black is in trouble.

26.♘e4

Now the white knight occupies a dominating position.

26...♖e6 27.♗b4 ♔g7

Black has no useful moves. He is standing with his back to the wall, as can be seen, for example, in the variation 27...♕b7 28.♗d6 ♘f8 29.h4.

28.♖c6!

Exploiting the insecure placing of the black pieces.

28...♘f6

Not 28...♖xc6? 29.♕xc6 and wins.

29.♖xe6 fxe6 30.♘xf6 ♔xf6 31.♖a1

It was also good to exchange: 31.♖xd8 ♗xd8 32.♕e4 ♔f7 33.♗d6 (or 33.♕xe5 ♕d7 34.♕f4+ ♗f6 35.h4) 33...♗f6 34.♕c6, and Black has problems.

31...♕b7?!

Black is worn out by the constant threats. The best try was 31...a5 32.♗c3 ♕d7 (d5 is an ideal position for the queen) 33.h3 ♕d5 34.♕a4 ♔g7, and Black is centralized.

32.♗c3 a5 33.♕a4

But now Black is too late.

33...g5

Black cracks under the pressure. After 33...♕d5 34.♕f4+ ♔e7 35.♕h4+ ♔f8 36.♕f6+ ♔g8 37.h4, I think that White must win, since there is nothing that Black can move.

34.h4 h6 35.♕g4 ♕h7 36.♕h5

36...♕g6?

This hastens the end. Better was 36...♖g8 37.hxg5+ ♖xg5 38.♕h3 h5 39.f4 ♖g4 40.♗xe5+ ♔e7 41.♖e1, and White would still have faced some technical difficulties.

37.♗xe5+ ♔f7 38.♕f3+ ♔g8 39.♕c6

Black resigned.

A complete game with opportunities for play from both sides of the board.

NOTES BY
Pavel Eljanov

Game 31   Queen's Gambit Accepted
Pavel Eljanov
Vladimir Tkachiev
Khanty-Mansiysk Olympiad 2010 (10)

It is no longer a secret to anyone that in modern chess the term 'opening preparation' is hope-lessly out of date and does not correspond to the objective picture. The analyses of some opening variations, not only by leading players but also by ordinary ama-teurs (with the required diligence and technical equipment) extend deep into the endgame, by-passing the middlegame. It is quite obvious that few relish the fate of being trapped in a net of computer variations, from which sometimes it is not possible to escape. Therefore many players prefer to deviate from the main lines, to take the opponent away from his preparation as soon as possible. In this light the following game seems to me to be quite interesting. The initial moves, at first sight in no way noteworthy, have a definite implication.

1.d4 d5 2.c4 e6!?
The first surprise. Vlad's main opening is the Slav, and usually he straightforwardly plays 2...c6. The move in the game leaves open the question of the name of the opening – various transformations are possible.

3.♘f3
In this position I have also played 3.♘c3. Possibly Vlad was nevertheless intending to take the play along Slav lines with 3...c6. I last played the critical gambit line 4.e4 (as well as 4.♘f3) at about the age of 13, while 4.e3 ♘f6 takes play into the Meran Variation and allows Black to avoid lines such as 1.d4 d5 2.c4 c6 3.♘f3 ♘f6 4.♘c3 e6 5.♗g5 or 5.g3!?.

3...dxc4!?
But this was the main surprise! To judge by my MegaBase, Vlad became disillusioned with the Queen's Gambit Accepted roughly at the end of 2002 and nowadays he employs it only sporadically. In fact, his choice has a clear and logical explanation: in recent times, in reply to the 'Accepted', I have been playing the variation with e2-e4 (1.d4 d5 2.c4 dxc4 3.e4). As regards 4.e4 in this position, it would appear that Black has a normal game after 4...b5!. Incidentally, the previous occasion when the position after 3...dxc4 occurred with me was in a game with the chief improviser of modern chess – Vasyl Ivanchuk

(Jermuk 2009). Vasyl has the ability, like no one else, to deflect an opponent from his preparation – believe me! If anyone doesn't believe this, I advise them to study a couple of his recent games from the Olympiad: with Beliavsky and Sokolov.

4.e3 ♘f6 5.♗xc4 a6 6.0-0 b5

A rather rare variation.

7.♗d3

I remembered that somewhere I had seen/heard that it was best to retreat the bishop to d3 and then advance e2-e4. With that, unfortunately/fortunately, my knowledge came to an end.

7...♗b7 8.a4 b4 9.♘bd2 c5

10.♕e2

It is very difficult to give any specific evaluations of individual moves – the position is a fresh one, although quite typical.

10.e4 is the most logical, but I was concerned that the black knight would retreat to d7 followed by ...♗d5 – 10...cxd4 11.e5 ♘fd7 12.♘b3 (12.♘c4 ♘c5) 12...♗d5!?.

My computer does not like this move, but how White is to claim an advantage after 13.♘bxd4 ♘c5

14.♗e2 (14.♗g5 ♕d7 15.♗c2 ♘c6) 14...♘bd7 it does not know.

10...♘bd7

The position after 10...cxd4 11.exd4 ♗e7 12.♘b3!? suited me, although I am not sure that White can hope for anything serious.

11.e4 cxd4 12.e5 ♘d5 13.♘b3!

I was happy, both with the position and with the fact that Vlad began thinking for a long time.

13...♘c5 14.♘xc5 ♗xc5 15.♗d2

Here I also spent quite a lot of time, although what I was thinking about I don't understand. Nothing is given by 15.♘g5 ♗e7 16.♕h5 g6 17.♕h6 ♗f8 18.♕h3 ♗e7.

15...♗e7

I was rather concerned about the piece sacrifice 15...♘c3!?. In such positions, where one side is aiming to attack and is methodically bringing up his reserves, a sharp change of course can be extremely unpleasant! Nevertheless, White should be better, but I am not sure that I would have liked such changes! After 15...♘c3!? play might continue 16.bxc3 dxc3 17.♗e3 (17.♗f4 b3) 17...♕c7 18.♗c2 ♗xc3 (18...♗d5!?) 19.fxe3! h6 (19...0-0?

Pavel Eljanov, one of the pillars of the Ukrainian team, won silver on Board 3, with a 7 out of 9 score and a 2737 performance.

19...♘c7
Interesting was 19...♖ac8!? 20.♖xc8 ♗xc8 21.♘f3 ♘c3! 22.bxc3 bxc3 23.♗xh7+ ♔xh7 24.♗xc3 ♕d3 with adequate compensation.
20.♗e4
Bad was 20.♗xb4? ♗xb4 21.♖xb4 ♘d5 and Black is better.
20...♗xe4 21.♕xe4 ♘b5 22.♘f3 b3 23.♖ac1 ♖ac8 24.♕e3 ♖xc4 25.♖xc4

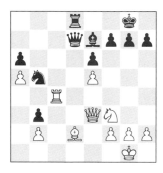

25...h6?
Up to this point Vlad had played slowly but well, and the evaluation of the position had not gone beyond the bounds of 'White has slight pressure'.
Black had two worthy continuations here.
The most obvious was 25...♕d3!? 26.♕xd3 ♖xd3 27.♖c8+! (in my preliminary calculations I had been intending 27.♔f1 h6 28.♔e2 ♖d5 but here it is not apparent how White can successfully regroup his forces – the ♗a3 resource does not allow him to calmly develop his plans: 29.♖c6 ♗a3!) 27...♖d8 28.♖c6 ♖a8! 29.♔f1 ♗a3! 30.♗c1 ♗b4 31.♘d2 ♗xa5 32.♘xb3 ♗c7 33.f4 and again White retains some pressure, but

20.♗xh7+ ♔xh7 21.♘g5+ and wins) 20.a5 with a white plus.
16.♖fc1
A move aiming for a small plus.
I think that greater practical problems would have been posed by 16.♕e4!? ♕d7 17.♕g4 g6 18.♗h6, with a long-term initiative.
16...0-0 17.♘xd4 ♕d7 18.a5 ♖fd8 19.♖c4

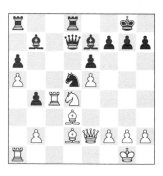

Black should be able to hold the position.

There is also the more complicated 25...♕d5!? 26.♕xb3 ♗c5 27.♕c2 ♘d4 28.♘xd4 ♗xd4, which would appear to solve all Black's problems, but here too White retains a minimal initiative with 29.♖c8! h6 30.♖xd8+ ♕xd8 31.b4 ♗xe5 32.♗e1! (32.♗e3 ♕d5) and, strangely enough, Black has to be very careful – the b4-b5 breakthrough is on the agenda and in some cases the a-pawn may cost him his bishop: 32...♕d7 33.♕e2 ♕d6 34.g3 with the initiative for White.

26.♕xb3

Now the game enters the technical phase – Black has no compensation at all.

26...♕b7 27.♕c2 ♖d7 28.h4 ♖c7 29.h5

My moves hardly deserve any particular approval – when the opponent has no counterplay,

it is very easy and pleasant to strengthen the position.

29...♗d8 30.♖xc7 ♗xc7 31.♕c4 ♗d8 32.♘e1! ♕d7 33.♘d3 ♗e7 34.♗e3 ♕b7 35.♗b6 ♕d7 36.b4 ♕b7 37.f3 ♘a3 38.♕c7!

Now, when everything is ideally placed, White can go into the endgame!

38...♕xc7 39.♗xc7 ♔f8 40.♗d6 ♘b5 41.♗xc7+ ♔xe7 42.♘c5 ♘c7 43.♔f2 g6 44.g4 gxh5 45.gxh5 f6 46.f4 f5

47.♔f3

There are various ways to win; there is also the forcing line 47.b5 axb5 (47...♘xb5 48.♘xa6) 48.a6 b4 49.a7, and Black is powerless.

47...♔d8 48.♔e2 ♘d5

Otherwise after ♔d3-c4 and ♘d3 my king penetrates into Black's position.

49.♘xe6+ ♔e7 50.♘d4 ♘xf4+ 51.♔f3 ♘d5 52.b5 axb5 53.a6 ♘c7 54.a7 b4 55.♔f4 1-0

CHAPTER VII

What's your Superpower? I'm Ukrainian!

Mykhaylo Oleksiyenko

Mykhaylo Oleksiyenko (born 1986 in Lviv) has been a grandmaster since 2005. He tied for first in the Bronstein Memorial in Minsk, 2014, and also in Jermuk 2015. One year later he became Ukrainian Champion. His peak rating was 2643 in both 2015 and 2017. In recent years, Mykhaylo, who also has a Ph.D in mathematics, has focussed on chess coaching rather than playing. He was the coach of Ukraine, Egypt and the Dutch Women's team, and is very active creating online chess courses. Some of his strongest pupils so far have been grandmasters Bassem Amin, Ahmed Adly, and Alexander Ipatov.

NOTES BY
Mykhaylo Oleksiyenko

This is one memorable game of mine. To understand why the game ended the way it did, I want to share a little story. Different national championships have different rules of when the board pairings become certain. In Israel, it is decided right before the game, meaning that the captain reveals the names of the players just before the round starts. Each team has a list of players and usually it is not allowed to change the order of players. In Israel, you could change the board order if the rating difference between the players was less than 100 points if I remember correctly. What does this all mean? It meant that it was very hard to guess who you were playing against. Our captain told me to prepare against Ilia Smirin

(2668) or Emil Sutovsky (2657). The rating difference between me (2546) and our second board Gad Rechlis (2460) was more than 100 points. In other words, everyone knew that I was playing board 1. Imagine my surprise when I saw Ilia Smirin walking into the playing hall and sitting down at board 4! Shortly after that, Emil Sutovsky walked in and sat on board 2! I was like: 'Oh my God, who on earth will I be playing?' I am not very good at hiding my emotions during the game, so Vugar Gashimov could easily tell that I had not expected to play against him. Think about my situation – I am playing against a World Top-10 player, he has prepared against me and I have not prepared against him at all, he has the White pieces, each board has at least 200 Elo points advantage over us. They were going to crush our team. On the other hand, it is easier to play under those circumstances, since everyone is expecting you to lose. I think this whole situation played a cruel trick on my super-GM opponent. He was pushing too hard for a win and did not take the chance to make a draw when the position demanded it.

Game 32   Sicilian Defence
Vugar Gashimov   2759
Mykhaylo Oleksiyenko   2546
Israel tt 2010 (5)

1.e4 c5 2.♘f3 d6 3.d4 cxd4 4.♘xd4 ♘f6 5.♘c3 a6
I had prepared this line for both Sutovsky and Smirin. The problem was that they played mostly 6.♗e3 here...
6.♗g5
Immediately after this move, I remembered that I had seen Gashimov's games in top tournaments with this line... luckily, recently I had studied a sideline that he probably had not prepared.
6...e6 7.f4 ♕c7
I used to play only 7...♗e7.
8.♗xf6 gxf6

9.♘b3
This move prepares 10.♕h5. Or at least I thought this was the idea. 9.♕h5? ♕c5! is the point! Black is better after the queen exchange because his king will be safe! 9.♕d2 is the main line, while 9.♕f3!? is also strong.
9...h5!? 10.♗e2 h4
If White occupied the h5-square then Black would be in strategic trouble.
11.♗g4
White is preparing the typical pressure on the e6-square.
11...♘d7 12.0-0 b5 13.f5

13...♘c5?!
I did not like the move 13...♘e5! since I thought I would not be able to hold the e6-square after ♗h3 + ♘d4 + ♘ce2 + ♘f4. It turns out I was wrong!
   A) If 14.fxe6 fxe6 15.♖xf6?? (the pawn is poisoned) 15...b4! 16.♘b1 (16.♘e2? ♘xg4−+) 16...♕g7 17.♗h5+ ♔e7 18.♖f2 Black has a winning attack after something like 18...♕g5. All his pieces are active, whilst the opposite is the case for White;
   B) 14.♗h3 ♔e7!? 15.♘d4 ♕c5!? 16.♘ce2 ♗h6 is unclear.

It turns out that the king can help defend the pawn!

14.fxe6 fxe6 15.♞d4?!

I calculated the following line: 15.♖xf6?! b4! 16.♗h5+ ♚d8! 17.♖f7 ♗e7! 18.♞b1?? ♞xb3 19.axb3 ♕c5+. 15.♗h5+ ♚d8!. My king is surprisingly safe here.

However, I would have been in trouble after 15.♕f3!+−. The queen is super active, f6 is hanging, e4-e5 is coming, the queen can go to h3...

15...b4! 16.♞d5

Vugar was clearly in a very aggressive mood!

16...exd5 17.exd5

This is a typical sacrifice. White has only one pawn for the knight, but he dominates on the light squares, and my king will never be safe now.

17...♕g7!? 18.♗xc8?

18.♕e2+! ♚d8 19.♖ae1 ♚c7 was my plan! The king runs away to relative safety; 20.♗e6!? is still interesting.

18...♖xc8 19.a3 b3!?

This is one typical way to keep the rook on a1 passive.

20.cxb3

Now I needed to activate my pieces.

20...h3!? 21.g3 ♕g5

The queen comes into play.

22.♕e2+ ♕e5

I chose a forcing option where I get to play several moves quickly.

A) 22...♚f7! was winning according to Stockfish. I was low on time and was afraid to put the king in front of a rook;

B) 22...♚d7!? was also winning, apparently.

23.♕g4 ♚d8! 24.♞c6+ ♖xc6!

25.dxc6 ♕xb2?!

How can you not threaten mate in one? 25...♗h6! (I needed to develop my bishop) 26.♖ae1 ♗e3+ (and then pin it to the queen!) 27.♚h1 and then just keep it cool with 27...♚c7−+ or possibly 27...♕xb2!? 28.♕f3 ♖e8! (all my pieces are in the game) 29.b4 ♞d3!−+.

26.♕f3 ♚c7

My king was safe and I have an option of trading queens on g2. That is all I knew in this time trouble phase.

27.♖ae1?!

I believed that the main continuation was 27.b4! ♞d3 28.♖ad1! ♞e5 29.♕d5!∓ and I thought that I would survive here. In fact, Black is even better. The knight on e5 shelters the king.

27...♘d3!

The queen cannot capture the knight!

28.♖e2 ♕d4+ 29.♔h1 ♘e5 30.♕xf6

We played this series of moves almost instantly. I had about 3 minutes left on my clock. I realized that my position was not worse because of my amazing knight on e5. I pretended I wanted a draw with a quick repetition.

30...♕d5+!?

It turns out the rook is not hanging! I could not find 30...♗h6!! with just a couple of minutes on my clock, which is why I decided to repeat the position to get an extra minute and check my opponent's intentions.

A) 31.♕xh8?

analysis diagram

31...♕d5+! 32.♔g1 ♗e3+!!. There is a checkmate literally on the next move! 33.♖xe3 ♕g2# or 33.♖ef2 ♕g2#;

B) It is also critical to see that my king can escape from a couple of checks: 31.♕e7+ ♔xc6! 32.♖c2+ ♔d5! 33.♕b7+ ♔e6! – no more checks. Black can exchange the queens and start pushing the passed pawn, with a winning advantage.

31.♔g1 ♕d4+

My opponent spent a lot of time here and chose:

32.♖ef2?

This was a bad way to play for a win! The objective evaluation was that White is in big trouble and a draw would be a great outcome for him. And yet, the rating difference between the players, the color of the pieces, the time on the clock, and the fact that I had not expected to play this opponent were all yelling that White should win this game!

During the game, I felt that the text move had to be a big mistake and yet I did not have enough time to see the win. That is why I quickly moved my 'hanging' rook.

32...♖g8 33.♕f5 ♖h8

And then I instantaneously moved the rook back to give an impression that I wanted a draw. Vugar Gashimov thought for some time and then reluctantly played:

34.♕f6

The time my opponent spent on his last move was enough for me to see that my rook was not really hanging! It meant that I could finally develop my bishop on move 34!

34...♗h6!! 35.♕e7+

35.♕xh8

analysis diagram

35...♘f3+!! 36.♔h1 ♕xh8 and Black wins.

35...♔xc6

It is over. Black has a material and a dynamic advantage.

36.♕h4 ♘f3+ 0-1

Our team ended up drawing the match 3-3! No draws! We definitely put up a good fight!

Yuriy Kryvoruchko

Yuriy Kryvoruchko (born 1986 in Lviv) won the bronze medal in the European U18 Championship, 2004, and became a Grandmaster in 2006, earning bronze in the World Junior Championship in the same year. He became Ukrainian Champion in 2013, edging out Ruslan Ponomariov on tiebreak. His peak rating was 2717 which made him the strongest Ukrainian player for a while. He was a member of the Ukrainian team that won bronze at the European Team Championship in Novi Sad, 2009.

NOTES BY
Yuriy Kryvoruchko

Game 33   Ruy Lopez
Yuriy Kryvoruchko
Fabiano Caruana
Plovdiv Ech 2012 (11)

1.e4 c5 2.♘f3 ♘c6 3.♗b5 a6 4.♗a4 ♘f6 5.0-0 b5 6.♗b3 ♗c5 7.a4 ♖b8 8.c3 d6 9.d4 ♗b6 10.♘a3 0-0 11.axb5 axb5 12.♘xb5 ♗g4 13.♗c2 exd4 14.♘bxd4 ♘xd4 15.cxd4 ♗xf3 16.gxf3 ♘h5 17.♔h1 ♕f6 18.♗e3 ♖a8 19.♖xa8 ♖xa8 20.♖g1 ♘f4 21.♗b3 g6

22.e5!?
A novelty. 22.♖g4 ♘e6 23.♗xe6 ♕xe6 24.♖g1 ♖a2 25.♕d2 ♕h3 26.♕e2 ♖xb2 27.♕xb2 ♕xf3 28.♖g2 ♕d1 gives equal play.
22...dxe5 23.dxe5
Now Black has a choice, but there is no continuation that promises clear equality.

23...♕f5
Perhaps the best choice was 23...♕xe5 24.♗xf7 ♔h8 (24...♔xf7 25.♗xf4 ♕e6 26.♖e1 ♖d8 27.♕c1 ♕d5 28.♔g2, with a slight advantage for White) 25.♕d2 ♘h3 (25...♗xe3

26.fxe3 ♕f6 27.♗c4, with a slight advantage for White) 26.♖f1 ♕f6 27.♕c3 ♕xc3 28.bxc3 ♔g7 29.♗d5 ♖a5 30.c4 g5 31.♔g2 ♘f4 32.♗xf4 gxf4 33.♔h3 ♗c5 34.♔g4 ♖a2 35.♖b1, after which the position is objectively a draw, but in a practical game White still has some chances to win.

24.♗xf7+

24...♔g7

24...♕xf7 didn't promise Black an easy life. After 25.♗xf4 ♗xf2 26.♖f1 White's king is much more secure, and Black faces a difficult fight.

25.♗d5

An inaccuracy. It was better to play 25.♗b3, e.g. 25...♘h3 26.♖g2 (26.♖f1? ♖a1 27.♕e2 ♖xf1 28.♕xf1 ♕xf3 29.♕g2 ♕f5, with attacking play) 26...♕h5 27.♗c2 ♗xe3 28.fxe3 ♕xe5 29.♖e2 (29.♗e4!?), with a slight advantage.

25...♘xd5

25...♘h3!? gives equal play, both after 26.♖g5 ♕c8 27.♗xa8 ♗xe3 and after 26.♗xa8 ♗xe3 27.♖f1 ♘xf2 28.♖xf2 ♗xf2.

26.♕xd5 ♖a5 27.♕c6

27...♖xe5?!

Now Black's position is rather unpleasant. After 27...♗xe3 28.♕f6+ (28.fxe3 ♖xe5= 29.♕xc7+ ♔h6) 28...♕xf6 29.exf6+ ♔xf6 30.fxe3 ♖c5 (30...♖b5) 31.h3 ♖b5 he should have held without much difficulty.

28.♗xb6 cxb6 29.♕c3 ♕f6 30.♖d1 ♔h6 31.♖d4 ♖e7 32.♔g2 ♖f7 33.♕e3+ ♔g7 34.♖b4 ♖b7 35.h4

35...h5

35...h6!? takes away the g5-square from the white queen, but the position of the black monarch would be weakened.

36.b3 ♖f7 37.♖e4

An alternative was 37.♖xb6 ♕xh4 38.b4 ♖e7 39.♕d2, but I decided not to force things.

37...b5 38.♖d4 ♖e7 39.♕d3 ♖f7 40.♖d6 ♕f5 41.♕d4+

41...♔h6

Probably the decisive mistake.
41...♖f6 42.♖xf6 ♕xf6 43.♕d7+ ♔f8
44.♕xb5 ♕xh4 45.♕c5+ would have
given White a winning endgame,

but the rook endgame after 41...♔h7
42.♕e4 (42.♕e3, defending the
position, is not so easy either)
42...♕xe4 43.fxe4 ♖f4 44.f3 ♖xh4
45.♖d5 b4 46.♖b5 ♖f4 doesn't
promise White too much.

42.♕h8+ ♖h7 43.♕c3 ♖f7

Also 43...♕f4 44.♕d3 ♖g7 45.♕e3
♖f7 46.♖b6 ♔h7 47.♕d3 wouldn't
help Black.

**44.♖b6 ♖g7 45.♕c6 ♕f4 46.♕e4
♕c7 47.♖xb5 ♖e7 48.♕d4 ♔h7
49.♖d5 ♕b7 50.b4 ♖f7 51.b5 ♕c7
52.♖d8 ♖g7 53.♕f6 ♕c5 54.♕c6**

Black resigned.

Anton Korobov

Anton was born in Siberian Russia (Mezhdurechensk 1985). Korobov's family found themselves in Ukraine after the collapse of the Soviet Union and chose to stay. Anton graduated with a degree in foreign languages from Kharkiv University and won his first of four Ukrainian Championships in 2002. When he next won in 2012, after a few years when he had almost quit chess, it took his rating above 2700 for the first time, and he also claimed the title in 2018 and 2020. Other individual successes include winning the Poikovsky Tournament in 2014 and 2016 and reaching the quarterfinals of the 2013 World Cup, where he lost to eventual winner Vladimir Kramnik.

As part of the Ukrainian team, Anton Korobov narrowly missed out on gold as Ukraine tied with the USA in the 2016 Olympiad. Two years later he won individual gold on Board 5, while in the 2013 World Team Championship he claimed gold on Board 2 as Ukraine took bronze. As a coach he helped Ukrainian GM Anna Ushenina win the Women's World Championship.

NOTES BY

Anton Korobov

Game 34   Sicilian Defence
SP Sethuraman   2640
Anton Korobov   2675
Baku Olympiad 2016 (9)

1.e4 c5 2.♘f3 d6 3.d4 cxd4 4.♘xd4 ♘f6 5.♘c3 ♘c6

The main criterion in my choice of opening was my opponent's limited experience. In my preparations, the decision was taken to play as audaciously as possible and to adopt an aggressive approach from the very first moves.

6.♗g5 e6 7.♕d2 a6 8.0-0-0 ♗d7 9.f4 ♗e7 10.♘f3 b5 11.♗xf6

The first fruit of the correct opening choice. Compared with the Panchenko Variation – 9...b5 10.♗xf6 gxf6 11.♘xc6 ♗xc6

12.♗d3 – an additional pair of knights remains on the board, affording Black a greater number of constructive ideas in the subsequent play.

11...gxf6 12.♔b1 ♕b6

13.g3

White's main strategic idea is to attack the e6-point, with the aim of provoking a favourable change in the pawn structure. With this aim in mind, 13.f5! was very logical and strong. It is not easy to put forward any arguments after 13...b4! 14.♘e2 ♕f2 15.♘fg1!!.

13...♘a5!?

A move that is in accordance with the chosen strategy. Generally speaking, classical manuals do not recommend initiating a conflict without first completing the mobilization of the forces (especially with Black!), but here the smell of blood is clearly felt already.

Black is ready for a series of attacking moves: ...b5-b4, ...♘c4, followed by ...♘a3+. It is time to discard false modesty.

14.f5 b4 15.fxe6 fxe6 16.♘e2 ♘c4

17.♕d4?!

White caves in. He takes the opponent at his word, although in the event of the critical 17.♕h6! he would have invited Black to demonstrate what compensation he had for the sacrificed piece (and apparently, it is insufficient): 17...♘a3+!. It is already too late to sound the retreat. With his king stuck on e8 and his rooks disconnected, it is time for Black to forget generally-accepted rules and to try and attack with those forces which he has available. During the game I was not in fact able to work out the variations, but I trusted that there would be a knock-out. 18.bxa3 bxa3+ 19.♔c1 ♖c8 20.♔d2 (20.♖d2 – initially this move frightened me more than the prospect of paying alimony, but after 20...♕b2+ 21.♔d1 ♕xa2 the presence of the expensive passed a3-pawn instils great financial potential in Black's position) 20...♕b4+ 21.♔e3 ♕c5+ 22.♘ed4 e5 23.♗h3! ♗xh3 24.♕xh3 f5 25.♕xf5 ♖f8 26.♕e6 ♖b8!, and in a practical game it is obvious that three results are possible. However, the soulless automaton promises White an advantage after 27.♔d3

exd4 28.♘xd4 ♖b4 29.♘f5!! ♖xf5
30.♕xf5 ♖d4+ 31.♔e2 ♕xc2+

analysis diagram

32.♔e3!! (it is not easy to calculate
as far as such geometry!) 32...♖xd1
33.♕h5+ ♔d7 34.♕xd1.

17...♕xd4 18.♖xd4
The capture with either of the
knights would have allowed Black
the advantage of the two bishops in
classical form after 18...♘e3.

18...♘e5
After the exchange of queens,
the dynamic potential has been
sharply reduced, which is to Black's
advantage. It is time for White to
forget about aggressive intentions
and adjust to the opponent's actions.

**19.♗g2 a5 20.♖e1 ♖c8 21.♖dd1 ♔f7
22.♘f4**

22...♘g6!

The correct conception! Black
forces the opponent to come to a
decision: either retreat, or allow
a transformation of the pawn
structure favourable for Black.

23.♘xg6!
A non-trivial approach: White
himself opens up the position,
despite his opponent possessing
the two bishops. The play revolves
around one factor: the presence of
the black king in the centre – is
this an advantage or a drawback?
In the endgame it is recommended
to keep the king in the centre, but
here the position has not yet lost its
middlegame features and the king
comes under attack.
If 23.♘d3 there follows 23...♖c7, and
Black can endlessly strengthen his
position with moves such as ...♖hc8,
...♗e7-f8-h6 and ...♔e7.

23...hxg6 24.e5!

24...d5?!
An incorrect evaluation of the
position. I was under the illusion
that I already held a big positional
advantage. All that remained was
to obtain stability, and the two
bishops would have their weighty
say. But in fact the position is a very
concrete one, and the way to get an

advantage was with the positional pawn sacrifice 24...♖hd8!, and now:

A) 25.exd6 ♗f8. Compared with the game Black has retained a three-day stubble in the form of the g6-, f6- and e6-pawns, which seriously restrict the white knight and do not allow it to come close to the black forces. The d6-pawn is in fact a weakness and it should soon be lost;

B) 25.exf6 ♗xf6 26.♖xd6 ♗a4! 27.♖xd8 ♗xc2+ 28.♔c1 ♗xd8 29.♔d2 ♗f5 30.♖c1 ♖xc1 31.♔xc1 ♔f6, and White faces a difficult defence. It is important for Black not to allow a transposition into an ending with opposite-coloured bishops, and then he will be able to endlessly torment his opponent in this position.

25.exf6

25...♗xf6?!

Here also, it was better to refrain from the immediate regaining of the material – 25...♗d6!, and here White would have to make a series of only moves: 26.♖f1 ♔xf6 27.♗h3! ♗b5 28.♗xe6 ♗xf1 29.♗xc8 ♗e2 30.♖xd5 ♗xg3 31.♗g4! ♗xh2 32.a3 bxa3 33.♘xh2 ♖xh2 34.♗xe2 ♖xe2 35.♖xa5, gaining a draw.

26.h4 ♖h5

Objectively, this is a step in the wrong direction. Black wants to retain the two bishops and defend against the check on e5. However, such an obvious striving to retain the advantages of the position could have led to the loss even of equality.

Here I realized that in this game I would not be able to manage without an exchange sacrifice on f5. And this prophecy came true!

27.♗h3 ♖c4 28.♖e3

Here, for the first time in the game, I experienced a feeling of chilling horror – the opponent is preparing to put pressure on me at a sore point, which I had thought was healthy. What to do...?

28...d4!?

The path to victory runs via complete loss of control.

29.♖e2

29...♖hc5?

The first real chess mistake. Now the rook on c4 has no moves and it comes under all sorts of attacks. 29...♖c7! was much stronger. The tactical justification is 30.♘xd4?? e5!, and Black remains a piece up.

30.♘e1?!

30.♖f2! was much more forceful, aiming with the rook at the king and vacating the diagonal for the bishop: 30...♔e7 31.♗f1 d3 32.♗xd3 ♖g4.

30...♖e5

An exchange of rooks certainly falls in with Black's plans, since with an exchange of pieces his central pawns immediately acquire mobility.

31.♖f2

31...♖f5!!??

The dream is realized! I made this move with a 'firm hand' and with a confident air I began pacing around the board. My confident air obviously unsettled my opponent. At any event, I gained the impression that he did not even consider winning the exchange.

32.♖e2?

The same psychological mistake as on the 17th move. White does not display the required decisiveness and goes along with his opponent. And yet, winning material would evidently have led also the winning of the game: 32.♗xf5 gxf5 33.g4! e5 34.♘f3! e4 35.♘d2! ♖c5 36.♘xe4!

fxe4 37.♖df1 ♗xg4 38.♖xf6+ ♔e7 39.♖6f4 ♗f3 40.♖e1 and wins.

32...♗c6!

To remove the rook from the attack is pointless: the opponent is not intending to take it. The rejection of the sacrifice gave me a considerable psychological boost, and I began playing increasingly confidently.

33.g4

The remainder of the game took part in a time scramble.

33...♖e5 34.♖f2 ♔e7 35.g5 ♗h8 36.♘d3 ♖e3

37.♗f1?

37.♘f4! ♔d6 38.♗g2 ♗e8 39.♗f3! was stronger, when Black appears to have no normal ways of improving his position. Apparently he would have had to make use of a tested

device – an exchange sacrifice:
39...♖c8 40.♘g2 ♖xf3 41.♖xf3 ♗c6
42.♖f2 e5 43.♖df1 ♔e6, when all
three results are possible.

**37...♗e4 38.♘f4 ♖c8 39.♗d3 ♖g8
40.♘g2**

Another inaccuracy, this time on
the 40th move. White's striving for
clarity results in him losing the
coordination of his pieces.

40...♖f3!

The smoke has cleared, and the
waves have died down. Black has
obviously been successful, and his
audacious approach has triumphed:
White is lost.

41.♖e2 ♗d5 42.♗e4 ♗xe4 43.♖xe4

43...♔d6!

Black's plan is simple: with the
support of his king (for whom a

brilliant career is now in prospect,
in contrast to his white opponent)
he sets about advancing his central
pawns. White's downfall is caused
by the bad position of his knight
and the lack of real living space for
his king.

44.♘e1 ♖f1 45.c3

Agony.

**45...bxc3 46.bxc3 ♖b8+ 47.♔c2 ♖f2+
48.♔d3 ♖xa2 49.♘c2**

If 49.cxd4 there follows 49...♖b3+
50.♔c4 ♖aa3 with an aesthetic
finish.

49...dxc3 50.♖de1

50...♖d8!

An ambush.

**51.♖1e2 ♔c5+ 52.♔e3 ♖d6 53.♖h2
♗g7 54.h5 gxh5 55.♖eh4 ♖d5
56.♖xh5 ♔c4 57.♖h7 ♖xg5 58.♔e4
♔b3 59.♖xg7**

Pre-death convulsions.

**59...♖xg7 60.♘d4+ ♔a3 61.♘b5+
♔b4**

White resigned.

(PS: I would like to thank my friend
*National Master Alexey Yarovinsky for
his assistance in writing the text and for
his fantastic creativity!*)

Alexander Areshchenko

Born in Luhansk 1986, Alexander Areshchenko was another star of the Kramatorsk chess school that produced World Champions Ruslan Ponomariov and Anna Ushenina and many more top players. In 2000 he won the World U14 Championship ahead of Wang Yue, Hikaru Nakamura and Pentala Harikrishna, while in 2005, as a 19-year-old, he won the Ukrainian Championship. He came closest to repeating that feat when he finished second in 2012, the same year he achieved his peak rating of 2720.

Alexander took individual silver in 2007 at the European Team Championship as well as bronze twice with Ukraine in the 2011 and 2013 World Team Championships. In 2015 he knocked Levon Aronian out of the Baku World Cup, but although he also played the 2021 World Cup he has otherwise only featured in league games since announcing his retirement in 2017.

NOTES BY
Alexander Areshchenko

This game was played in the World Cup. One mistake and you can be eliminated. After losing the first game of the match this was exactly the situation that occurred. How to play for a win when a loss and a draw means the same? Fortunately, having White helps a bit to put pressure on the opponent.

Game 35   Scotch Opening
Alexander Areshchenko   2664
Dmitrij Jakovenko   2736
Khanty-Mansiysk 2009 (3)

1.e4 e5 2.♘f3 ♘c6

3.d4!?

After 3.♗b5 Dmitrij plays the rock-solid Berlin Defence. 3...♘f6. Probably he also expected 3.♗c4. In such situations, the Scotch is an interesting choice. Maybe objectively White does not have an advantage according to the modern theory. But it was the least expected choice and the position becomes unbalanced – a nice combination of factors when you need to win at any cost!

3...exd4 4.♘xd4 ♞f6 5.♘xc6 bxc6 6.e5 ♛e7 7.♕e2 ♞d5 8.c4 ♝a6

9.♘d2!?

Another small surprise.

One of the reasons why the Scotch Opening became popular again was that Garry Kasparov played it. First he prepared it for his match against Karpov in Lyon 1990 and later he continued to successfully play it in tournament games. However, his choice 9.b3 has been very well analysed by now, with some lines ending in a forced draw.

9...0-0-0

This is one of the options here for Black apart from 9...g6, 9...♞b4 or 9...f6.

In general, Black should try to play energetically to exploit the fact that White's king is still in the centre, to compensate for the defects in his pawn structure. Somehow such play is not exactly in Jakovenko's style – he is better known for his brilliant technique, squeezing points in the endgame.

10.b3 f6!?

Black immediately attacks the enemy pawn on e5.

Another top game went 10...g5 11.♝b2 ♝g7 12.0-0-0 ♞b6 13.h4! g4 14.f4 gxf3 15.♘xf3 c5 16.♕e1 ♝b7 17.♝d3± and Black didn't solve all of his problems in Radjabov-Topalov, Nanjing 2009.

11.♝b2 fxe5 12.0-0-0

This is a typical pawn sacrifice for such a type of position. Quick development is important! At the same moment Black still hasn't solved all his problems. For example, the ♞d5 and ♝a6 can be active, but at the same time they are unstable, and potential targets.

12...♞f6?!

Too passive. Black is ready to return the pawn, but it will leave him with a slightly inferior endgame.

More principled and more risky was 12...♜e8!?. White still has to prove that he has enough compensation for the pawn, for example 13.g3 (13.♘f3?! e4 14.♘e5 ♛g5+ 15.♕d2 e3! 16.fxe3 ♝b4 17.♕d4 ♛xe3+ 18.♔b1 ♛xd4 19.♝xd4 c5∓) 13...♞f6 14.♝h3 ♔b8 15.♜he1 ♛f7 (15...d6 16.♝g2 ♝b7 17.b4! with initiative) 16.♕f3 and now it seems an appropriate moment for Black to return the extra pawn: 16...♗b7 17.♖xe5 ♖xe5 18.♗xe5 ♗a3+ 19.♔c2 ♖e8 20.♕f4 d6 21.♗xf6 gxf6 with good play for Black, Brodda-De Oliveira, cr 2016. Of course it's easy to suggest this in the calm situation after the game, but it is another thing when you need to play actual moves over the board. Playing some solid moves when you just need a draw looks like a logical strategy, doesn't it?

13.♕xe5 ♕xe5 14.♗xe5 ♘g4 15.♗g3

In future games White preferred 15.♗d4 c5 16.h3 cxd4 17.hxg4 ♗b7 18.f3 h6 19.♗d3 ♗b4 20.♔c2 with a complex endgame, Yu Yangyi-Stefansson, Reykjavik rapid 2013. How to keep the tension and which move to choose is probably a matter of taste.

15...♗a3+

16.♔b1

If White manages to complete his development smoothly, then he will enjoy a stable advantage, thanks to his superior structure. However, Black's temporary initiative still gives him counterplay.

Another option was 16.♔c2 ♖hf8 17.♘f3 ♗c5 18.♖d2 ♗b4 but here the rook has fewer squares on the second rank: 19.♖d4 ♘f6 20.♗d3 c5 21.♖f4 ♗b7 is unclear.

16...♖hf8 17.♘f3 ♗c5 18.♖d2 ♘f6

Another tame move.

After 18...d5? 19.♖c2 Black will have serious problems along the c-file, but it was worth considering the more active 18...♖de8!? 19.♗d3 g6 and if 20.h3± ♘f6.

19.♗d3 ♖de8 20.♗f5 ♖e7

21.♘e5

If 21.♖hd1 there is the slightly unpleasant 21...♗b4 22.♖d3 ♘d5! and many pieces are under attack: 23.♘d4 ♘c3+ 24.♖xc3 ♗xc3 25.♘xc6 ♖e1 26.♗xd7+ ♔b7 27.♔c2 ♖xd1 28.♔xd1 ♔b6 and this endgame should be fine for Black because White's pieces lack coordination, e.g. 29.♘e7 ♗b7 30.♘d5+ ♗xd5 31.cxd5 ♗b4 32.f3 ♗d6 33.♗f2+ ♗c5 34.♗e1 a5=.

21...♗b7 22.♖hd1 ♗d6 23.♘g4

Suddenly, even without queens, the position becomes sharp and it is not so easy to calculate all of the lines.

23...♗xg3?!

Instead, Black had two satisfactory continuations:

A) 23...♗b4 24.♘xf6 (probably a better try is 24.♖c2 if you need to play for a win) 24...♗xd2 25.♗xd7+ ♔b8 26.♘xh7 ♖d8 27.♖xd2 ♖exd7 28.♖xd7 ♖xd7 and once again White does not have enough time to consolidate the position: 29.♔c2 ♖e7 30.♔d2 ♖d7+ 31.♔e2 ♖e7+=;

B) 23...♘e4 24.♗xe4 ♗xg3 25.♗xh7 ♗f4 26.♘e3 (26.♖d3?! c5 27.f3 g6! 28.♗xg6 ♖g7 29.♗h5 ♖g5∓) 26...c5 27.♘d5 ♗xd5 28.♖xd5 ♗d6 29.f3 ♖h8 30.♗e4 ♖xh2 and Black's position is very solid, with opposite-coloured bishops.

24.♘xf6

Stockfish prefers 24.fxg3 but after 24...♘d5! 25.♖f1 ♔d8! it seems that Black can create enough counterplay after e.g. 26.♖df2 (26. cxd5 g6 27.dxc6 ♗xc6 28.♘h6 gxf5) 26...g6 27.♗c2 ♖xf2 28.♖xf2 ♘b4 29.♖f8+ ♖e8 30.♖xe8+ ♔xe8.

24...♖xf6?

This is probably the last and decisive mistake. Somehow Black still had a chance to create some counterplay with 24...♗d6!

25.♗xd7+ ♔b8 (25...♖xd7 26.♘xd7 ♔xd7 27.c5+−) 26.♘xh7 ♖h8 27.♗f5 ♗c8! 28.♗c2 (28.♗xc8 ♔xc8 29.♘g5 ♗f4) 28...♔b7!. Black is two pawns down, but the pair of bishops can be good compensation.

Instead of this, Jakovenko goes for a passive defence; he was hoping to create a fortress in the bishop ending.

25.♖xd7 ♖xd7 26.♗xd7+ ♔b8 27.fxg3 c5 28.♖d2 ♖d6 29.♔c1!

Obviously White doesn't want to have a passive bishop just to save the pawn: 29.♖xd6? cxd6 30.♗h3 ♔c7=.

29...♗xg2 30.♗f5 ♖xd2

Hardly better was 30...g6 31.♖xg2 gxf5 32.♖f2 and Black has too many weak pawns.

31.♔xd2

31...g6

Some annotators thought that this was the decisive mistake. The pawns on light squares will become a target later on, so they suggested instead 31...h6!?. But I think White still should be winning here thanks to the active king. Let's have a look: 32.♔e3 g5 (the only temporary way to stop the king from advancing)

33.♗e4 ♗h3 34.♔f3 ♗e6 (34...♔c8
35.g4! ♔d7 (or 35...♗f1 36.♔f2 ♗h3
37.♗f3 ♔d7 38.♗e2 etc) 36.♗d3
♔e6 37.♔g3, trapping the bishop)
35.♗g6 ♔c8 36.♔e4 ♔d7 37.♔e5
♔e7 38.♗f5 ♗g8 39.♗e4 and Black
can't stop the white king going
either to d5 or f5 at some moment:
39...♗e6 40.♗d5 ♗g4 41.♗g8 ♗f3
(41...c6 42.♗h7 ♗f3 43.♗f5 ♗g2
44.♗d3 ♗f3 45.♔f5 ♔f7 46.♗c2
♗g2 47.♗d1) 42.♔f5 ♗h5 43.♗d5
♗e8 44.♗e4 ♗f7 45.♗c6 ♗h5 46.g4
♗f7 47.h3 and Black ends up with
no good moves.
**32.♗c2 ♔c8 33.♔e3 ♔d7 34.♔f4
♔e6**
Black controls the e5-square, but it's
only temporary.
**35.♔g5 ♔f7 36.♔h6 ♔g8 37.h4 ♗f3
38.♗d3 ♗d1 39.♗e4 a5 40.♗d5+
♔h8**

The move 40 time control has
passed and now it's possible to
calmly look for the decisive plan.
**41.♗e4 ♔g8 42.♗d3 ♔h8 43.♔g5
♔g7 44.g4 ♗f3 45.♔f4 ♗b7 46.♗e4
♗c8 47.g5 ♔f7 48.♔e5**
Now it's clearly winning for White.
**48...♔e7 49.♗f3 ♗e6 50.♗c6 ♗f7
51.♗d5 ♗e8 52.♗e4 c6**
52...♗f7 53.h5!.
53.♗f3 ♗d7 54.♗g2 ♗e8 55.♗h3 ♗f7

56.a4! ♗g8
56...♗e8 57.♗e6+– zugzwang.
57.♗g2
White wins the c6-pawn and gets
the crucial d5-square for the king.
The rest is easy.
**57...♗e6 58.♗xc6 ♗f5 59.♔d5 ♗c2
60.♔xc5 ♗xb3 61.♔b5**
And Black resigned. Surprisingly,
this time, when he needed only to
make a draw, endgame technique
played a joke on Jakovenko.

Andrei Volokitin

Andrei Volokitin (born 1986 in Lviv) has been a grandmaster since he was 15 years old and by that time he had already won silver and bronze in World Youth Championships: under 12 and under U14 respectively. He is well admired for his sharp style. Andrei became Champion of Ukraine in 2004 and 2015. His peak rating was 2725 in March 2013. He has been a faithful member of the strong Ukraine team, playing in four Olympiads and winning several medals with the team. In the European Team Championship 2021, won by Ukraine, he was the top scorer on board two with 6/8, with a stunning 2824 performance.

NOTES BY
Andrei Volokitin

Game 36   Sicilian Defence
Andrei Volokitin   2724
Shakhriyar Mamedyarov   2748

Eilat tt 2012 (1)

This year in the European Cup for teams there was a strange pairing system. Our team Ashdod had to meet the rating favourites Socar in the very first round.

1.e4 c5

A surprise for me. Recently Shakhriyar had been playing 1...c6 and 1...e5.

2.♘f3 d6 3.d4 cxd4 4.♘xd4 ♘f6 5.♘c3 a6

Previously, my opponent had played the Najdorf about ten times.

6.♗e3

Here I thought for 7 minutes.

6...♘g4 7.♗c1 ♘f6 8.♗g5

The second attempt!

8...♘bd7

With this move Shakh selects a 'winning variation'.

9.♕e2

9...e6

The game Motylev-Wojtaszek from Poikovsky 2012 continued 9...h6!? 10.♗xf6 ♘xf6 11.0-0-0 e5 12.♘f5 g6 13.♘e3 ♗e6 14.g3 ♖c8 15.♘cd5 ♘xd5 16.♘xd5 h5 17.h4 ♖c5 and Black had no problems.

I have to say that 9...h6 is very interesting for Black.

My game against Al Sayed in the Istanbul Olympiad continued 9...b5 10.♘d5 ♗b7 11.♗xf6 ♘xf6 12.♘xf6+ exf6 13.a4 bxa4 14.♖xa4! and White was somewhat better.

10.0-0-0 ♛c7 11.f4 b5

Now we have ended up in the variation 6...e6 7.f4 ♘bd7 8.♛e2.

12.f5

The main move is 12.a3.

12...b4?!

In my opinion, 12...e5! is stronger than the game continuation. 13.♘d5 ♘xd5 14.exd5 is the main variation here.

13.fxe6 bxc3 14.exd7+ ♘xd7

After 14...♗xd7 15.♛c4! cxb2+ 16.♔b1 ♛xc4 17.♗xc4 ♗e7 18.♖he1 White has the slightly better endgame. The main idea is ♘f5.

15.♛c4! cxb2+ 16.♔b1 ♘c5

Instead of an endgame, Black wants to keep the queens on the board.

17.e5

Too early. During the game I could not remember my analysis, all I remembered was the evaluation of the variation as better for White, but not the specific moves.

The best move is 17.♗e2!. White develops his pieces, while on the

other hand Black cannot bring his bishop to e7: 17...♗e7? (17...h6 18.♗h4±; 17...♖a7 18.♖hf1 ♘e6 19.♗h4±) 18.♗xe7 ♛xe7 19.e5!±. So, after the quiet move 17.♗e2 White has a clear advantage.

17...♖b8!

The strongest reply. Other moves are weaker: 17...dxe5? 18.♘b5 axb5 19.♛d5 f6 20.♗xb5+ ♔e7 21.♛xa8! fxg5 22.♖hf1 and White has a very strong attack, for example 22...h5 23.♗c4 ♗e6 24.♗xe6 ♘xe6 25.♛a3+ ♔e8 26.♛a4+ ♔e7 27.♖d5 ♘f4 28.♖a5+−.

18.exd6 ♗xd6 19.♖e1+ ♔f8

20.♗d3

This looks logical. White also has other options:

A) 20.♗d2 – prophylaxis against ...♖b4 and ...h7-h6:

analysis diagram

A1) 20...♞e6! (Black must exchange queens, otherwise the position can become dangerous) 21.♞xe6+ ♝xe6 22.♛xc7 ♝xc7 23.♝xa6 h5! 24.a4 ♚g8 25.♝b5 h4 26.h3 ♜h5! and White is slightly better, but Black should be able to hold the draw;

A2) 20...h5? 21.♝d3! (21.♛c3 ♞e6! – Black should be able to hold the position without queens – 22.♛xc7 (22.♞c6 ♜b6 23.♞e5 ♛xc3 24.♝xc3 ♝xe5 25.♜xe5 f6 26.♜e3 ♜c6 with counterplay) 22...♝xc7 23.♞c6 ♜b6 24.♞e5 ♞d4=) 21...♞xd3 22.♛xd3 ♝d7 23.♜hf1 ♚g8 24.♞f5! ♝xf5 25.♜xf5 (this position looks dangerous. Black has major problems with the rook on h8, for example) 25...♝xh2 26.♜e4!:

analysis diagram

A21) 26...♛g3 27.♛e2! ♛g6 28.♜e8+ ♜xe8 29.♛xe8+ ♚h7 30.♛e4 ♚g8 31.♛a8+ ♚h7 32.♛f3 ♜c8 33.♜xh5+ ♚g8 34.♜h8+! ♚xh8 35.♛h3+ ♛h7 36.♛xc8+ ♛g8 37.♛h3+±;

A22) 26...♜d8 27.♜d5 ♜c8 28.♜ed4 g6 29.♜e4!±;

A23) 26...g6 27.♜d5 ♛g3 28.♛f1 ♛c7 29.♝a5 ♛c6 30.♛d3!±;

A24) 26...♜c8 27.g3! ♝g1 (27...♛xg3 28.♛d7! ♜f8 29.♜e8+−; 27...♝xg3 28.♜d4! g6 29.♜g5! ♝f2 30.♜f4+−; 27...h4 28.♝a5! ♛c6 29.♜e7 ♜f8 (29...f6 30.♜d5!+−; 29...♝xg3 30.♜fxf7 ♜h7 31.♝b4!+− a5 32.♛xh7+ ♚xh7 33.♜xg7+ ♚h6 34.♝d2+; 29...hxg3 30.♜fxf7 ♜h7 31.♛xh7+ ♚xh7 32.♜xg7+ ♚h8 33.♜h7+ ♚g8 34.♜eg7+ ♚f8 35.♝b4++−) 30.♜exf7! ♜xf7 31.♛d8+ ♚h7 32.♜h5+ ♛h6 33.♜xh6+ gxh6 34.♛d3+ ♚g8 35.♛g6+ ♜g7 36.♛e6+ ♚h7 37.♛f5+ ♚g8 38.♝c3+−) 28.♝b4! ♛d8 29.♜c4 ♜a8 30.♛f3±.

B) 20.♛c3 does not promise White anything: 20...♞a4! 21.♛xc7 ♝xc7 22.♝d2 ♝f4 23.♝a5 ♝c7=.

20...h6??

The decisive mistake. The only move was 20...♜b4! 21.♛c3! (after 21.♛xb4 ♞xd3 22.♛d2 ♞xe1

165

23.♖xe1 h6 Black has no problems)
21...f6! (once more, the only move.
21...h6? does not work here: 22.♗d2!
♘xd3 23.♕xd3 ♖a4 24.♖e4! ♗d7
25.♖he1 with an attack) 22.♕xb4
(White must take the rook, or
else ...♘a4 will follow) 22...♘xd3
23.♕b3 ♘xe1 24.♖xe1 fxg5 and here
one forced line goes: 25.♕f3+ ♗f4
26.g3 g6 27.♘c6! ♗d7! 28.♕c3 ♗e5
29.♕xe5 ♕xe5 30.♘xe5 ♗f5 31.♔xb2
♔g7 32.c4 h5 and Black should hold
the draw here.

Now there is a beautiful combination:
21.♗d8!! ♕xd8 22.♖hf1 ♖b7
22...f6 23.♘c6+−.
23.♗g6 f6
After 23...♕d7 I calculated this
variation: 24.♗xf7 ♕xf7 25.♖d5!
♕xf1 26.♖xf1+ ♔e7 27.♕f7+ ♔d8
28.♘c6#.

24.♕d5??
A blunder. I still had some 10
minutes left and was getting
nervous. I was only calculating two
moves: 24.♕d5 and 24.♘c6.
Of course, after 24.♖e3! Black could
have resigned straight away.
24...♖e7
Now the game starts afresh.

**25.♘c6 ♗b7 26.♕xc5 ♗xc5
27.♘xd8 ♗d5 28.♖d1**

28...♗e4! 29.♘f7 ♖xf7??
My opponent gives me a second
chance.
After 29...♗xg6! 30.♘xh8 ♗e8!
31.♖d8 ♖e4! 32.♘g6+ ♔f7 33.♘f4
♗b5 34.♘d3 ♗a3 Black has
sufficient compensation for the
exchange and good drawing
chances.
30.♖fe1!
My opponent had overlooked this
move. Now White wins very easily.
**30...♗xc2+ 31.♔xc2 ♔g8 32.♖d8+
♖f8**
32...♗f8 33.♖e6 a5 34.♗xf7+ ♔xf7
35.♖a6+−.
33.♖xf8+ ♗xf8 34.g4!

Black has no moves, so my
opponent resigned.

Yuriy Kuzubov

Yuriy Kuzubov (born 1990 in Sychyovka) became a grandmaster before his 15th birthday, in 2004, the same year he finished runner-up in the World U14 Youth Championship. He has since been live-rated 2700 and has won tournaments that include the Abu Dhabi Masters, the Chigorin Memorial and the Reykjavik Open.

In 2014 Yuriy became Ukrainian Champion, while he also won gold with Ukraine in the 2021 European Team Championships, after building up by taking bronze in 2017 and silver in 2019.

NOTES BY
Yuriy Kuzubov

This game was played in the Spanish club championship in 2020. My opponent, Igor Kovalenko, was then still representing the Latvian Chess Federation and was well-known to all for his sharp and uncompromising play. This game was no exception.

Game 37   English Opening
Igor Kovalenko   2645
Yuriy Kuzubov   2643
Linares tt 2020 (5)

1.c4 ♘f6 2.♘c3 e5 3.♘f3 ♘c6 4.g3 ♗b4 5.♗g2
5.♘d5.
5...0-0 6.0-0
6.♘d5 is also playable here, with a great deal of theory.
6...♖e8

Knowing the style and reputation of my opponent, I chose a quieter and more positional line of play. A very fighting position arises in the variation 6...e4 7.♘g5 ♗xc3 8.bxc3 ♖e8 9.f3 e3 (it is also possible to play 9...exf3 10.♘xf3 ♕e7) 10.d3 (or 10.dxe3) 10...d5.

7.♘e1
A quite rare move. White intends to take control of the square d5 by means of the manoeuvre ♘e1-c2-e3. Also possible is 7.♘d5 ♗c5 8.d3 h6 9.♘d2 d6 with roughly equal play.
7...♗xc3 8.dxc3

The alternative 8.bxc3 e4 9.f3 exf3 10.♘xf3 ♕e7 transposes to the variation with 6...e4.

8...h6

In my view, this is inaccurate. Better was 8...e4 9.♗g5 h6 10.♗xf6 ♕xf6 11.♘c2 d6 12.♘e3 a5 with counterplay.

9.e4! d6 10.h3

My opponent commits an inaccuracy in return, as this move could have waited.

Better was the immediate 10.♘c2, not losing time, e.g. 10...a6 11.♘e3 b5 12.b3, with a slightly more pleasant position for White.

10...a6 11.♘c2

White cannot close the position with 11.a4, because of the typical 11...♘a5 12.b3 ♗e6 with the idea of ...b7-b5, immediately or after the preliminary ...♕d7. Or even ...c7-c6, followed by ...d6-d5.

The thrust ...b7-b5 is also not prevented by the move 11.♕e2 because of 11...b5! 12.cxb5 axb5 13.♕xb5 ♘a5! with the threat ...♗a6, and after the forced 14.♕e2 ♘b3 15.♖b1 ♖xa2 Black seizes the initiative.

11...b5 12.♘e3

The exchange on b5 favours Black, since now the ♖a8 is already in play on its home square: 12.cxb5 axb5 13.♕d3 ♘e7 and then ...♗b7, preparing ...d6-d5.

12...bxc4 13.♕a4 ♗d7

More subtle was 13...♘e7 14.♕xc4 a5 15.♕d3 a4 with chances for both sides, or even 13...♘b8!? with similar ideas.

14.♕xc4 ♕c8 15.♔h2

Although the h3-pawn was not hanging, White will sooner or later have to play this king move anyway.

15...a5

With the idea of seizing some space with ...a5-a4.

16.b3 ♕b7

Preparing the manouevre ...♘c6-e7 and then ...♗d7-c6, creating pressure against square e4.

17.♕e2 ♘e7

18.f4

Just in time!

After the mediocre 18.♕c2 Black seizes the initiative: 18...♗c6 19.f3 d5 with a slightly more pleasant position for Black, in view of the passivity of the ♗g2 and the weakened kingside pawn cover.

18...♗c6 19.fxe5 ♘xe4

Of course not 19...dxe5?? 20.♖xf6! gxf6 21.♘g4 with a decisive attack for White.

20.♕h5?!

This is too optimistic.

Principled was 20.♘g4 ♘g6 (this move looks too risky) 21.♗xh6 ♖e6 followed by ...♘c5 and Black is fine. During the game, I was planning to take on e5 with the pawn: 21...dxe5 22.♕f3 ♖f8, and here I did not see how White can continue his cavalry charge, but even so the computer assesses the position in White's favour after 23.♖ad1 and now it is again difficult to appreciate that the move ...f7-f5 is not a threat, e.g. 23...f5 24.♘e3 ♘e7 (24...gxh6 25.♕h5 and Black's position collapses, e.g. 25...♘e7 26.♘xf5 ♘xf5 27.♖xf5 ♖xf5 28.♕g6+ ♔h8 29.♕xh6+ ♔g8 30.♕g6+ ♔h8 31.♕xf5+−) 25.♕h5 ♗e8 26.♕g5±.

The engine easily finds equality in the variation 20...h5:

A) 21.♘h6+ gxh6 22.♕f3 (22.♕xh5? ♘g6−+) 22...♘g5 23.♕f6 ♗xg2 24.♗xg5 ♗xf1 25.♖xf1 and again Black is saved by a queen jump: 25...♕d5! 26.♗xh6 ♕xe5 27.♕xf7+ ♔h8 28.♖f6 ♕e2+ 29.♔g1

♕e1+ 30.♔h2 ♕e2+ with perpetual check;

B) Or the prettier and more forcing 21.e6! fxe6 22.♘h6+ gxh6 23.♕xh5 ♕b5!! (all other moves lose) 24.♕f7+ (24.♕g4+ ♘g5 25.h4 h5 26.♕xg5+ ♕xg5 27.♗xg5 ♗xg2 28.♔xg2 with a roughly equal endgame) 24...♔h8 25.♗xh6 ♕e5!!. Over the board, such a move is extremely hard, if not downright impossible, to see. But the engine defends such positions easily and assesses everything as 0.00, for example 26.♗xe4 ♗xe4 27.♖f6 ♘f5 (the only move) 28.♗g7+ ♘xg7 29.♖h6+ ♔h7 30.♕g6 ♕e2+ 31.♔h1 ♕f3+ 32.♔h2 with perpetual check.

It is easy to find such variations in home analysis and with the computer, but at the board it is not very realistic to plumb down to the depths of such a variation!

20...♘g6

Now only White can have problems because of his undeveloped queenside and the weakness of his king.

21.♘g4

Things are extremely sad for White after 21.exd6 ♘xd6 22.♗xc6 ♕xc6∓.

21...♘xg3!

I also examined the exchange sacrifice 21...♖xe5 22.♘xe5 ♘xc5 with good compensation for Black, but decided the move in the game was stronger.

22.♔xg3

22.♗xc6 ♘xf1+ 23.♔g1 ♕xc6−+.

22...♗xg2 23.♖f2

23....♗e4

It was also possible to start with 23...♕c6 with the idea after 24.♗xh6 to take on e5 with the rook: 24...♖xe5 25.♘xe5 dxe5 with the better prospects for Black, e.g. 26.♖xg2 (26.♗d2 ♗e4 reaches a similar position to the game) 26...♕xc3+ 27.♕f3 ♕xf3+ (27...♕xa1?? 28.♕xa8++−) 28.♔xf3 ♘h4+ 29.♔g3 ♘xg2 30.♗g5 ♘f4 31.♗xf4 exf4+ 32.♔xf4 ♖d8 33.♖c1 and the endgame is probably drawn.

24.♗xh6?

In my calculations, I had considered the main variation to be 24.♘f6+ gxf6 25.exf6 ♖e6 (also not losing is 25...♕d5 26.♕xh6 ♕e5+ 27.♔g4 ♕e6+ 28.♔g3 ♕e5+ with perpetual check) 26.♕xh6 ♖xf6 27.♖xf6 ♕d5, with compensation. At the board, I considered my compensation to be sufficient, an assessment which the computer confirms.

24...♖xe5! 25.♘xe5 dxe5

Even stronger was 25...♘xe5∓.

26.♗e3 ♕c6∓

After all the adventures, White's hopes have crumbled. It will be hard to stop the advance of the

black central pawns, and for a human, the position is extremely unpleasant.

27.c4

Perhaps it was better to forget about the c-pawn and play 27.♖g1 with the idea after 27...f5 to take 28.♖xf5 ♗xf5 29.♕xf5∓ with good chances to escape. But here too, after 27...♕xc3 28.♕e2 f5 29.♔h2 ♕c6 White's position is far from all he could wish for.

27...f5

It is hard to offer White any good advice.

28.♔h2 f4 29.♗d2

29...♕b6?!

Over the board, I felt that this was the strongest continuation, but in our mutual time-trouble I failed to find 29...♔f7! (this move crowns Black's strategy) 30.♖g1 ♖h8 31.♕g5 ♕d7 32.♖g4 ♔g8 followed by 33...♗f5, winning.

30.♖e2

But now White gets breathing space and can organize control of the g-file.

30...♗d3 31.♖g2 ♖f8 32.♖ag1 f3

On 32...♖f6 it looks strong to reply 33.♗xf4! ♖xf4 (bad is 33...exf4??

34.♕d5++−) 34.♖xg6 ♗xg6 35.♖xg6 with an equal ending.

33.c5!
Igor is up to the mark!
Losing was 33.♖xg6 ♗xg6 34.♕xg6
(34.♖xg6 ♕f2+ 35.♔h1 ♕xd2−+)
34...♕xg6 35.♖xg6 f2 36.♖g1 fxg1♕+
37.♔xg1 a4.
33...♕f6 34.♖xg6?
The final mistake in the game.
After the accurate 34.♖f2 it would
have been extremely difficult for
Black to set his pawns in motion.
**34...♗xg6 35.♖xg6 ♕xg6! 36.♕xg6
f2 37.♗h6**

This is the move my opponent was counting on, but it transpires that after the banal
37...♖f7 38.♗xg7 f1♕
White has no perpetual check and his king falls under an irresistible attack.

**39.♗xe5+ ♔f8 40.♕h6+ ♔e7
41.♕e3 ♖f2+ 42.♔g3 ♖e2 43.♕d4
♕g2+ 44.♔f4 ♕h2+ 45.♔f5
♕xh3+ 46.♔f4 ♕h4+ 47.♔f3 ♕xd4
48.♗xd4 ♖xa2 49.♔e4 ♖a3 50.♗c3
a4 0-1**
A very tense game, with mutual inaccuracies and mistakes!

Anna Ushenina

Anna Ushenina (born in Kharkiv, 1985) was the Women's World Champion from November 2012 to September 2013. Her many successes in team chess reached an early pinnacle in 2006. At the Turin Women's Olympiad, she was a part of the victorious Ukrainian team and remained undefeated throughout the contest. Ushenina and her compatriots Natalia Zhukova (also undefeated), Kateryna Lahno and Inna Gaponenko each scored between 70% and 80% in a commanding performance, earning them team gold medals and much adulation in chess circles.

In the final of the Women's World Chess Championship 2012, Anna achieved a tie-break victory over Antoaneta Stefanova to become the 14th Women's World Champion. This automatically earned her the grandmaster title. She was Ukraine's first Women's World Champion. She lost her title against Hou Yifan in the World Championship match in 2013. In 2016, Ushenina won the European Women's Championship.

NOTES BY
Ruslan Ponomariov

Game 38　Nimzo-Indian Defence
Anna Ushenina　　　　　　　2452
Nadezhda Kosintseva　　　　2539
Khanty-Mansiysk Wch W k.o. 2012 (4.2)

Kharkiv is not just the second biggest city in Ukraine. At some moment in history, it was even a capital. But Kharkiv is also a big chess centre, and I think Anna benefited a lot from this. For example, Mikhail Brodsky, the coach of the national women's team, is from this city. At some moment Anna also worked with Anton Korobov, and this game illustrates quite well the benefits of this cooperation, as she played one of Anton's favourite lines in the Nimzo-Indian Defence.
1.d4 ♘f6 2.c4 e6 3.♘c3 ♝b4 4.e3 0-0 5.♝d3 d5 6.♘f3 c5 7.0-0 ♘c6
Black also decides to go for a complex strategic fight.

Calmer is 7...dxc4 8.♗xc4 cxd4
9.exd4 b6 as, for example, Anatoly
Karpov liked to play.

8.a3 ♗xc3 9.bxc3 ♛c7

Another main line is 9...dxc4
10.♗xc4 ♛c7.

10.cxd5

Anna goes for the main theory
and plays the most popular moves
according to Mega Database.
I have good memories myself with
Black here: 10.♗b2 ♖e8!? (this is
a point of not playing 9...dxc4,
somehow my opponent got
confused and very quickly ended
up in a bad position with White:
11.h3 ♘a5 12.cxd5 exd5 13.♘d2 ♗e6
14.♖c1?! (14.a4) 14...b5! 15.dxc5?! ♘c4
16.♖b1 ♛xc5 17.♘b3 ♛c7 18.♗c1
a6 and White's c1-bishop looks
very miserable, 0-1 (41) Nakamura-
Ponomariov, Dortmund 2011.

**10...exd5 11.a4 ♖e8 12.♗a3 c4
13.♗c2 ♗g4**

Theory regards 13...♘e4 as safer,
but let's leave this for further
investigation.

14.♛e1 ♗h5

Here it was possible to exchange
on f3: 14...♗xf3 15.gxf3 ♛d7 16.♔h1
♛h3 17.♛d1. Black has spoiled

White's pawn structure on the
kingside, but on the other hand
White has gained the two bishops,
so it will be a long struggle.

15.♘h4

Of course White should discourage
15...♗g6, with the exchange of the
light-squared bishops.

15...♘g4 16.g3 ♗g6 17.♘xg6 hxg6

18.♛d2

Here 18.e4?! does not promise
much: 18...dxe4 19.♛e2 (19.♗xe4
♘f6 20.f3 ♘a5 and ...♘b3 is coming,
with a perfect position for Black)
19...♘f6 20.♛xc4 ♖ac8∓ with
the idea ...b7-b6 and ...♘a5 with
occupation of the c4-square.

18...♘a5

The attempt to take the e4-square
under control with 18...f5 is too
slow: 19.♖ae1 ♘f6 20.f3 ♛d7 21.g4!
and White had the initiative in
Jussupow-Lobron, Munich 1994.

19.♖ae1 ♘f6

This natural move may be the cause
of Black's further problems.
As you will see later, it may have
been more accurate to play first
19...♘b3 to limit White's options,
e.g. 20.♛d1 ♛d7 (20...♘f6!? 21.f3
♛a5 22.♗b2 ♛xa4 – now the

queen is not so well placed on d1 –
23.e4 ♕a2 24.♗c1 dxe4 25.fxe4 ♘a1!
26.♖e2 ♘xc2 27.♖xc2 ♕b3 28.e5
♘d5 29.♖ff2 ♕b6 is unclear, but I
rather like Black's position here)
21.♗xb3 cxb3 22.♕xb3 ♖ac8 23.♗c1
♘f6 24.f3 ♖e6 (24...♖c4!? deserves
attention: 25.a5, for example
25...♖a4 26.♗d2 ♖xa5 27.c4 dxc4
28.♕xc4 b5 29.♕d3 ♖a4) 25.♗d2
♖b6 26.♕c2 ♖a6 27.♖a1 ♘e8 with
compensation, Del Rio Angelis-
Kurajica, Las Palmas 2005.
20.f3

20...♕c6
Another top grandmaster from
Kharkiv, Pavel Eljanov, had a game
here with Black: 20...♘b3 21.♕d1 (I
think Anna planned to play anyway
21.♕g2!?, the move that wouldn't
have been possible if Black had
played 19...♘b3 one move earlier,
e.g. 21...♕a5 22.♗b2 ♕xa4 23.e4
with transposition to 20...♕c6)
21...♕a5 22.♗b4 (22.♗xb3 ♕xc3!∓)
22...♕xa4 (Black has won a pawn,
and in addition the bishop on b4 will
be attacked soon) 23.e4 a5 24.♗d6
♖e6 25.♗e5 ♕d7?! (here I think
Black missed a chance to gain an
advantage with 25...dxe4! 26.fxe4

♕d7 and Black's idea is just to push
the a-pawn) 26.♗xf6 ♖xf6 27.e5
♖b6 28.f4 with mutual chances in
Gelfand-Eljanov, Astrakhan 2010.
21.♕g2!? ♘b3 22.e4 ♕xa4 23.♗b2!
23.♗d6?! ♖e6 24.♗e5 (24.e5 ♘e8
25.f4 ♘xd6 26.exd6 ♖xe1 27.♖xe1
♕c6∓) 24...♕a5 25.exd5 ♕xd5
(25...♘xd5?! 26.f4 ♖ae8 (26...♘xc3
27.f5 gxf5 28.♗xf5 ♖xe5 29.dxe5
♕b6+ 30.♔h1 ♘d4 31.e6 ♘xe6
32.♗xe6 fxe6 33.♕f3 ♕c6 34.♕xc6
bxc6 35.♖f4±) 27.f5 gxf5 28.♗xf5
with an attack) and it's hard to tell
where White's compensation for the
pawn is.

This is probably the position Anna
wanted to reach during her home
preparation. It looks very similar to
classical examples like Botvinnik-
Capablanca. Black has won a pawn,
but White has very powerful pieces
on the kingside plus a broad pawn
centre. All this promises a very
complex battle.
23...♕b5 24.♗b1!
It was tempting to play 24.e5!? but
Black has a very powerful shot:
24...♘xd4! (24...♘d7 25.♗a3 ♕a5
(25...♕a4 26.♗d6 ♕a5 27.♖e3)
26.♗b4 ♕b6 27.♗d6 ♖ad8 28.f4

♘f6 29.f5 with White's initiative)
25.♗b1 ♘b3 26.exf6 ♕b6+ 27.♔h1
♕xf6, when White's bishops are
not very active and at some point
Black's three pawns could be a more
important factor.

24...dxe4

24...♘d7 is too slow a try to
exchange one of White's bishops
(with the manoeuvre ...♘d7-b6-a4):
25.e5 ♘b6 (25...♕c6 26.f4) 26.f4 ♘a4
27.f5! with an attack, e.g. 27...gxf5
(27...♘xb2 28.fxg6+−; 27...g5 28.f6)
28.♗xf5 ♘xd4 (28...♘xb2 29.♕h3!;
28...g6 29.e6 gxf5 30.♖xf5 ♖xe6
31.♖xe6 fxe6 32.♖g5+ ♔f7 33.♕f2+
♔e7 34.♖g7+ ♔d6 35.♕f4+ ♔c6
36.♕c7#) 29.cxd4 ♕xb2 30.♕xd5
♘b6 31.♕e4+−.
If 24...a5, 25.e5 ♘d7 26.f4 ♕c6 27.f5
b5 28.e6 also promises White an
attack.

25.fxe4 ♖e6?!

Too slow. Instead, the prophylactic
25...♕c6!? (to prevent 26.e5)
deserved serious attention: 26.g4 b5
27.g5 ♘h5 with mutual chances.

26.♖e2

More direct was the immediate
26.e5!? and now:

A) If 26...♘d5 27.♖e4 and White
can play actively against Black's
king: 27...♖ae8 28.♕h3 f5 29.♖h4
♖xe5 (29...♘e3 30.♗a3 ♘xf1
31.♗xf5±) 30.dxe5 ♕c5+ 31.♔h1
♖xe5 32.♗xf5 gxf5 33.♖xf5 ♖e1+
34.♖f1±;

B) 26...♖ae8 27.♖e2 ♘d5 (27...♕b6
– with the idea to take on e5 –
28.♕f2 ♕c7 29.♕f4 29...♘d5 30.♕f3
and White is better) 28.♕f3 ♕d7
29.♗e4, with a strong initiative.

26...♖ae8 27.e5 ♘d5

Here Black missed what was
probably the last chance to create
some counterplay and change the
direction of the game. But for a
human player it is really difficult
to find 27...♘c5!! White's centre is
so powerful that Black is happy to
return some material. The main
idea is 28.dxc5 ♖xe5 29.♖xe5 ♖xe5
30.♗a3 ♕e8! (White's bishops are
slightly out of play and now it's
Black who creates active play on
the kingside with just a few pieces)
31.♕xb7 ♖e7 32.♕f3 ♖e3 33.♕f4 ♖e2
with chances for both sides.

28.♕f3 f5

28...♖8e7 29.♖ef2.

29.g4!

Now White's attack is unstoppable.
The good thing about bishops is
that they can work from a long
distance, something we cannot say
of Black's knight on b3.
29.exf6? ♘xf6 30.♖xe6 ♖xe6
31.♗xg6 ♘d2 32.♕f5 ♕xf5 33.♖xf5
♖a6 34.♖c5 ♘d7 35.♖c7 ♖xg6
36.♖xd7 ♖b6 37.♗a3 ♘e4∓.

29...f4 30.♗e4 ♖d8

30...♘e3? 31.♖xe3 fxe3 (31...♘d2
32.♕xf4 ♘xf1 33.♖f3!+−) 32.♕f7+
♔h7 33.♖f3+−.

**31.♗xd5 ♕xd5 32.♕xf4+− ♕d7
33.♗a3 ♖a6 34.♗b4 ♕e6 35.♕e4**

**b5 36.♖ef2 ♖a1 37.♖xa1 ♘xa1
38.♖a2 ♘b3 39.♖xa7 ♘c1 40.♖e7
♕a6 41.♕f3 ♔h8**

41...♖f8 42.♖xg7+ ♔xg7
43.♕xf8++−.

**42.♕f7 ♖g8 43.♖a7 ♕c8 44.♕xg6
♘e2+ 45.♔f1 ♘f4 46.♕g5 1-0**

I think this was a very instructive
game. It's hard to tell where Black
made the decisive mistake that cost
her the game.

With this victory, Anna reached
the semi-finals, where Ju Wenjun
waited for her. And later in the final
she beat Antoaneta Stefanova to
become World Chess Champion.

Anna Muzychuk

Anna Muzychuk was born near Lviv (1990) and introduced to chess as a 2-year-old by her parents, who were both professional chess coaches. She played her first tournament when she was five and, spurred on by the similar success of her younger sister Mariya, went on to claim countless Ukrainian and European Championships, before crowning her junior career by winning the World Girls U20 Championship in 2010. In July 2012 she became only the fourth woman in history to cross the 2600 mark.

Anna came closest to winning the classical Women's World Championship when she lost the final match to Tan Zhongyi in Tehran in 2017, but she has been the Women's Rapid (2016) and Blitz (2014 and 2016) World Champion. Since representing Ukraine in team events she's won Olympiad silver in 2018 and bronze in 2014 and 2016, while in 2016 she also won individual gold on top board.

NOTES BY
Anna Muzychuk

I consider this to be one of my best games. But it's the first time I have annotated it.

Game 39   Sicilian Defence
Anna Muzychuk   2555
Gunay Mammadzada   2438
Porto Carras 2018 (2)

1.e4 c5 2.♘f3 d6 3.♗b5+
The main direction is of course 3.d4, leading to different variations of the open Sicilian. 3.♗b5+ has a tendency to lead to quieter positions but as this game showed it doesn't mean that ♗b5 is a 'boring' move. In general, I can say that I have quite a lot of experience after both 3.d4 and 3.♗b5+.

3...♗d7
Another tabiya starts after 3...♗d7. It leads to quite a different type of position. 3...♘c6 is less popular nowadays.

4.0-0 a6

5.♗d3
This manoeuvre looks a bit artificial, but it is quite typical. You can see a similar plan not only in this line or other Sicilian lines but also in some other openings, for example in the Petroff: 1.e4 e5 2.♘f3 ♘f6 3.♘e5 d6 4.♘f3 ♘e4 5.♗d3. The idea is that White is protecting the e4-pawn (in case of the coming ...♘f6), and also slowly regroups the bishop to c2. After

c2-c3, ♗c2, d2-d4 White gets a space advantage.

5...♘gf6 6.c3 g6

The most popular move is 6...b5. Sometimes Black develops the bishop to e7 after 6...e6 but 6...g6 is also very reasonable and it has been played by many strong grandmasters.

7.♗c2 ♗g7 8.d4 0-0

9.e5

A very sharp and commital decision. One year before this game was played I tried 9.a4 in my game vs Ian Nepomniachtchi. The idea of the move is to prevent ...b7-b5. After 9...b6 10.♖e1 e5 11.dxe5 ♘xe5 12.♘xe5 dxe5 13.♕xd8 ♖xd8 14.c4 I got a slightly more pleasant endgame as the b1-knight is closer to the d5-outpost than Black's knight is to its favourable d4-square, though that game later ended in a draw, A.Muzychuk-Nepomniachtchi, Jerusalem 2018.

9...♘e8

9...♘d5 is a blunder due to 10.dxc5; And 9...dxe5 10.dxe5 ♘e8 is a much worse version compared to the game in view of 11.e6 fxe6 12.♘g5.

10.e6!?

10.♕e2 ♘c7 or 10.♖e1 cxd4 11.cxd4 ♘c7 is not so clear. After ...b7-b5 and ...♗b7 White will start to feel pressure on the e5-pawn.

10...fxe6 11.♘g5

Very energetic and straightforward.

11...♘c7 12.dxc5!

An important move. The immediate 12.♘xh7 does not work in view of 12...♔xh7 13.♕h5+ ♔g8 14.♗xg6 (14.♕xg6 ♖f6) 14...♘f6 and Black successfully parries the attack.

12...d5!

A good answer. My point was that if Black recaptures with the knight, she would no longer have the chance to play ...♘f6:

A) 12...♘xc5 13.♘xh7 ♔xh7 14.♕h5+ ♔g8 15.♗xg6 ♘f6 could be very helpful but now the knight is a bit too far away, so 15...♖f6 is the only move but here White wins the queen after 16.♕h7+ ♔f8 17.♗h6 ♖xg6 18.♕h8+ ♔f7 19.♕xd8;

B) 12...dxc5 looks ugly as it leaves the doubled e-pawns very weak: 13.♕e2+−.

13.f4!?

I remember that I was thinking for quite a long time before playing this move. The idea of 13.f4 is to take control over the e5-square. However, there were also many other interesting options:

A) 13.♕g4!? ♘f6 (13...♖f6 also deserves attention: 14.♕h4 h6 15.♘f3 g5 16.♘xg5 (16.♕g3 e5 17.h4 g4 18.♘h2 h5) 16...hxg5 17.♗xg5 e5) 14.♕h4 e5 15.♘xh7 ♘xh7 16.♗xg6 ♘f6 17.f4 e4 (17...exf4!? 18.♗xf4 ♗d7 planning ♗e8) 18.f5 e5, always with very unclear positions;

B) 13.♘xh7 does not look so convincing after 13...♔xh7 14.♕h5+ ♔g8 15.♗xg6 ♘f6 16.♕h4 ♗d7, again with the idea of ...♗e8, and I believe White does not have enough resources to continue the attack;

C) 13.♗e3, protecting the pawn on c5, looks slow. Now Black occupies the centre with 13...e5 and gets a preferable position.

13...e5!
Pawn structure is more important than material!
13...♘xc5 was possible but after 14.♕e1 with the idea of 15.♕h4 (or simply 14.♗e3) White's position looks better.
14.♘xh7!
I had planned this sacrifice before playing 13.f4.

In case of 14.fxe5 ♘xe5 Black takes over the initiative.
14...♔xh7 15.♕h5+ ♔g8 16.♗xg6 ♘f6 17.♕h4
All this was pretty much forced up to here and now Black has to take a decision. 18.fxe5 is a serious threat, so there seem to be two logical moves: 17...e4 and 17...exf4.

17...e4!
Perhaps after 17...exf4 Black can maintain equality but opening the f-file looks much more scary compared to 17...e4. Additionally, after 17...exf4 Black has to play very precisely – the engines claim that in a number of lines Black can defend only by finding various only moves:

A) 18.♖xf4 is logical but after 18...♗d7 the sacrifice on f6 is not winning, viz. 19.♖xf6 ♖xf6 20.♕h7+ ♔f8 21.♗h6 ♖xg6 22.♕xg6 ♘e6 23.♘d2 (if only we had a chance to make one more move, bring the last piece into the game and play ♖f1, White would celebrate the victory, but... the moves are made one by one) 23...♗xh6 24.♕xh6+ (24.♖f1+ ♗f4) 24...♔g8. After lots of complications and exchanges things have calmed down. White has two pawns for the piece and some compensation but I believe it can be enough only for a draw;

B) 18.♗xf4 ♗d7 19.♗e5 (19.♘d2!? ♗e8 20.♗c2 (20.♗f5 ♘h5 (20...♗d7!?) 21.♗g5 ♖xf5 22.♖xf5 ♕d7 is unclear) 20...♘e6 21.♗e3 (21.♗h6 ♖f7 22.♗g6 ♘xc5 is unclear; 21.♖ae1?! ♘xf4 22.♖xf4 e6∓) 21...♕c7 22.♖ae1 (22.♘f3 ♘e4 unclear) 22...♘xc5 23.♗d4 unclear) 19...♗e8 (only move again) and now:

B1) 20.♗c2!? ♘e6! 21.b4 ♘e4 (there are also other moves but 21...♘e4 is the most concrete) 22.♘d2 ♗xe5 23.♘xe4 dxe4 24.♕g4+ ♘g7 25.♕xe4 ♖xf1+ 26.♖xf1 ♗f6 27.♕h7+ ♔f8 (27...♔f7? 28.♗g6+ ♔e6 29.♕h3++−). All this was forced and now White should sooner or later agree to the repetition: 28.♕h8+ ♔f7 29.♕h7=;

B2) 20.♗f5 ♗d7! (20...e6?! 21.♗c2 and now there is no 21...♘e4 '!' because of 22.♖xf8+ ♔xf8 23.♕f4+ ♔g8 24.♗xc7; 20...♘h5? 21.♗xg7 ♖xf5 22.♖xf5 ♘xg7 23.♕g3 with a white attack) 21.♗c2 ♘e6! 22.♘d2 (22.b4 ♕e8! (a very strong defensive idea) 23.♘d2 ♕h5 24.♗xf6 ♕xh4 25.♗xh4 ♗xc3∓) 22...♘xc5 and here again there are many options. According to the computer, the evaluation is 0.00 but in my opinion it's quite dangerous to play this position with Black. During the game I also considered 17...♕d7 with the idea of trading the queens after ...♕g4. But after the prophylactic 18.h3! the queen

is misplaced on d7: 18...e4 (18...exf4 19.♗xf4±) 19.♘d2±.

18.f5

Preparing g2-g4; 18.g4? ♗xg4−+.

18...♗d7?

A logical move, finishing development and preparing ...♗e8, but the position is so concrete that pure calculation is much more important than common sense.

A) 18...e5! 19.fxe6 (19.g4 d4 (19...♕e7!? 20.g5 (20.♗h7+=; 20.b4 ♗d7 21.g5 ♗e8) 20...♕xc5+ 21.♔h1 e3 22.gxf6 ♖xf6) 20.g5 e3 with a complete mess! Btw, 21.♘d2 is the strongest here! For the engine all this is clear ☺) 19...♘xe6 20.♗e3 ♗d7 21.♘d2 (21.♘a3 d4! 22.cxd4 ♗e8∓) 21...♗e8 22.♗f5 ♗d7=;

B) 18...e6 is also possible but if we compare 18...e5 and 18...e6, 18...e5 looks 'more human'. After 19.fxe6 we may simply have a transposition but there are also other options like 19.g4, 19.♘d2, 19.♘a3 etc.

19.g4

19.♗h6 doesn't achieve much, e.g. 19...♗xh6 20.♕xh6 e5 21.♔g5 ♗b5 and despite the fact that White has some discovered check options, her position is nearly lost.

19...♗e8?!

Once again 19...e5 was better but Black did not play it on the previous move and now it was even much harder to do so: 20.g5 ♕e7 21.gxf6 ♗xf6 22.♕g4 ♕g7 23.♘a3±.

20.g5 ♗xg6 21.fxg6 ♘h5?

And even here, 21...e5 was the only move to stay in the game but I believe the position is already quite bad for Black after 22.♘a3 ♕e7 23.♘c2, maintaining a strong attack.

22.♖xf8+

22.♘d2 was even stronger but 22.♕xh5? could be a serious mistake: 22...♖xf1+ 23.♔xf1 d4 and the position becomes unclear. White is very much behind in development after 24.♗f4 ♕d5.

22...♕xf8

22...♔xf8 23.♕xh5 d4 24.♗f4+−.

23.♕xh5 ♕f5 24.♗e3 ♘e6

25.♘d2

I saw the let's say objectively best move which was 25.♕h7+ but preferred to finish my development instead of winning material: 25...♔f8 26.♘d2 ♘xg5 27.♗xg5 ♕xg5+ 28.♔h1 ♕xd2 29.♖f1+ ♔e8 30.♕g8+ ♔d7 31.♕xa8. Somehow I

was afraid to put the queen on h7 and then move it to the other side of the board (a8) in a position when my king is very exposed. I still believe that the move I chose in the game is safer and more practical.

25...♘f8 26.♖f1 ♕e6

26...♕xg6 runs into the simple trick 27.♖xf8+, winning the queen.

27.♘b3 ♘xg6 28.♘d4 ♗xd4

29.♗xd4 ♖f8

29...e3 was more tenacious but it should not have saved the game: 30.♕e2 and after taking on e3 White would simply be two pawns up.

30.♖f6!

The last important nuance. I saw this idea when I played 25.♘d2. If there was no 30.♖f6, the position would not have been so clear.

30...♖xf6

30...♘f4 31.♖xe6 ♘xh5 32.♖xe7+−; 30...exf6 31.♕xg6+ ♔h8 32.♗xf6+ ♖xf6 33.gxf6+−.

31.gxf6 ♕f7 32.fxe7

The rest is easy:

32...♕e6 33.e8♕+ ♕xe8 34.♕xd5+ ♔h7 35.♕h5+ ♔g8 36.♕d5+ ♔h7 37.♕xb7+ ♔h6 38.♗e3+ 1-0

Mariya (above) and Anna Muzychuk (photos Lennart Ootes).

Mariya Muzychuk

Mariya Muzychuk (born: Lviv 1992) had the best possible chess upbringing. Not only did her parents, both professional chess coaches, start teaching her the game from a very young age, but she had her older sister Anna to inspire her. Mariya played her first tournament at the age of six and won the Girl's U10 European Youth Championship in 2002. She won the Ukrainian Women's Championship in both 2012 and 2013 and claimed the top women's prize, and a grandmaster norm, at the 2014 Gibraltar Masters.

Mariya's crowning achievement so far came in 2015, when she defeated Monika Socko, Antoaneta Stefanova, Humpy Koneru, Harika Dronavalli and Natalia Pogonina to become the Women's World Chess Champion. She then played a World Championship match in her home city of Lviv, but lost 6:3 to Hou Yifan. Mariya's illustrious career for the Ukrainian team includes individual gold at the Olympiad, World and European Team Championships, and also team gold in those last two events.

NOTES BY
Mariya Muzychuk

This game was played in the last round of the Women's Candidates Tournament. I am pleased to annotate it as this game got a prize for the most beautiful game of the event.

Game 40   Caro-Kann Defence
Mariya Muzychuk   2563
Alexandra Goryachkina   2522

Kazan Women's Candidates 2019 (14)

1.e4 c6 2.d4 d5 3.e5 ♗f5 4.♘f3 e6 5.♗e2 c5 6.♗e3 ♕b6 7.♘c3 ♘c6
A sharp and principled variation of the Caro-Kann Defence. For me this line did not come as a surprise because Alexandra had chosen it several times before and the last time she had played it was exactly in this tournament, in the 12th round against the Chinese player

Tan Zhongyi. That game continued with 8.♘a4 – it is less known but also interesting.
In my game I chose 8.0-0 after which we kept on following the forced line:
8.0-0 ♕xb2 9.♕e1 cxd4 10.♗xd4 ♘xd4 11.♘xd4 ♗b4 12.♖b1 ♗xc3 13.♖xb2 ♗xe1 14.♖xe1 b6

15.h4
Up to here, everything had been played quite fast by both sides. It is a well-known line where the game goes from the opening into the endgame.

In the current position Black is a pawn up but the pieces on the kingside are undeveloped. The move 15.h4 isn't a new one but is rarely played. 15.♗b5+ is a far more popular move: 15...♔f8 16.♘xf5 exf5 and now 17.♖b3 and 17.c4 have been tested many times. Also there are games with 17.♖d1. All these continuations are interesting for analysis but for this game I had prepared another direction.

15...♗e4

Fortunately, my hopes assigned to 15.h4 proved justified. Alexandra wasn't familiar with this continuation and immediately made a mistake which most probably turned out to be a decisive one. It was correct to play 15...h5 with an approximately equal position, and this is much better than 15...h6 as after 16.♘xf5 exf5 17.♗b5+ ♔f8 18.c4 dxc4 19.♗xc4± Black cannot play ...♖h6, which was possible if Black had started with 15...h5, I hadn't checked 15...♗e4 before the game, so from now on both Alexandra and myself started to play on our own.

16.♗b5+

The best decision. White rules out Black's option of castling and plans to manoeuvre the rook from e1 to the seventh rank.

A) Less good but also quite strong was 16.♘b5 ♔f8 (16...♔e7 17.h5 (the threat is to trap the bishop with f2-f3; just not 17.♘d6? in view of 17...♘f6= and Black develops the kingside with the help of this tactical trick; 17.c4±) 17...h6 (17...d4 18.♘xd4 ♗b7 19.a4±) 18.c4+− and here we see that the insertion of h4-h5 and ...h7-h6 is in White's favour as now there is no ...♘h6 due to the pawn on h6) 17.h5 h6 18.♘d6 and White's position is much better;

B) The same position could arise if we start with 16.h5 h6 and then get into the variation you can see above: 17.♘b5 ♔f8 18.♘d6±;

C) Likewise it was possible to play first 16.f3 ♗g6, transposing to the game after 17.♗b5+ ♔f8 18.♖e3.

16...♔f8 17.f3

If we manoeuvre the rook to c7 immediately with 17.♖e3 then it's necessary to take into account the possibility of the pawn sacrifice 17...g5!? with the idea of clearing the g7-square for the king (17...♘e7 18.f3 ♗g6 19.♖c3, transposing to the game): 18.f3 ♗g6 19.hxg5±. The material is equal and obviously White possesses a strong initiative, but now Black has a chance to finish development with ...♔g7 and ...♘e7).

17...♗g6 18.♖e3 ♘e7

If 18...♖c8 then 19.♖a3 ♖c7 20.♗f1 followed by ♘b5.

19.♖c3

During the game I also considered another possibility of playing on the queenside: 19.♖a3. The idea is to retreat the bishop from b5 and to attack the a7- and b6-pawns. But objectively it is less strong as at the cost of the lost pawns on the queenside Black gets time to move the king to h7 and to develop the pieces. This can be seen in the following lines: 19...h5 20.♗e2 (20.♗a6 ♔g8 21.♗b7 ♖b8 22.♖xa7 ♔h7 23.♗a6 ♖a8 24.♖xa8 ♖xa8 25.♖xb6 ♘c8 26.♗xc8 ♖xc8 27.♔f2±; obviously White is fighting for the win but I tend to think that with precise play Black can hold a draw) 20...♔g8 (20...♘f5 21.♘c6±) 21.♖xb6 ♘f5 22.♘xf5 (22.♘c6 ♔h7 23.♖ba6 ♖ac8 24.♗b5 ♘xh4 25.♖xa7 ♔h6±) 22...♗xf5 23.♖b7 ♗xc2 24.♖axa7 ♖xa7 25.♖xa7 ♔h7 26.♖c7 ♗f5 27.a4 ♖a8 28.g4 hxg4 29.fxg4 ♗xg4 30.♗xg4 ♖xa4 31.♗h5 ♖xh4 32.♗xf7 ♖e4 with a theoretically drawn position.

19...h5

It was possible to stop the penetration of the rook to c7 only by playing 19...♖c8 but after 20.♖xc8+

♘xc8 21.♖b3 the other rook goes to c7 after which the entire black queenside crumbles.

20.♖c7

The plan is fulfilled and due to the active position of her pieces White has a decisive advantage, even with a pawn minus.

20...a6

Now it's hard to suggest a good move for Black, as in every line White forcibly creates serious problems, e.g. 20...♘f5 21.♘xf5 ♗xf5 22.♗c6 ♖b8 23.♖xa7 g6 24.♖a6 ♔g7 25.♖axb6 (equally strong is 25.a4 ♖hc8 26.♖axb6 ♖xb6 27.♖xb6 ♗xc2 28.a5 ♖c7 29.a6+−) 25...♖xb6 26.♖xb6 ♗xc2 27.a4 d4 28.♔f2!; the last important move, with a winning position.

Or 20...a5 21.♗e2 ♖b8 22.♖a7 and White wins.

21.♗d7 b5 22.a4

22...bxa4

The best defence was 22...♘f5 and now White has to find a series of precise moves: 23.♘xf5! (23.♘c6?! ♔g8 (23...bxa4 24.♖a7+−) 24.a5 ♔h7±) 23...♗xf5 24.♘c6! ♖d8 (24...♖b8 25.♖a7+−) 25.a5!+− and after the fall of the a6-pawn, the passed a-pawn becomes unstoppable.

23.♗xa4 ♘f5

One more critical moment. I understood that I had to play concretely here because Black threatens to move the king to h7 with possible counterplay against the weak c2-pawn.

24.♖a7!

It is very pleasant to make such a move, moreover this continuation is not only beautiful but also the strongest one.

24...♖d8

The exchange sacrifice after 24...♖c8 25.♗d7 ♘xd4 is interesting but doesn't save the game: 26.♗xc8 ♔g8 27.♖c7+− or 27.♗xa6 ♘xc2 28.♖c7 ♘d4 29.♖b4 ♘c2 30.♖b8+ ♔h7 31.♖xh8+ ♔xh8 32.♔f2+−, while 24...♖xa7 loses immediately to 25.♖b8+ ♔e7 26.♘c6+ ♔d7 27.♘xa7+ and White wins a rook.

25.♘c6

25...♖e8

Almost the same position as in the game could have arisen after 25...♖c8 26.♖c7! (an important move continuing tough play based on using the weakness of the back

rank) 26...♖e8 (26...♖a8 27.♘b8! ♔g8 28.♗c6+−) 27.♘e7! ♖d8 28.♘xg6+ fxg6 29.♖bb7+−.

26.♘e7!

One more beautiful move.

26...♖d8 27.♘xg6+ fxg6 28.♗d7

I could have won more quickly and forcibly by continuing 28.♖bb7 ♔g8 29.g4 hxg4 30.fxg4 ♖xh4 31.gxf5 ♖xa4 32.♖xg7+ ♔f8 33.♖af7+ ♔e8 34.fxe6 with inevitable mate.

28...♔g8 29.♗xe6+

29...♔h7

Here I considered three possibilities: 30.♗f5, 30.♖bb7 and 30.♗f7. After calculation I decided to retain the advantage of the bishop versus the knight and to try to advance the e-pawn.

30.♖bb7

The last thing I wanted was to get into the rook endgame and to undouble the g6- and g7-pawns by means of 30.♗xf5 gxf5 31.♖bb7 ♖hg8 32.♖xa6 ♖c8 33.♖f6 ♖c4 34.♖xf5 ♖xh4 35.♖d7. White's position seems winning here but it is well known that many rook endgames have a drawing tendency. 30.♗f7!? with the idea of e6-e7 was also interesting, but there is a defence: 30...♘h6, after which I have to get into the rook endgame again (31.♖bb7 ♘xf7 32.♖xf7 ♖hg8 33.♖xa6+−) or move back with the bishop: 31.♗e6.

30...♘d4

Another option is 30...♘xh4 31.♖xg7+ ♔h6 and here several moves leads to a win but I liked best 32.f4, creating a mating net and keeping the black rook on h8.

31.♗d7!

Black could get theoretical chances of salvation after 31.♖xg7+ ♔h6 32.♗h3 ♘c6 33.♖ac7 ♘xe5, winning the c5-pawn. From here on, White has to play very precisely again: 34.♔f2!+−.

31...♖b8 32.e6 ♘f5 33.♗a4 ♖bc8 34.e7 ♘d6 35.♖b6 ♘e8

35...♘b5 36.♖axa6+−.

36.♖bxa6 ♔g8

There are several paths that led to a win but the simplest for me was to get into the winning pawn endgame.

37.♖a8

  A) 37.♗d7 ♖b8 38.♗e6+ ♔h7 39.♗xd5+−;

  B) 37.♖b6 ♔f7 38.♗d7 ♖xc2 39.♗e6+ ♔f6 40.♗xd5+ ♔e5 41.♗f7+−.

37...♖xa8 38.♖xa8 ♔f7 39.♔f2

Black resigned in view of 39...♔xe7 40.♔e3 ♖f8 41.♖xe8+ ♖xe8 42.♗xe8 ♔xe8 43.♔d4 and White wins.

NOTES BY
Mariya Muzychuk

Game 41   Petroff Defence
Mariya Muzychuk   2563
Humpy Koneru   2580
St Louis 2020 (2)

1.e4 e5 2.♘f3 ♘f6

The Petroff Defence is a very
solid opening choice. Just to
remind you, both Caruana and
Nepomniachtchi chose it in their
World Championship matches
against Magnus Carlsen. Humpy
also played it in the second game
of her World Championship match
versus Hou Yifan.

3.d4

3.♘xe5 was played in the first round
of the same tournament: 3...d6
4.♘f3 ♘xe4 5.♘c3 ♘xc3 6.dxc3 ♗e7
7.♗e3 ♘c6 8.♕d2 ♗e6 9.0-0-0 ♕d7
10.h3 h6 11.♔b1 0-0-0 12.♘d4 ♘xd4
13.♗xd4 ♖hg8 14.♕e3 a6 15.c4±
and White's pieces are more active
but Black's position is pretty solid.
Slowly she managed to equalize,
½-½ (40) M.Muzychuk-Ju Wenjun,
St Louis 2020.

3...♘xe4 4.♗d3 d5 5.♘xe5 ♘d7

6.♘c3!?

An interesting option that became
trendy recently. It was also
recommended by Gawain Jones in
his book *Coffeehouse Repertoire 1.e4
Volume 2*, published in 2021. It looks
like White isn't worried about the
doubling of his c-pawns and is
playing for fast development.
6.♘xd7 ♗xd7 7.♘c3!? has a similar
idea.

6...♘xc3 7.bxc3 ♗d6 8.0-0 0-0

9.♖e1

The main move nowadays. 9.♘xd7
♗xd7 10.♕h5 is just a transposition
to the very well investigated
opening lines. Next time it would
be interesting to try 9.♗f4!? which
has been played in just a few games
so far: 9...♗xe5 10.♗xe5 ♘xe5
11.dxe5 f5. This pawn structure
reminds one of the game Carlsen-
Shirov, Douglas 2019. Here Black is
probably solid and benefits more
from the exchange of dark-squared
bishops but there is still lots of play
ahead.

9...♗xe5

Black's problem from a practical
point of view is the wide choice of
different options White has.

A) 9...♘xe5 10.dxe5 ♗c5 doesn't look very logical as Black could have exchanged knights on the 7th move; after 11.♕h5 g6 12.♕h6± having the rook on e1 is beneficial for White;

B) Black could also play 9...c5!? but after 10.♕f3!? it's still too early to say that Black has solved all the problems, e.g. 10...c4 11.♗f5 ♘xe5 12.dxe5 ♗c5 13.♗xc8 ♖xc8 14.♗e3 ♗xe3 15.♕xe3 b6 16.♖ad1 ♕d7 (Shankland-Rapport, Wijk aan Zee 2022), and now instead of 17.e6?!, which only simplifies the position, it's interesting to try 17.f4!?, maintaining pressure in the centre with an initiative on the kingside.

10.dxe5 ♘c5

11.♖b1?!

Beginning an interesting plan of attacking on the kingside, which worked perfectly.

However it might be stronger to play 11.♗f1!, keeping the pair of bishops which can be a long-term advantage in this open position. A logical continuation is 11...♖e8 (11...♗f5 12.♗e3 b6 13.♗b5±) 12.♗a3 (12.♗e3 b6 13.c4 ♖xe5 14.♗xc5 ♖xe1 15.♕xe1 bxc5 16.cxd5 ♗f5! 17.c4

♕d6=) 12...b6 13.c4 d4 14.♗xc5 bxc5 15.♖b1 (or 15.♕f3!? ♖b8 16.♕a3! ♕e7 17.♕xa7 ♗e6 18.♗d3±) 15...♗d7 16.f4 ♖b8 17.♖xb8 ♕xb8 18.♗d3 and White is better, as played in Steinkellner-Zajontz, cr 2013.

11...♘xd3 12.cxd3 b6?!

Black doesn't sense the danger and is just thinking how to finish her development on the queenside. She should have opted for 12...d4! in order to prevent White's plan of regrouping the pieces: 13.c4 (13.cxd4 ♕xd4 14.♕c2 b6 15.♗e3 ♕d5=) 13...b6. Now it's not so easy to bring the rook on b1 into play and therefore White's attack on the kingside is not so dangerous: 14.♕f3 ♗e6 15.♕g3 ♕d7 16.♗g5 ♔h8 17.♖e4± ♗f5 18.♖h4 ♖ae8.

13.♖b4!

This is the main point of 11.♖b1. Despite equal material the existence of the opposite-coloured bishops benefits the attacking side.

13...♗f5

Black needs to do something against ♕h5 and ♖h4, but now the bishop comes under attack.

14.♕f3 c5 15.♖f4 ♗g6 16.h4! h5 17.g4!?

This is the most logical move from the human point of view.
However the engine suggests 17.d4 with the idea 17...♖c8 18.e6 ♕d6 19.exf7+ ♖xf7 20.♖xf7 ♗xf7 21.♗f4 ♕f6 22.♕h3, keeping the initiative.

17...♕xh4 18.♔g2!

Threating to capture Black's queen after g4-g5. No wonder that Black collapses under such pressure.

18...♕e7??

Probably the decisive mistake. It was really hard to find 18...♕g5!. Black's queen is not safe here, but after 19.e6 (19.♖a4 ♕h4! 20.♖f4 ♕g5=) 19...♖fe8! is another only move which doesn't lose: 20.♕h3 (or 20.♗d2 d4 21.cxd4 cxd4) 20...hxg4 21.♖xg4 ♕f6 22.♗g5 ♕f5 and there is nothing really decisive for White, e.g. 23.♖e3 ♖xe6 24.♖f3 ♕e5 25.♖h4 (25.♖e3 ♕f5=) 25...♕xg5+ 26.♖g3 ♕xh4 27.♕xh4 ♖e5 28.♖h3 ♖h5 with counterplay for Black.

19.gxh5 ♗xh5

19...♗xd3 20.♖g4 ♗e4 21.♖xg7+ ♔h8 22.♕g3+−.

20.♖e3!

Bringing all the pieces into the attack.

20...♖fe8 21.♕h2

21.♖h3 was also good enough, e.g. 21...♕xe5 22.♗e3+−; or 21.e6 fxe6 (21...f6 22.♖h4+−) 22.♖h3 ♖f8 23.♖xh5+−.

21...g6

21...d4 22.♖g3 ♕xe5 23.♖e4 ♕f5 24.♖g5+−.

22.♖f5 ♗g4

22...♔g7 23.e6+−.

23.♖f4 ♗h5

24.e6!

The following line was forced, but still from the aesthetic point of view the sacrifice of the second pawn and the whole attack in the style of AlphaZero is very beautiful.

24...fxe6 25.♖g3 ♔h7

25...♕h7 26.♖g5 e5 (26...♖f8 27.♖h4 ♔f7 28.♖hxh5 gxh5 29.♕c7++−) 27.♖h4 ♔f7 28.♖xe5 ♕g7 29.♖hxh5 gxh5+ 30.♖g5+−.

26.♖h4 ♕f7 27.♖g5 ♖g8 28.♔f1!

Another quiet move in the middle of the attack.

**28...♕f3 29.♖hxh5+ gxh5 30.♕c7+!
♔h8 31.♕e5+ ♔h7 32.♖xh5+ ♔g6
33.♕g5+ ♔f7 34.♖h7+**

And just one move before the checkmate, Black resigned.

Kirill Shevchenko

Kirill Shevchenko (born: Kyiv 2002) became a grandmaster at the age of just 14 years and 10 months, but it was in 2021 that the teenager really shot to prominence by winning the Tal Memorial Blitz that followed the Grand Swiss in Riga. He put in a final run of 7½/8 to finish half a point clear of both Arjun Erigaisi and Fabiano Caruana.

Kirill's debut for the Ukrainian national team couldn't have gone better as he scored 4½/8 to help Ukraine to surprise gold medals in the 2021 European Team Championship — like the team as a whole, he didn't lose a game. Kirill was in his native Kyiv when Russia attacked in February 2022 and has taken a leading role since in fund-raising and representing the Ukrainian chess community.

NOTES BY
Kirill Shevchenko

This game was played in a decisive match against Russia in round 7. We met on board 3 and I decided to choose the English Opening to create a mess on the board.

Game 42   English Opening
Kirill Shevchenko   2647
Kirill Alekseenko   2710
Terme Catez European Team Championship 2021 (7)

1.c4 e5 2.♘c3 ♗b4
Instead of 2...♘f6, Kirill chose another interesting sideline.
3.♘d5 a5 4.a3 ♗c5 5.♘f3 d6 6.e3 ♘d7
6...c6 7.♘c3 ♘d7 8.d4 ♗a7 is just a transposition.
7.d4 ♗a7 8.♗e2 c6 9.♘c3 ♘gf6

10.g4
A slightly unusual move here, which was my novelty. This move wasn't new for Kirill, as I had played it at the European Clubs two months earlier vs Ivanisevic. Ivan was not afraid to accept the sacrifice and after wild complications the game ended in a draw.
10.0-0 0-0 11.b4 ♗b8 12.♗b2 ♕e7 was the normal continuation, leading to standard position with different plans for both sides.

10...0-0

10...♘xg4 is of course the principled move: 11.♖g1 f5 (11...♘f8 was Ivanisevic's choice: 12.dxe5 ♘g6?! (if 12...♘xe5, 13.♘e4 is also strong) 13.♕xd6 ♗d7 14.♘e4 gave me a big advantage, but in time trouble I missed the win and Ivan escaped to a draw) 12.h3 e4 13.hxg4 exf3 14.♗xf3 fxg4 15.♗xg4 0-0 leads to a messy position, but I would prefer White, because after ♗c1-d2, ♕d1-e2 and 0-0-0 his pieces can develop an initiative.

11.g5 ♘e8

12.♕c2

I think Alekseenko expected 12.h4, which looks more logical, but 12.♕c2 makes some sense, as it helps me finish development. After 12.h4 ♕e7 13.h5 f5 14.c5 d5

the two sides have created a crazy pawn structure which is hard to evaluate.

12...♘c7

12...f5 was logical, e.g. 13.gxf6 (13. g6!? is also worth considering, and can lead to a very unclear position after 13...e4 (13...h6 14.h4) 14.gxh7+ ♔h8 15.♘g1 ♕h4) 13...♘dxf6 (13...♕xf6 14.♗d2 was my idea, but taking with the knight is stronger) 14.♗d2 ♘g4 and ...♗f5. Black has a bright future.

13.h4 ♕e7 14.♗d2

14...b5?!

Again, 14...f5 was the right plan, but it wouldn't have bothered me because I already have good development: 15.gxf6 ♘xf6 16.dxe5 dxe5 17.♖g1 ♔h8 18.0-0-0 and my pieces are ready for battle.

15.dxe5 dxe5 16.♗d3?!

16.♘e4! was the better option. I did not see how to continue after 16...♘e6 but the attacking move 17.♖g1 ♘ec5 18.cxb5 cxb5 19.♗xa5 ♗b7 20.♗b4 leaves White just a pawn up and with more space. Of course Black's counterplay should not be underestimated, but it lacks targets to create threats.

16...bxc4

I saw the option 16...f5!, but
considered it inferior to 16...bxc4.
However, after 17.gxf6 (17.♗xf5?
♖xf5 18.♕xf5 ♘c5 and ...e5-e4 on
the next move is bad for White, of
course) 17...♘xf6 18.♘g5 h6 19.♘ce4
b4! 20.c5 ♘cd5 things become very
complicated, as I don't have any
quick attacking ideas, while Black is
going to finish his development.

17.♗xc4?

17.♗xh7+ ♔h8 18.♘e4 would have
given me an enormous advantage
according to the engine! The white
pieces have great coordination, and
do now allow the black knight to
come to c5. Next comes ♗d2-c3,
long castling and an attack with
h4-h5 and g5-g6 or h5-h6. 18...♘e6
19.♗c3 ♗b8 20.♗f5 ♘ec5 21.♘xc5
♘xc5 22.h5 is the first line, but still
Black's pawns are weak, his king
is weak and his pieces have poor
coordination. White is much better.

17...♗a6?

17...♘c5 could have pointed out
my mistakes and given enough
counterplay. Of course I saw this
line, but I had planned 18.g6.
Unfortunately, this leads only

to an unclear position, not to an
initiative after 18...hxg6 19.♕xg6
♗e6 20.♗xe6 ♘7xe6 21.♕f5 ♖ad8
22.♖g1. Still I think my position is
slightly more pleasant to play, but a
fight lies ahead.

18.♘e4

Now the position is consolidated
and I can continue my attack.
White is again much better!

18...♗xc4 19.♕xc4 ♘e6

20.0-0-0

Finally castling! But not on the
kingside as usual ☺.

20...♘b6

20...♘ec5 21.♗c3 ♕e6 22.♕xe6 fxe6
23.♘fd2 ♘d3+ 24.♔b1 ♘xf2 25.♘xf2
♖xf2 26.♘e4 ♖f7 27.♖he1 doesn't
improve Black's position a lot, but it
was a better chance.

21.♕c2

Black lacks pieces on the queenside to create counterplay, so my king is completely safe. My plan is easy to find, but Kirill didn't know what to choose, so he just exposed his king.
21...f5
Agony, but strategically Black's position is hopeless.
22.gxf6 gxf6 23.♗c3 ♗b8 24.h5 ♘d5 25.♘h4 f5 26.♖dg1+ ♔h8 27.♘g3

All the pieces take part in the attack. Black has no defence.
27...♘xc3 28.♕xc3 ♕c5 29.♕xc5 ♘xc5 30.♘gxf5
There is no defence against 31.♘g6+, so Alekseenko resigned.
A very tense game, but thanks to this win Ukraine won the match against Russia and took the sole lead. Next, in the 8th round we made a peaceful draw vs Azerbaijan and in the 9th round, thanks to the efforts of Korobov and Volokitin, we beat Armenia and, in addition, won the gold medals ☺.

CHAPTER VIII

Ukrainian nuggets

Most chess fans will not know their names, but their studies deserve a broad audience. **Jan Timman** presents the leading study composers from Ukraine and treats you to some of their finest compositions.

The Ukrainian endgame study composer Sergiy Didukh has had a website for donkey's years, which he constantly manages to improve. One of his novelties is a database in which experts can judge and comment on studies from many decades – instructive for every study fan. Didukh also comments on recent awards in study tournaments, always with a critical eye; he is a great expert of the history of endgame studies. There is also room for discussions on other topics; sometimes politics, sometimes even football – which I personally find least interesting.

And then the website of Sergiy Didukh went blank, only showing the word CLOSED.

When the Russian government decided to recognise the rebellious regions around the cities of Luhansk and Donetsk as sovereign states, the world anxiously watched to see if the conflict would escalate. Didukh didn't seem too worried then. When asked, he observed that 'the Russian bear had bitten off two rotten pieces of our country'. He also said that he didn't read newspapers and didn't watch TV. He trusted what Bismarck had said: the United States was blessed with its geographical position: its neighbours to the south and north were no threat, and for the rest it is only bordered by oceans. I must say that this viewpoint reassured me somewhat. But it didn't take long: the dreaded war did come about, and Didukh's website could no longer be reached: 'CLOSED', it said in red letters, giving Bismarck's words sinister connotations. There must have been personal suffering behind those red letters. It is also an illustration of what a war can destroy in the cultural sphere: a platform full of hidden cultural assets can no longer function.

It seemed like a good idea to delve more deeply into the history of the chess study in Ukraine. Its tradition is admittedly less rich than the Russian one with Troitzky, Kubbel, the Platov brothers and Liburkin, yet Ukraine has put its own stamp on chess study history. This was largely due to Sergei Tkachenko, who is a renowned study composer himself. Besides his well-known book *Alekhine's Odessa Secrets*, Tkachenko has written twelve books on endgame studies.

The first notable Ukrainian study composer was **Lazar Zalkind** (1886-1945), an economist. In 1930 he was accused of being part of a plot to infiltrate the Bolshevik government with pro-Mensheviks. The notorious Krylenko personally led the trial against Zalkind. Zalkind was sent to the Gulag and released in 1938. In that time of the great purge, new 'evidence' against

Lazar Zalkind (1886-1945), the first notable Ukrainian study composer, spent years in the Gulag.

him was found, and he was sent to an even more severe camp and only released in 1943, a broken man. He died of heart failure two years later. Zalkind has composed all kinds of fine studies, often based on minor promotion. I think this is his best one, composed a year before his first banishment:

Lazar Zalkind

1/2. prize Troitzky ty 1929

White to play and win

I have modified the study by removing the black f7-pawn. This makes it a bit more economical. **1.c7 a5!** Threatening mate in 1. White has only one move to prevent this, but it's a very nice one: **2.♖d4! ♖xf3** What now?

3.♖f4! The rook returns to its post. The alternative 3.♖d2 is insufficient; after 3...♔xd2+ 4.♔b2 ♖c3! Black has perpetual check.

3...♖g3 The black rook couldn't return. 3...♖d3 is met by 4.♖f2, and wins. The fall of the f-pawn has made square f2 available, which is why Black puts his rook on the g-file, enabling him to withdraw it to g8.

4.♖g4! Again the same principle.

4...♖h3 Without the rook on g4, White would be able to queen now. But how to get rid of the rook?

5.♖h4! ♖g3 6.♖h3! This is the answer: a fifth rook sacrifice.

6...♖xh3 7.c8♕ 1-0.

Tigran Gorgiev (1910-1976) was one of the greatest composers of all time.

Tigran Gorgiev (1910-1976) was originally from Armenia, as may be inferred from his first name. He was born in Dagestan, close to the Chechen border. At the start of World War II, he fled to Kazakhstan, and then, after the war, settled in Ukraine, where he made a great name for himself as a microbiologist. Gorgiev was one of the greatest composers of all time. He has worked with all kinds of themes, and it wasn't easy to settle on his best study. In the end I decided on this one:

Tigran Gorgiev

1. prize USSR Team Championship 1956/57

White to play and win

Both sides have an advanced passed pawn. Black is threatening to take the bishop with check, making White's first move forced:

1.♗f3+ ♔d4! Other king moves would lose at once: 1...♔d3 2.♗xd5+ ♘xh3 3.♗b3 or 1...♔e5 2.♖h5+, and White wins.

2.♖h4+!

Certainly not 2.♗xd5? in view of 2...c2, and the c-pawn becomes unstoppable.

2...♘e4!

A Novotny: the knight causes interference on the bishop's diagonal and the rook's fourth rank.

3.♖xe4+

Not 3.♗xe4 in view of 3...♖c5! 4.♔g6 ♔e3, and Black keeps the draw.

3...♔d3 4.♖c4!

A magnificent move, yielding White control of the c-file.

4...♖d6+

Black obviously can't take the rook. Nor will 4...♖d8 help: in that case, White will win with 5.c7 ♖c8 6.♗g4 (or 6.♗b7).

5.♔g5!

The correct square for the king, which must remain close in case the position is liquidated to an endgame.

5...♔xc4 6.c7

6...♖c6!

A beautiful counter-sacrifice that echoes White's fourth move. Black blocks the c-file.

7.♗xc6 c2

Threatening to queen with check. White will have to sacrifice his bishop with check.

8.♗b5+!

Only like this. After 8.♗d5+? ♔c3! 9.c8♕+ ♔d2! White will be unable to win. The bishop is blocking the d-file.

8...♔b3 9.c8♕ ♔b2! 10.♕h8+

The only check. But it wins!

Sergey Tkachenko has written a book about **Nikolai Rezvov** (1921-2013) entitled *From Child Burglar to Grandmaster*. The story of Rezvov's youth is indeed miraculous. He grew up in poverty in 1920s Odessa. At about six years of age, he was recruited for a special job. There was a group called 'noble thieves' in those days, which employed young boys to sneak into houses, helped by their tiny stature. The young Rezvov was caught while burgling the house of a jeweller. The jeweller gave him a thorough beating and then decided – probably for this reason – not to hand him over to the police. He did something else: he employed him as an apprentice jeweller. And he taught him to play chess. Rezvov continued to compose studies till an advanced age. The following was composed together with his biographer.

Nikolai Rezvov / Sergey Tkachenko

1. prize Dvoresky-60 JT 2007

White to play and win

A confusing starting position because of the many hanging pieces.

1.♗f6! The only move. White must keep his bishop and stop the b-pawn. After 1.♘xe6? b2 2.♗g5+ ♔f2 White will be unable to win.

1...b2! Black's best chance. After 1...♘xc5+ 2.♔xa3 the knight will stand no chance against the white bishop pair.

2.♗xb2 ♘c4 3.♗h8! The only good square for the bishop, which must stay out of the reach of the black knights. After 3.♗c1+? ♔f2! 4.♗d5 ♘xc5+ 5.♔b5 ♘d3 it's a draw; the same goes for 3.♗a1? ♘xc5+ 4.♔b4 ♘d2.

3...♔f2!

4.♗h1!

The second bishop also needs to go to a corner square. But it has to be the right one! After 4.♗a8? ♘xc5+ 5.♔b5 ♘d7! 6.♗d4+ ♘e3! 7.♗e4 ♘f8! 8.♔c6 ♘e6 the draw is a fact. 4.♗h3? is also insufficient in view of 4...♘xc5+ 5.♔b4 ♔g3!.

4...♔g1!

Again Black's best chance. After 4...♘xc5+ 5.♔b5 ♘e3 6.♔xc5 ♘g2 7.♗d4+! ♔g3 8.♗g1 White will win easily.

5.♗a8!

Now it's the right one! The white bishop pair stays out of the reach of the knights.

5...♘xc5+

Or 5...♘b6+ 6.♔b5 ♘xa8 7.♘xe6, and the black knight is encircled.

6.♔b5! ♘d7

A last-ditch attempt.

7.♗d4+! 1-0.

Stanislav Belokon (1939-1984) had a good name for a chess player, as Belokon means 'white horse'. When he was 10 he had a terrible accident and lost both hands. I am a great fan of his studies, for example this one:

Stanislav Belokon

1 prize. Krasnaya Gazeta 1977

White to play and win

At the age of 10, Stanislav Belokon tragically lost both hands in an accident.

In the original version, the rook was on a1 instead of d1. But in that case, there's an ancillary solution.

1.♖b8+ ♘d8

The only move; otherwise Black will soon be mated.

2.♖xd8+ ♔h7 What now?

3.♖g8!!

White sacrifices his rook without allowing the king to escape. After 3.♖h8+ ♔g6 4.♖g8+ ♔f5! 5.♖f8+ ♔g6 6.♖f6+ ♔xf6 7.d8♕+ ♔e5 White will be unable to win.

3...♖h1+ 4.♔g5 ♖g1+ 5.♔f6 ♖xg8

And now comes the point of the manoeuvring:

6.d8♘+! 6.d8♕+? would have been insufficient in view of 6...♔h8, and Black wins.

6...♔h6 7.♘f7+ ♔h7 8.♘g5+ ♔h8

Or 8...♔h6.

9.♖h7+! ♝xh7 10.♘f7 Mate. White has sacrificed both rooks to give mate with the promoted knight.

Mikhail Zinar (1951-2021) was an absolute master of pawn endings – in Nikolai Grigoriev's footsteps. Zinar was surrounded by a veil of mystery for a while. Before 1990 he composed around 300 studies, virtually all of them pawn endings. In that same year, he published a book entitled *Harmony in Pawn Studies*.

After that, silence descended; no new studies were published. Years later, it turned out that he had moved from the Crimea to a little village 300 km from Odessa, where he worked as a teacher. Tkachenko visited him in 1997. Zinar told him that financial troubles had prevented him from composing more studies. Three years later, Zinar visited the Odessa Chess Club to sell his extensive chess library. Shortly afterwards, news came out that he had died, which was shown to have been a false alarm some years

Mikhail Zinar (1951-2021) was an absolute master of pawn endings.

later. The pawn artist was still alive, and after 2005 he started publishing studies again, now also featuring different themes besides pawn endings. After his resurrection, Zinar composed hundreds of studies – until he really died last year. His studies are characterised by a combination of simplicity and profundity.

Mikhail Zinar

2. prize Moscow ty 1983

White to play and draw

In such endgames White must always find the correct route for the king.

1.♔b7! Certainly not 1.♔d7? c5 2.d3 c4!, and Black queens with check.
1...c5 2.d3 Forced. Now the issue becomes clear: Black's c-pawn can crash through at any moment, but Black is in no rush. It will always mean he will queen first, and what matters then is which positions will be drawn with the white pawn on c7.
2...♔g6! A subtle retreat. After 2...c4 3.dxc4 d3 4.g6! ♔xg6 5.c5 d2 6.c6 d1♕ 7.c7 a draw is inevitable. Look at White's fourth move: it is indispensable to make the eventual

stalemate possible – with the queen on b6 and the white king on a8.

3.♔a7!

Vintage Zinar. As we'll see later, White must keep his king on the seventh rank in order to be able to reach square b8. After 3.♔b6? c4 4.dxc4 d3 5.c5 d2 6.c6 d1♕ 7.c7 ♕d7 8.♔b7 ♔f5! White will be mated because he still has his g-pawn.

3...♔f7

After 3...♔xg5 White would go 4.♔b6 after all, e.g. 4...c4 5.dxc4 d3 6.c5 d2 7.c6 d1♕ 8.c7 ♕d7 9.♔b7, with a draw.

The immediate breakthrough 3...c4 would lead to a draw after 4.dxc4 d3 5.c5 d2 6.c6 d1♕ 7.c7 ♕d7 8.♔b8.

4.g6+!

Again, White must get rid of the g-pawn.

4...♔g8 5.g7! ♔xg7

6.♔b6! The same principle as before. Without the g-pawn, the white king can get onto the sixth rank. 6.♔a6 would have worked as well.

6...c4 7.dxc4 d3 8.c5 d2 9.c6 d1♕ 10.c7 ♕d7 11.♔b7 ♔f6 12.♔b8 Draw.

Alexander Stavrietsky (born 1959) is a representative of what you could call *magic realism* in the art of study composition. I myself can also compose such studies, but he is a past master of the genre. An example:

Alexander Stavrietsky

1. prize Babich MT Olimpiev MT 2017

White to play and draw

A cluttered position, which is nevertheless not overly unnatural. White is behind in material and his king is exposed; but he has many resources.

1.♘d5 ♖c4+ 2.♔b1!

The only square for the king. After 2.♔b2? ♖xe4! 3.♘xe7 ♖f2+ Black would capture the white queen.

2...♖c1+!

A venomous rook sacrifice.

3.♔b2!

White could not accept the offer. After 3.♔xc1? ♕a3+ 4.♔d2 ♕b2+ 5.♔e1 ♖f1+! the white queen is lost again.

3...♖f2+

The second rook sacrifice.

4.♘xf2 ♖b1+!

With this third rook sacrifice, Black ends up winning the queen after all.

5.♔xb1 ♕h7+

The point of the last two rook sacrifices. Black now wins the queen for real.

6.g6!

The start of a fantastic combination. After 6.♔b2? ♗xh5 7.♗xe5+ ♘g7 8.♘e7 hxg5 White's position would be hopeless.

6...♗xg6+

7.♗c2!!

The amazing climax of the study. White sacrifices another piece. Insufficient was 7.♔b2? ♗xh5 8.♗xe5+ ♘g7, and White is finished.

7...bxc2+ 8.♔c1

Now the black c-pawn will restrict the black queen's elbow-room.

8...♗xh5 9.♗xe5+ ♘g7

10.♘e7!

The deeper intention behind the combination starts getting clear. The black queen has no squares.

10...♗g4!

A dangerous winning attempt that White must deal with accurately.

11.h4!

Only like this! 11.♗f4? would have been met by 11...♗h3!, creating room for Black on the kingside.

11...h5 12.♗f4

An incredible position. White has only a knight for the queen, but he will hold.

12...♞e8 13.♗e5+ ♞g7 14.♗f4 ♗d7

15.♗d2!

The only way to continue to dominate the black queen. After 15.♗e3? ♞f5 and 15.♗g5? ♞e8 Black would free himself.

15...♞e6 16.♗c3+

The knight is repulsed every time.

16...♞g7 17.♗d2 ♗a4 18.♗f4! Draw.

Vladislav Tarasiuk (born 1968) is a physician. At the time of writing, he is working under extremely difficult circumstances in a hospital near Kharkiv, fearing for his life and that of his family.

Tarasiuk has composed very good studies, winning several first prizes.

Vladislav Tarasiuk

1. prize Ukraine Team Championship 2018

White to play and win

To rein in the black passed pawns, White has to sacrifice his queen.

At the time of writing, Vladislav Tarasiuk is working under extremely difficult circumstances in a hospital near Kharkiv, fearing for his life and that of his family.

1.♕c1+ The alternative 1.♕d6? was insufficient, since Black then has an intermediate check. After 1...♗h6+ 2.♔e4 ♔g2! 3.g7 ♗xg7 4.♕g6+ ♔h1! 5.♕a6 ♔g2 6.♕g6+ ♔h1 White cannot make progress. **1...♔g2 2.♕h1+!** The point. White sacrifices his queen to force the black king into the corner.
2...♔xh1 3.♔xf2 ♗d4+! The start of a fascinating struggle on the long diagonal.

4.♔f1! It goes without saying that White must not capture the bishop in view of stalemate. **4...♗c3!** Black keeps pressing. **5.♗b2!** Well done. Now Black has no other option than to capture the bishop. **5...♗xb2 6.c4**

The black bishop can no longer stop the white passed pawn. But Black has a back-up plan: aiming for stalemate.
6...♗d4 7.c5 ♗g1! 8.g7 f2

The stalemate construction is finished. But White has a ready-made answer:
9.♔e2! Avoiding the stalemate, since the g-pawn will queen with check. 1-0.

I regard **Sergiy Didukh** (born 1976) as the most talented composer Ukraine has ever known. Interestingly enough, he found a lot of inspiration in Zinar's *Harmony in Pawn Studies* as a young man. Didukh has garnered many first prizes, and his studies feature a broad variety of themes. This made it a hard choice for me, but I think the following study is his best one:

Sergiy Didukh
1. prize Bilek-75 JT 2007

White to play and win

The first move is clear:
1.f7 ♗d6
Black sacrifices his bishop to get his rook to the f-file. The alternative 1...♖a3+ would lose hopelessly after 2.♖xa3 ♗d7+ 3.♔b3 ♗e6+ 4.♔c2 b3+ 5.♔b1 ♗xf7 6.♖a7, and one of Black's bishops will fall.
2.♖xd6 ♖f3

3.♗d3+!
Forcing the black king to a less favourable square. Insufficient for the win was 3.♗g6?. After 3...♗f5 4.♗h5 ♗g4 5.♖d3 ♖f2! 6.♗g6 ♗e6 Black will win the f-pawn.
3...♔e1
The king could not have gone to the g-file: 3...♔g1 4.♗g6 ♗f5 5.♗h5 ♗g4 6.♖g6!, and White wins.
4.♗g6

4...♗f5!
A fantastic resource, forcing more subtleties out of White.
5.♗h5!
Not 5.♖d1+?, in view of 5...♔f2 6.♗h5 ♗c2+.
5...♗g4 6.♖d1+!
Now it's OK!
6...♔f2 7.♖d3!
It's an ingenious mechanism.
7...♖f6
7...♖f4 would have been met decisively by 8.♖d4.
8.♗g6 ♗f5
Again the same defence, this time with the rooks at the other side – on the f-file.

9.♖d6!
A brilliant echo of the seventh move.
9...♗c2+ 10.♔a5!
The only square for the king. Remarkably enough, White won't be able to win after 10.♔b5? ♖xf7 11.♗xf7 b3.
10...♖f4 11.♖d2+ 1-0.

Explanation of symbols

**The chessboard
with its coordinates:**

<table>
<tr><td>❏</td><td>White to move</td></tr>
<tr><td>■</td><td>Black to move</td></tr>
<tr><td>♔</td><td>King</td></tr>
<tr><td>♕</td><td>Queen</td></tr>
<tr><td>♖</td><td>Rook</td></tr>
<tr><td>♗</td><td>Bishop</td></tr>
<tr><td>♘</td><td>Knight</td></tr>
</table>

±	White stands slightly better
∓	Black stands slightly better
±	White stands better
∓	Black stands better
+−	White has a decisive advantage
−+	Black has a decisive advantage
=	balanced position
!	good move
!!	excellent move
?	bad move
??	blunder
!?	interesting move
?!	dubious move
#	mate
ch	championship
zt	zonal tournament
izt	interzonal tournament
ct	candidates tournament
tt	team tournament
ol	olympiad
m	match
cr	correspondence